COMPARATIVE INCOME TAX DEFERRAL:
THE UNITED STATES AND JAPAN

Comparative Income Tax Deferral: The United States and Japan

by

CHRISTOPHER H. HANNA
Professor of Law
School of Law, Southern Methodist University

KLUWER LAW INTERNATIONAL
LONDON / THE HAGUE / BOSTON

Library of Congress Cataloging-in-Publication Data
Hanna, Christopher H.
Comparative income tax deferral of the United States and Japan / by Christopher H. Hanna.
p. cm.
Includes bibliographical references and index.
ISBN 9041197710 (HB: alk. paper)
1. Deferred compensation–Taxation–Law and legislation–United States. 2. Deferred compensation–Taxation–Law and legislation–Japan. 3. Deferred compensation–Taxation. I. Title.
K4506. H36 2000
343.5205'23–dc21 00-039090

ISBN 90-411-9771-0

Published by Kluwer Law International
P.O. Box 85889, 2508 CN The Hague, The Netherlands

Sold and distributed in North, Central and South America
by Kluwer Law International,
675 Massachusetts Avenue, Cambridge, MA 02139, USA

In all other countries, sold and distributed
by Kluwer Law International, Distribution Centre
P.O. Box 322, 3300 AH Dordrecht, The Netherlands

Printed on acid-free paper

To my parents

Table of Contents

Acknowledgments

I need to thank a lot of people. The members of the SMU Alumni Association in Japan who have been particularly kind to me include: Professor Hide Ara (a wonderful mentor to me), Justice Hideo Chikusa and his family, the late Judge Kazuo Fujii, Hideki Kojima, Fujio Matsumuro and his family, Haruhiro Nakatsu, Justice Shigeharu Negishi, Judge Yukio Nozaki and his family, and Muneo Ohta. At the University of Tokyo where I began this book, I owe many thanks to the following professors: Masahito Inouye, Mitsuaki Usui and his family, Minoru Nakazato (my host), and Yoshihiro Masui. At Meiji Gakuin University, I thank Professors Fumihiro Tamakuni (my host) and his family, Masamitsu Sakamoto, Kanji Kawamura, Norihisa Kyoto, and Taiichiro Tsuji. I also thank Professor Hiroshi Kaneko for allowing me to participate at his very informative Tax Research Group meetings. All of the members of his group have treated me as one of their own. At the Japanese Ministry of Finance, I thank Hiroshi Watanabe, Eimon Ueda, Yasuhito Suzuki, Jiro Tamura, and Isao Watanabe. I also thank Rex Coleman, Justice Shigemitsu Dando, the Honorable Thomas S. Foley, Glen S. Fukushima, Yoshiko Hiwano, Takashi and Sumiko Inaba, Dr. Chalmers Johnson, Akiko Kato, Fumihiro Komamiya, Hisako Matsumuro, the Honorable Walter F. Mondale, Mark Ramseyer and Morio Uematsu for their advice and kindness during my visits to Japan.

I should also mention that after completing my year at the University of Tokyo, I was very fortunate to spend the summer of 1997 at Harvard Law School under the guidance of Professor Daniel Halperin. Every time I met with him, I learned an incredible amount about tax deferral. His reputation for being incredibly intelligent and always right is accurate.

At the Fiscal Affairs Division of the Organisation for Economic Co-operation and Development, I thank Masahiro Kan and his family, Naoki Matsuda, and Katsumi Shinagawa and his family for helping me with my understanding of Japan. Shinagawa-san was of tremendous help in discussing Japanese tax issues with me. Professor Hugh Ault was kind enough to arrange my appointment at the OECD, and Jeffrey Owens, head of Fiscal Affairs, graciously approved my appointment. I also thank the following people at the OECD for their collegiality during my stay: Chiara Bronchi, Steven Clark, Elizabeth Conway, Bernard Damsma, Flip de Kam, Michael Engelschalk, Torsten Fensby, Michael Hardy, Susan Himes, David Holland, Fran Horner, M. Milliet-Einbinder, Grace Perez-Navarro, Suzanne Sansade, Jacques Sasseville, and Andrew Scott.

At SMU Law School and the Dallas community, I thank Dean John Attanasio, Jonathan Blacker, Jeffry Blair, Professor Alan Bromberg, Professor Regis Campfield, Brett Enzor, Mary Lynn Kime, Professor Henry Lischer, Cym Lowell, Professor George Martinez, Professor Joseph McKnight, Professor John Mylan, Dr. Norman Neureiter, Professor Joseph Norton, Scott Parel, Professor Roark Reed, Dean Paul Rogers, Professor Marc Steinberg, Charles Thompson and Carolyn Yates. At the University of Texas Law School, I thank Professors Joseph Dodge, John Dzienkowski, Mark Gergen, and Calvin Johnson.

Lastly, and most importantly, I thank my parents for their love and support.

Foreword

A number of reviewers of this book have commented how unusual but interesting it is to find a book on tax deferral with an emphasis on Japanese tax law (as well as American tax law) written by an American law professor. Let me explain briefly how this book came to be written as well as the purpose of the book. In mid-1993, after three years of teaching tax law at Southern Methodist University School of Law in Dallas, Texas, I found myself focusing on time value of money and tax deferral issues. I found it to be a very interesting and extremely challenging field. Later that year, Ambassador Robert Strauss gave a luncheon speech at my law school. I was fascinated by his discussion of international business and globalization and decided that I wanted to devote more time to issues in the international arena. I was also very fortunate to have had the opportunity to meet Ambassador Strauss, and he has graciously helped me with my career.

In the spring of 1994, Professor Harold Koh gave an endowed lecture at the law school. His terrific lecture on public international law cemented my interest in international issues and in the concept of globalization. As a result of his visit to SMU, I have been very lucky to count Harold as a friend and mentor to me.

During the 1996–1997 academic year, I was a visiting research scholar at the University of Tokyo Faculty of Law. I studied the Japanese tax system with a particular focus on time value of money and tax deferral issues. I gave a number of presentations on tax deferral and found that Japanese professors, practitioners, and business people were very interested in tax deferral. It was, however, a relatively new area in Japan. The Japanese government had not yet implemented a number of measures to counter tax deferral.

It was during this time that I decided to write this book. The book begins with a general discussion of tax deferral. Then comparisons are made between the U.S. and Japanese tax systems with respect to deferral opportunities. The book concludes with a discussion of how the U.S. has eliminated many of the deferral opportunities in the U.S. system and how Japan may want to consider some of the same deferral prevention methods. The intended audience is primarily academics and government officials, but I think there is something of interest to practitioners and business people as well. The book also includes an appendix on the history of the Japanese income tax system, which gives the reader an idea as to what issues were important in the development of the income tax.

Chapter 1

Introduction

I. Background and Purpose of the Study

One of the leading tax professors in the United States, William Andrews, wrote a number of years ago that "Deferral of gain is not as serious as outright exemption, but it is the next best thing, as sophisticated taxpayers and their counsel are now well aware."[1] This statement seems as true today as it was when it was made in 1983. In fact, it seems more appropriate today in the sense that there is greater awareness of tax deferral not just in the United States, but in many countries throughout the world. This is probably due in part to the overused but generally accurate term "globalization." For example, in recent years, it has become increasingly easier for many investors to shift funds overseas into a tax haven jurisdiction and receive the time value of money benefit of tax deferral. But another reason for the growing awareness of the importance of tax deferral is simply the increasing sophistication of tax counsel and their clients as well as government tax administrators.

In this book, the focus will be on tax deferral and the associated time value of money issues – more specifically, deferral of income and acceleration of deductions. The focus is on the benefit that is achieved by deferring income (or accelerating deductions) even if tax rates and interest rates remain constant during the deferral period. This time value of money benefit is one of the driving forces behind the explosive growth of derivatives that has taken place in the last ten years. As many commentators have noted, there are three principal issues involved in taxing derivatives: timing, sourcing, and character. Almost all would agree that the timing issue is of overwhelming importance while sourcing and character are generally considered of secondary importance, although certainly not insignificant.

The key to understanding time value of money and tax deferral is the Cary Brown model. As will be explained in later chapters, Dr. Edgar Cary Brown, an economics professor at the Massachusetts Institute of Technology, published his model as a

---

[1] William D. Andrews, "The Achilles' Heel of the Comprehensive Income Tax," in *New Directions in Federal Tax Policy for the 1980s* 278, 280 (Charls E. Walker and Mark A. Bloomfield eds., 1983).

chapter in a small book published in 1948.[2] Although the model is now 50 years old, it really is the fountainhead of learning on the subject of tax deferral and will be referred to constantly throughout the book.

Much has been written in the American tax law literature on time value of money and tax deferral. Some of the insights have been truly brilliant. But it appears that many of these insights can be explained by Dr. Brown's model developed 50 years ago. In this book, many of these recent brilliant observations on tax deferral will be revisited in light of the Cary Brown model. It will be demonstrated that many of these observations are variations on the Cary Brown model. This is not meant in any way to belittle the more recent insights into tax deferral but rather to show how important it is to understand the original Cary Brown model.

The United States has devoted a lot of attention to time value of money issues and the prevention of tax deferral. Much of this is probably due to the late Professor Stanley S. Surrey. Professor Surrey, who started his career in academia at the University of California at Berkeley and then moved to Harvard University, was appointed Assistant Secretary of the Treasury for Tax Policy by President John F. Kennedy in 1961. He would serve in this role until 1969 when he returned to Harvard. During Professor Surrey's tenure at the Treasury Department, he devoted a lot of attention to tax deferral and time value of money issues. In fact, he really was responsible for making the United States government aware of the tremendous benefits that taxpayers enjoyed through tax deferral. He, along with Professor William Andrews, was responsible for popularizing the Cary Brown model among American tax law academics. As a result of Professor Surrey's tenure at the Treasury Department, a number of provisions were enacted by the United States Congress to eliminate the benefits of tax deferral. For example, in 1962, the U.S. Congress passed controlled foreign corporation legislation addressing issues of tax deferral in the international arena.[3] In 1969, the U.S. Congress enacted legislation requiring annual accrual of original issue discount on a zero coupon bond even if the holder of the bond is on the cash method of accounting.[4] In fact, throughout the 1970s, 1980s, and 1990s, the United States has continued to address issues of tax deferral, and whenever possible, prevent the time value of money benefit of tax deferral.

While the focus of the book is on principles of tax deferral and time value of money, the income tax systems of both the United States and Japan will be selectively analyzed and compared. The United States has been at the forefront in recognizing the time value of money benefit of tax deferral and devising various methods to attack deferral. In fact, much of the complexity of the United States income tax system can be linked to the numerous provisions designed to prevent the benefits of tax deferral. As a result, even though the United States has been the pioneer in attacking tax deferral through various methods, it can be argued that this has led to

---

[2] E. Cary Brown, "Business Income Taxation and Investment Incentives," in *Income, Employment and Public Policy: Essays in Honor of Alvin H. Hansen* 300 (1948). It has been reprinted in American Economics Assn., *Readings in the Economics of Taxation* 525–37 (Richard A. Musgrave and Carl S. Shoup eds., 1959).

[3] Pub. L. No. 87–834, section 12(a) (1962).

[4] Pub. L. No. 91–172, section 413(a) (1969).

too much complexity in the U.S. income tax system. In other words, as NYU Professor James Eustice has been known to say, "While there is a time value of money, there is also a money value of time."

Japan has the second largest economy in the world behind the United States. Like the United States, it collects a major portion of its taxes through its income tax system.[5] But unlike the United States, Japan has not historically placed much emphasis on tax deferral. This is understandable when one understands the history of the Japanese income tax system. The modern Japanese income tax system can, in some sense, be traced to the system set up by the United States immediately after World War II.[6] In 1949 and again in 1950, Dr. Carl Shoup of Columbia University led a delegation of leading American tax scholars (including Professor Surrey) to Japan to help the Japanese government in setting up its tax system. After studying the Japanese tax system for a number of months, the Shoup Mission released its first report on the Japanese tax system in 1949 in four volumes. The Japanese government adopted almost all of the recommendations although by 1953 it had repealed or substantially modified many of the adopted recommendations. Nonetheless, the spirit of the Shoup Mission recommendations continued on in the Japanese tax system and still does to the current day. Unfortunately, but certainly understandable given the year, the Shoup Mission devoted very little attention to time value of money issues in the Japanese tax system. As a result, it is quite understandable that these issues were not considered of much importance to the Japanese government for many years.

But change, although gradual, is taking place in Japan. The Japanese government is placing greater emphasis on tax deferral issues. It recognizes the tremendous benefit that can be achieved by a taxpayer in deferring taxes. This is true even though Japanese interest rates are currently incredibly low. Deregulation has allowed Japanese taxpayers to more easily invest money overseas and to take advantage of the higher returns that can be earned, for example, in the United States. Deregulation has also allowed foreign companies to enter the Japanese market taking advantage of the many provisions of the Japanese income tax law allowing deferral of taxes. In addition, new financial products are constantly being introduced in Japan to take advantage of the timing rules of the Japanese income tax system.

The academic community in Japan is also beginning to appreciate the advantages of tax deferral. It should be noted that in the early 1960s the University of Tokyo Faculty of Law established one of the first positions in a Japanese university for a tax law professor. That position was filled by Professor Hiroshi Kaneko, who is considered the dean of Japanese tax law professors. Prior to Professor Kaneko's appointment, there were very few tax specialists in the Japanese academic world. In fact, even today, it is not uncommon to find a Japanese university faculty of law that does not have a professor specializing in tax law. As a result, the study of tax law at Japanese universities is still a relatively new phenomenon.

Professor Kaneko, who was a student of Professor Surrey, has been focusing on tax deferral for a number of years and has recommended, for example, an interest

---

[5] See Appendix. [6] See *id.*

charge regime on unrealized appreciation.[7] But he has been the pioneer in the field and only in more recent years have others begun to build on Professor Kaneko's innovative work. As a result, it is quite understandable that the United States has developed a lead over Japan with respect to tax deferral and time value of money issues. But as the Japanese government and tax academics devote more time to tax deferral issues, this lead will narrow. In fact, it is possible that in the next 10–20 years, the Japanese government will begin to develop various methods of eliminating tax deferral in a manner similar to the United States government of the 1960s through the current day.

II. Methodology

The layout of the book is designed to first introduce the reader to the Cary Brown model, then to compare various provisions in the United States and Japanese income tax systems, and finally discuss solutions to preventing tax deferral. In Chapter 2, the Cary Brown model will be described and explained. The importance of the model in understanding tax deferral cannot be overemphasized. Once one has a thorough understanding of the model, all tax deferral situations can be easily analyzed.

Chapter 3 will discuss three prominent American tax scholars' interpretation of the Cary Brown model. Professors Surrey, Andrews, and Daniel Halperin have all devoted considerable attention to the model and their interpretations will be discussed and analyzed. Professor Surrey was at the forefront in analyzing tax deferral and focusing on the Cary Brown model.[8] Professors Andrews and Halperin have each written ground breaking articles on tax deferral that are still considered years ahead of their time.[9] In addition, two significant U.S. Treasury studies[10] and a U.K. tax study[11] will be discussed with respect to deferral.

Chapter 4 will introduce a different way of looking at the Cary Brown model.[12] It is not entirely accurate to say that it is a new view of the Cary Brown model but rather an expansion of an old view that was presented in Dr. Brown's book chapter over 50 years ago. It is hoped that this alternative view, because of its simplicity, will become part of the standard literature in analyzing and describing tax deferral.

---

[7] See Hiroshi Kaneko, "Capital Gains Kazei No Kaikaku" in *Kazei Tann'i Oyobi Johto Shotoku No Kenkyu*, 288–320 (1996) (this article is written in Japanese and was originally published in 1986).

[8] See Stanley S. Surrey, "The Tax Reform Act of 1969 – Tax Deferral and Tax Shelters," 12 *B.C. Indus. & Com. L. Rev.* 307 (1971); Stanley S. Surrey, *Pathways to Tax Reform* (1973).

[9] See William D. Andrews, "A Consumption-Type or Cash-Flow Personal Income Tax," 87 *Harv. L. Rev.* 1113 (1974); Daniel I. Halperin, "Interest in Disguise: Taxing the Time Value of Money," 95 *Yale L.J.* 506 (1986).

[10] See David F. Bradford and the United States Treasury Tax Policy Staff, *Blueprints for Basic Tax Reform*, (1st ed., 1977 and 2d ed., 1984); United States Department of the Treasury, *Tax Reform for Fairness, Simplicity and Economic Growth* (November 1984).

[11] See Institute for Fiscal Studies, *The Structure and Reform of Direct Taxation: Report of a Committee Chaired by Professor J. E. Meade* (1978).

[12] See Christopher H. Hanna, "Demystifying Tax Deferral," 52 *S.M.U. L. Rev.* 383 (1999). Chapter four is partially adapted from this article.

Chapter 2

The Cary Brown Model

I. Introduction

Issues relating to tax deferral and time value of money are probably the most important areas of tax study for several reasons.[1] First, they cut across all areas of tax law, whether one is focusing on individual income tax, international tax, corporate tax, partnership tax, or any other area. Second, they are the keys to understanding how to properly tax financial instruments, including derivatives.[2] Finally, tax deferral and time value of money issues are important in understanding the differences among the numerous flat tax and consumption tax proposals that have been introduced in the last few years.[3]

---

[1] See, e.g., William D. Andrews, "The Achilles' Heel of the Compehensive Income Tax," in *New Directions in Federal Tax Policy for the 1980s* 278, 280 (Charls E. Walker and Mark A. Bloomfield eds., 1983) ("Deferral of gain is not as serious as outright exemption, but it is the next best thing, as sophisticated taxpayers and their counsel are now well aware. Deferral for a generation, in a six percent world, is tantamount to three-fourths exemption. In a twelve percent world, it is tantamount to fifteen-sixteenths exemption."); Daniel I. Halperin, "Interest in Disguise: Taxing the 'Time Value of Money,' " *95 Yale L. J.* 506 (1986) ("Questions of timing – such as the correct period for reporting income or claiming deductions – present some of the most critical and vexing issues in the design of an income tax."); Stephen B. Land, "Defeating Deferral: A Proposal for Retrospective Taxation," 52 *Tax L. Rev*. 45, 46 (1996) ("The next best thing to not paying tax is putting it off. This principle, more than any other, has motivated tax planning over the years.").

[2] See, e.g., David A. Weisbach, "Tax Responses to Financial Contract Innovation," 50 *Tax L. Rev*. 491, 492 (1995) ("Changing from a realization-based income tax to another system may be the only complete solution to problems raised by financial innovation."); Deborah H. Schenk, "Taxation of Equity Derivatives: A Partial Integration Proposal," 50 *Tax L. Rev*. 571, 572 n. 1 (1995) ("In a pure accrual system that did not distinguish among income sources, financial instruments would pose little threat."); Daniel Shaviro, "Risk-Based Rules and the Taxation of Capital Income," 50 *Tax L. Rev*. 643, 651 (1995) ("The workability of a tax regime for capital income that, in so many respects, uses risk-based rules recently has come under severe and widely recognized challenge. This challenge, has resulted from the recent development of a broad array of new, widely marketed financial products, commonly called derivatives."); Jeff Strnad, "Taxing New Financial Products: A Conceptual Framework," 46 *Stan. L. Rev*. 569 (1994) (describing different frameworks for taxing financial instruments with the focus overwhelmingly on timing issues).

[3] See The National Commission on Economic Growth and Tax Reform, "Unleashing America's Potential," reproduced in 70 *Tax Notes* 413 (January 22, 1996) at 425. ("In order to end these biases [against work, saving, and investment] the tax system must either *let savers deduct their savings or exclude the returns on the savings from their taxable income.* It must *end double-taxation of business and their owners and permit expensing of investment outlays*.")

Chapter 5 will introduce eleven different tax deferral patterns that can arise under both the United States and Japanese income tax systems. Comparisons will be made between the United States and Japanese tax systems, the tax deferral benefit that is being achieved, and also briefly introduce how the United States has eliminated the tax deferral benefit that is being achieved. In this chapter, the Haig-Simons definition of income[13] will be discussed, as will Samuelson depreciation (sometimes referred to as economic depreciation).[14] If one has a thorough understanding of the Haig-Simons definition of income, Samuelson depreciation, and the Cary Brown model, then any provision in the income tax laws can be analyzed in terms of whether it is sound from a tax policy standpoint. Also in this chapter, Professor Alvin Warren's contribution to tax deferral in a short but brilliant tax article published in 1987 will be discussed and analyzed.[15]

Chapter 6 will discuss in detail five different methods that the United States government has introduced to eliminate the time value of money benefit of tax deferral.[16] The strengths and weaknesses of each method will be discussed. In addition, some thoughts for Japan will be given if it decides to adopt one of the five methods in its income tax system.

Chapter 7 will summarize some of the advantages and disadvantages of each of the five methods the U.S. has used in preventing tax deferral. In addition, some thoughts will be given on some proposed methods of eliminating deferral that have recently appeared in the academic literature.

Chapter 8 will offer some concluding thoughts on tax deferral with respect to both the United States and the Japanese income tax systems.

---

[13] See Robert M. Haig, "The Concept of Income – Economic and Legal Aspects" in *The Federal Income Tax*, 1, 7 (Robert M. Haig ed., 1921); Henry C. Simons, *Personal Income Taxation*, 50 (1938).

[14] See Paul A. Samuelson, "Tax Deductibility of Economic Depreciation to Insure Invariant Valuation," 72 *J. Pol. Econ.* 604 (1964).

[15] See Alvin C. Warren, Jr., "The Timing of Taxes," 39 *Nat'l Tax J.* 499 (1987).

[16] See Christopher H. Hanna, The Virtual Reality of Eliminating Tax Deferral, 12 Amer. J. Tax Pol'y 449 (1995). Chapter six is partially adapted from this article.

My research in the last few years has led me to conclude that the key to understanding tax deferral and corresponding time value of money issues is to have a thorough understanding of the Cary Brown model. The Cary Brown model, sometimes referred to as the MIT model, is named after its founder, Dr. Edgar Cary Brown. Dr. Brown, an economics professor at the Massachusetts Institute of Technology, published his model as a 17-page article in 1948 in a book containing a collection of essays, *Income, Employment and Public Policy, Essays in Honor of Alvin H. Hansen*.[4] It has been reprinted since then.[5] The Cary Brown model, as it is currently understood today, is discussed in less than one and a half pages of the article.[6] The model will be discussed in Section II. below. [7]

The Cary Brown model, although it has been in existence since 1948, did not seem to attract much attention in either the tax law or economic literature until the late 1960s and then throughout the 1970s.[8] In fact, the awareness in the late 1960s seemed to be primarily by public finance experts with a limited number of tax experts focusing on the Cary Brown model. Not until the 1970s and 1980s, did a number of tax articles appear discussing the Cary Brown model.

Much of the early awareness of the Cary Brown model may have been due to the appointment of Professor Stanley S. Surrey to the post of Assistant Secretary of the Treasury for Tax Policy in 1961 by President John F. Kennedy. Professor Surrey,

---

See also John S. Nolan, "Erwin N. Griswold Lecture: The Merit of an Income Tax Versus a Consumption Tax," 12 *Amer. J. Tax Policy* 207, 208 (1995) ("The key to understanding the basic equivalence of these two systems [the Nunn-Domenici USA Tax and the Armey flat tax] as being solely taxes on consumption is that the *economic effect* of not taxing an amount received, but taxing the investment returns on that amount, as in the USA Tax, is exactly the same as taxing the amount received but not taxing the investment returns, as in the Armey flat tax."); Martin D. Ginsburg, "Taxing the Components of Income: A U.S. Perspective," 86 *Geo. L. J.* 123, 132 (1997) (questioning whether the legislative sponsors of the USA Tax and the Armey flat tax understand the equivalence described by the Cary Brown model).

As to the flat tax and the USA Tax, see Robert E. Hall and Alvin Rabushka, *The Flat Tax* (2d ed. 1995) reprinted in *Special Supplement, Tax Notes* (4 August 1995) and "USA Tax System: Description and Explanation of the Unlimited Savings Allowance Income Tax System," 66 *Tax Notes* 1483 (10 March 1995).

[4] See E. Cary Brown, "Business Income Taxation and Investment Incentives," in *Income, Employment and Public Policy: Essays in Honor of Alvin H. Hansen* 300, 309–310 (1948).

[5] See American Economics Assn., *Readings in the Economics of Taxation* 525–37 (Richard A. Musgrave and Carl S. Shoup eds., 1959).

[6] See Cary Brown, *supra* note 4, at 309–310.

[7] This discussion of the Cary Brown model has been partially adapted from Christopher H. Hanna, "The Virtual Reality of Eliminating Tax Deferral," 12 *Amer. J. Tax Pol'y* 449 (1995).

[8] See, e.g., Carl S. Shoup, *Public Finance* 302 (1969); Stanley S. Surrey, "The Tax Reform Act of 1969 – Tax Deferral and Tax Shelters," 12 *Bost. Coll. Ind. & Comm. L. Rev.* 307, 313 (1970); United States Treasury Department, Tax Depreciation Policy, 116 Cong. Rec. E6963–6975 (23 July 1970); Stanley S. Surrey, *Pathways to Tax Reform* 123 (1973); William D. Andrews, "A Consumption-Type or Cash Flow Personal Income Tax," 87 *Harv. L. Rev.* 1113, 1127 (1974); Alvin C. Warren, Jr., "Fairness and a Consumption-Type or Cash-Flow Personal Income Tax," 88 *Harv. L. Rev.* 931 (1975); Institute for Fiscal Studies, *The Structure and Reform of Direct Taxation: Report of a Committee Chaired by Professor J. E. Meade* 37 (United Kingdom 1978); Michael J. Graetz, "Implementing a Progressive Consumption Tax," 92 Harv. L. Rev. 1575, 1602 (1979).

For an earlier work by a public finance scholar, see Richard A. Musgrave, *The Theory of Public Finance* 262–67 (1959).

who was one of the members of both the 1949 and 1950 Shoup Missions, continued to serve as Assistant Secretary of the Treasury for Tax Policy until 1969, when he returned to the Harvard law faculty. During his tenure at the Treasury Department, Professor Surrey raised Congress' and taxpayers' awareness of the benefits of tax deferral. His tenure at Treasury culminated in the Tax Reform Act of 1969, a large tax reform package that began to seriously address issues of tax deferral.[9] The awareness of the benefits of tax deferral increased during the late 1970s and early 1980s, partly as a consequence of the persistence of high interest rates.[10]

Professor William Andrews should also be given credit for developing interest in the Cary Brown model among American tax academics. In 1974, Professor Andrews wrote what some scholars consider to be the finest tax article in the American legal literature.[11] In the article, he discussed the time value of money benefit of tax deferral and spent a substantial portion of the article discussing the Cary Brown model and its importance to understanding tax deferral.

During the 1980s and 1990s, a number of articles have appeared in the American tax literature discussing the Cary Brown model. Unfortunately, much of it has focused on its application to expensing and depreciation and very little to its application to other areas of the income tax laws, for example, prepaid income and installment sales. This is unfortunate because the model can be applied to an almost endless number of areas of the income tax laws. In fact, one leading American tax commentator has remarked that all or almost all of the time value of money provisions in the income tax laws can be described through the Cary Brown model.[12]

As stated previously, this chapter will discuss the model in two parts. In a later chapter (Chapter 5), the model will be applied to a number of traditional areas, such as expensing, depreciation, and investment tax credits in both the United States and Japanese income tax systems. It will then be applied to some less traditional areas because they seemed to have caused a lot of confusion among tax commentators, some of whom are even familiar with the original Cary Brown model. The Cary Brown model can be applied not only to the deduction side, where it has traditionally applied, but also to the income side, for example, to unrealized appreciation.

II. Present Value of Tax Savings

The critical passage from the Cary Brown article is as follows:

> As they [the taxpayers] telescope the depreciation deduction, the present worth of the tax rebates from the depreciation increases as the rebates are shifted closer to

[9] Pub. L. No. 91–172 (1969).

[10] See generally Lawrence Lokken, "The Time Value of Money Rules," 42 *Tax L. Rev.* 1 (1986).

[11] See Andrews, *supra* note 8.

[12] See Interview with Martin D. Ginsburg, Professor of Law, 12 *ABA Section of Taxation Newsletter* 6, 10 (Fall 1992). ("One of Dan Halperin's greater achievements has been to generalize what I just described [applying the Cary Brown model to installment sales] and to show that it fairly explains almost everything in the tax law dealing with time value of money issues".)

> the present. In the limiting case, the asset could be written off in one year. In such an event, the tax rebate from depreciation would be proportional to the tax. Investment incentives would be restored to the pretax level, since the tax would proportionately reduce both the prospective net receipts from investment and its cost. By paying the entrepreneur the tax on the asset's cost, the Government would literally be a partner in the firm. It would make a capital contribution on new investments at the same rate at which it shared in the future net receipts of the enterprise. The contribution would be made at the same time the investment was undertaken. In contrast, the full-loss-offset system with economic-life depreciation would spread the Government's contribution out over the life of the investment, and would require the firm to carry a larger debt and interest cost until this contribution was finally received.[13]

In the above passage, the author is describing the tax effect when the cost of an asset can be spread (or recovered) over a shorter period than its economic life or, in the extreme case, be immediately deducted in computing taxable income. By shortening the period during which an asset's cost can be recovered, the present value of the tax savings is increased. For example, assume an asset used in business has an economic life of 10 years. The cost of the asset is 10,000*u*. If the asset is depreciated over its economic life of 10 years, using straight line depreciation, and a tax rate of 40 percent, the taxpayer would have 1000*u* of depreciation each year for 10 years. This would save 400*u* in taxes each year for 10 years. Using a discount rate of six percent, the present value of 400*u* each year (beginning with the current year) for 10 years would be 3120.68*u*.

If, however, the asset can be depreciated over four years, then the taxpayer would have 2500*u* of depreciation each year for four years. This would save 1000*u* in taxes each year for four years. Using a discount rate of six percent, the present value of 1000*u* each year (beginning with the current year) for four years would be 3673.01*u*, which is greater than the present value of the tax savings if the asset were depreciated over 10 years. This difference in present value is what Cary Brown is referring to when he states that "the present worth of the tax rebates from the depreciation increases as the rebates are shifted closer to the present."[14]

If the cost of an asset can be deducted immediately, or "expensed," the amount of tax saved is equal to the tax rate times the cost of the asset. In the above example, if the asset's cost of 10,000*u* could be deducted immediately, the taxpayer would save an immediate 4000*u* in taxes. Of course, the present value of the tax savings would also be 4000*u* because of the immediate deduction.

The taxpayer could take this immediate tax savings and invest it. If this additional 4000*u* capital investment could also be deducted, the taxpayer would save another 1600*u* in taxes, which could be invested in another deductible capital investment. By expensing the cost of the investment, the investor can increase the investment to $I/(1-t)$, where I is the amount of income to be invested and t is the tax rate. In this case, it would be $10{,}000u/(1-0.40)$ equaling 16,667*u*.

---

[13] See Cary Brown, *supra* note 4, at 309–310.

[14] See *id.*

III. Investment Incentives Returned to Pretax Level

Expensing, or immediate deduction of an expenditure, is the classic situation to which the Cary Brown model has been applied.[15] Taking the above analysis one step further, expensing the cost of an asset is equivalent to exempting from income the future annual return on the asset. This is what Cary Brown is referring to when he states that "[i]nvestment incentives would be restored to the pretax level, since the tax would proportionately reduce both the prospective net receipts from investment and its cost."[16] To illustrate this equivalence in its most basic form, assume investor A has received 16,667*u* in salary income. Assume that A is subject to tax at a 40 percent tax rate and that any tax liability is due immediately. Also assume that A has three investment options. First, she can invest in a tax-free municipal bond paying 10 percent interest annually. Second, she can invest in a regular bond paying 10 percent interest annually. Finally, A can invest in a regular bond paying 10 percent interest annually, and the cost of the bond is immediately deductible, i.e., expensed.

Under the first option, investing in a tax-free municipal bond, A will only have 10,000 *u* to invest because she has to pay 6667*u* (40 percent multiplied by 16,667*u*) in taxes on her salary income of 16,667*u*. Using a rate of return of 10 percent annually, A will earn 1000*u* of tax-free interest income each year until maturity. At maturity, A will not recognize gain or loss because her basis in the bond is 10,000*u*.

Under the second option, investing in a regular bond, A again will only have 10,000*u* to invest because she must pay 6667*u* in taxes on her salary income of 16,667*u*. A will earn 1000*u* of interest income each year until maturity. At a 40 percent tax rate, A will pay 400*u* in taxes on the 1000*u* of interest income leaving A with 600*u* in cash. At maturity, A will not recognize gain or loss because her basis in the bond is 10,000*u*.

Under the third option, investing in a regular bond in which the investment is deductible, A will have 16,667*u* to invest because the amount is fully deductible. By investing 16,667*u* in a deductible bond, A can utilize the deduction to offset A's salary income of 16,667*u* leaving A with zero taxable income at the time of the original investment. A will earn 1667*u* in interest income each year until maturity (10 percent multiplied by 16,667*u*). At a 40 percent tax rate, A will pay 667*u* in taxes on the 1667*u* of interest income leaving A with 1000*u* in cash. By immediately deducting the cost of the bond, A will receive 1000*u* after-tax each year – the exact same position A would be in by investing in a tax-free municipal bond. When A collects 16,667*u* on the bond's maturity, A will have gain of 16,667*u*. At this time, A will owe taxes of 6667*u* (40 percent multiplied by 16,667*u*).

---

[15] For a thorough discussion of the Cary Brown model as it applies to expensing, see Calvin H. Johnson, "Soft Money Investing Under the Income Tax," 1989 *Ill. L. Rev.* 1019 (1990).

[16] See Cary Brown, *supra* note 4, at 309–310.

The following table summarizes the three options:

	Tax-exempt bond	Taxable bond	Deductible taxable bond
Gross income	16,667*u*	16,667*u*	16,667*u*
Deductions	0	0	16,667
Taxes (40%)	6667	6667	0
Cash to invest	10,000	10,000	16,667
Return at 10%	1000	1000	1667
Taxes (40%)	Exempt	400	667
Net return	1000	600	1000

By allowing A to deduct immediately the cost of the bond, the government, according to Cary Brown, "would literally be a partner in the firm."[17] According to the Cary Brown model, it is as if the government had contributed 6667*u* toward purchase of the bond. Because the government contributed this amount, which is 40 percent of the cost of the bond (6667/16,667), it seems only fair that the government collect 40 percent of the interest on the bond. As a result, the government will collect 667*u* of each interest payment on the entire investment (667/1667) and will recoup its "investment" when the bond matures (or is sold). At maturity, the investor will have gain of 16,667*u* resulting in taxes of 6667*u* assuming that the tax rate remains at 40 percent. The government will therefore receive 6667*u* in taxes from the investor, which is equal to the amount that the government originally "contributed."

By expensing the cost of the investment, the investor can increase the investment to $I/(1-t)$, where I is the amount of income to be invested and t is the tax rate. In the above example, the investor would only have 10,000*u* to invest if the investment were not deductible. By being allowed to immediately deduct the cost of the investment, the investor would have 16,667*u* to invest (10,000*u*/(1−0.40)). Another way of looking at this is that the investor can increase the amount to be invested by the tax savings generated by expensing the cost of the investment.

IV. Assumptions Underlying the Model

A number of assumptions or conditions must be made in order for the Cary Brown model to apply.[18] At first glance, these conditions appear to make the Cary Brown

[17] See *id.*

[18] See, e.g., Michael J. Graetz and Deborah H. Schenk, *Federal Income Taxation: Principles and Policies* 306–07 (1995); Michael J. Graetz, "Implementing a Progressive Consumption Tax," 92 Harv. L. Rev. 1575, 1602 (1979); Musgrave, *supra* note 8, at 262–67; Myron S. Scholes and Mark A. Wolfson, *Taxes and Business Strategy* (1992); Johnson, *supra* note 15 at 1031–1036; Shoup, *supra* note 8, at 266–69; Alvin C. Warren, "Accelerated Cost Recovery, Debt and Tax Arbitrage," 38 *Tax Law.* 549, 552 n. 12.

model very limited in scope. But this is very deceptive. The conditions are in some cases not unreasonable as a practical matter, and as a result, the Cary Brown model has a lot of practical application. In addition, even if some of the conditions are relaxed, much can still be learned by utilizing principles derived from the Cary Brown model.

The following list is taken from Professor Michael Graetz' excellent treatment of the subject in his textbook.[19] First, the applicable tax rates must remain constant. They can neither increase nor decrease over the time period in question. Second, interest rates must also remain constant. Like tax rates, they can neither increase nor decrease over time. Third, the deduction (or exclusion) must produce an immediate tax savings equal to the deduction (or exclusion) multiplied by the tax rate. This also means that the deduction must offset income from other sources and is not lost or delayed. In other words, the deduction results in an immediate tax benefit.

Fourth, taxpayers must be concerned with their after-tax position and can invest the tax savings from the deduction at a rate of return equal to the original investment. The opportunities for investment at the original rate of return are assumed to be unlimited. Fifth, "where borrowing is involved (again with constant tax and interest rates), the equivalence would hold only if the ratio of borrowing to after-tax investment were the same under a yield exemption and an immediate deduction. If speculative investment opportunities (or borrowing opportunities) were limited, after-tax differences between winning and losing taxpayers would be lessened under the immediate deduction method."[20] Sixth, "the system must be closed. Tax is collected at an identical rate on the earnings from an asset immediately deducted and on amounts received at the close of the transaction (whether by the disposition of the asset or by some other event, such as the taxpayer's death."[21]

---

[19] See Graetz and Schenk, *supra* note 18, at 306–07. [20] See *id.* at 307. [21] *Id.*

Chapter 3

Interpretations of the Cary Brown Model

I. Introduction

Probably, the most widely accepted interpretation of the Cary Brown model today is that immediately deducting (or expensing) the cost of an asset is equivalent to excluding (or exempting) the future annual return of the asset from income.[1] Although Cary Brown's article does not state the model in these exact words, this is

[1] See, e.g., William D. Andrews, "A Consumption-Type or Cash Flow Personal Income Tax," 87 *Harv. L. Rev.* 1113, 1126 (1974) ("[W]here rates are constant, deferring the tax is the equivalent of imposing the tax initially, but exempting any subsequent profit due to continued investment of what is left after payment of the tax."); Martin D. Ginsburg, "Teaching Tax Law After Tax Reform," 65 *Wash. L. Rev.* 595, 604 (1990) ("Assuming stability of tax rates and investment yields, deduction at initiation of the cost of an investment is the equivalent of excluding from gross income the taxpayer's future annual return on her investment."); Michael J. Graetz and Deborah H. Schenk, *Federal Income Taxation: Principles and Policies* at 304 (1995) ("The tax savings that occur when the cost of an investment is immediately deductible, under certain conditions, can be described as equivalent to disallowing the deduction initially but exempting from tax the income from the investment."); Jane C. Gravelle, "The Economics of Taxing Capital Income" in *Tax Conversations: A Guide to the Key Issues in the Tax Reform Debate* 223, 241 (1997) ("Early on, it was recognized, for example, that deducting the cost of an investment when purchased eliminated any tax on the investment."); Daniel I. Halperin, "The Time Value of Money – 1984," 23 *Tax Notes* 751, 752 (14 May 1984) ("The concept that deferral is equivalent to immediate taxation accompanied by the avoidance of tax on the continued investment of the after-tax earnings ... "); Calvin H. Johnson, "Soft Money Investing Under the Income Tax," 1989 *Ill. L. Rev.* 1019, 1022 ("Under the Cary Brown thesis, the ability to make an investment with untaxed soft money is usually as valuable as exempting subsequent investment income from tax."); Richard A. Musgrave, "Clarifying Tax Reform," 70 *Tax Notes* 731, 735 (5 February 1996) ("By allowing immediate deduction of the investment cost against other income, the government in effect renders an interest-free loan to the investor. In the course of continuous reinvestment, this loan will generate an income stream the present value of which, after tax, equals the tax on the normal return on the initial investment."); Carl S. Shoup, *Public Finance* at 302 n. 20 (1969) ("The fact that completely accelerated depreciation, when coupled with complete loss offset, is equivalent to exemption of net return from the asset, under an income tax, was discovered by E. Cary Brown."); C. Eugene Steuerle, "Zero Tax Rates on Returns to New Investment & Learning," 72 *Tax Notes* 1311 (2 September 1996) ("If tax rates are constant throughout time – admittedly a strong assumption – pure *ex ante* and pure *ex post* taxes leave the taxpayer in exactly the same position when all is said and done."); Alvin C. Warren, Jr., "Accelerated Capital Recovery, Debt, and Tax Arbitrage," 38 *Tax Law.* 549, 551 (1985) ("An immediate deduction for the cost of a capital asset, which is often called expensing, can produce the same results as exempting the income produced by the asset under certain conditions ... .").

the generally accepted interpretation. Some alternative descriptions of the Cary Brown model have also been used over the years.[2] Many of these alternatives are really nothing more than restating the currently accepted interpretation in slightly different words. For example, the U.S. Treasury Department in 1970 stated that "permitting the capital cost of an asset to be expensed has the effect of exempting the income from ownership of the asset from taxation."[3] This appears to be substantively the same as the general accepted interpretation.

II. Professor Surrey's Explanations of Tax Deferral and the Cary Brown Model

A. *Introduction*

Professor Surrey, in his brilliant 1973 book *Pathways to Tax Reform*, has written a number of slightly different interpretations (focusing more on tax deferral rather than specifically the Cary Brown model) that are still extremely useful in terms of understanding the Cary Brown model. These interpretations include: (1) expensing the cost of an asset is analogous to an interest-free, non-recourse loan without collateral from the U.S. Treasury to the taxpayer;[4] (2) "the *exclusion* from tax of a percentage of a given amount of income provides the same benefit as deferring the tax on that income," with the particular percentage depending on the taxpayer's marginal tax rate, rate of return on investments, and period of deferral;[5] (3) "the *after-tax* rate of profit on what is *left at risk* under the tax expenditure of immediate deduction and deferral of tax is equal to the *before-tax* rate of profit *on the entire investment* as counted under financial accounting;"[6] (4) "immediate expensing of an investment is the equivalent of allowing the investor a tax-free return of the income yield from what he has left at risk in the venture – his initial investment less the tax benefit of its write-off through the immediate deduction;"[7] (5) "permitting the capital cost of an asset to be expensed has the effect of exempting the income from ownership of the asset from taxation;"[8] and (6) reinvesting the total tax savings from immediately deducting the cost of an asset will be equivalent to full exemption of the entire income from the original investment.[9] The first three interpretations are important steps in

[2] See Stanley S. Surrey, *Pathways to Tax Reform* 120–25 (1973).

[3] United States Department of the Treasury, *Treasury Department Study on Tax Depreciation Policy* (1970) at 116 Cong. Rec. 25, 684–25, 695.

[4] See Surrey, Pathways, *supra* note 2, at 109–10, 120. Professor Surrey gives the following example: the immediate deduction of $100 gives A an immediate tax savings of $60 (using a 60 percent tax rate). The $60 tax will be postponed until the asset is sold. One way to describe the result is to say that the Government has made a loan of $60 to A without asking for interest, collateral, or a definite time for payment of the loan, since it will wait until A decides to sell the asset. The higher A's tax bracket, the larger the interest-free loan. See Surrey, Pathways, *supra* note 2, at 120.

[5] See Surrey, Pathways, *supra* note 2, at 121.

[6] See *id.* at 121–22.

[7] *Id.* at 122–23.

[8] *Id.* at 123.

[9] *Id.* at 123–24.

thoroughly understanding the Cary Brown model. Interpretations four and five are the Cary Brown model while interpretation six is a slight variation on the model.

B. Interest-free Non-recourse Loan Analogy

Professor Surrey's first interpretation of expensing, analogizing it to an interest-free non-recourse loan, is not an interpretation of the Cary Brown model. It is, however, an important first step in thoroughly understanding the model because it demonstrates the role of the Government when expensing takes place. Assume investor A has received 16,667*u* in salary income. Assume that A is subject to tax at a 40 percent tax rate and that any tax liability is due immediately. Also assume that A has three investment options. First, she can invest in a tax-free municipal bond paying 10 percent interest annually. Second, she can invest in a regular bond paying 10 percent interest annually. Finally, A can invest in a regular bond paying 10 percent interest annually, and the cost of the bond is immediately deductible, i.e., expensed.

Investor A selects the third option and therefore immediately deducts the cost of the bond. A will hold the bond for 10 years, at which time A will sell it for 16,667*u*. Under the third option, investing in a regular bond in which the investment is deductible, A will have 16,667*u* to invest because the amount is fully deductible. By investing 16,667*u* in a deductible bond, A can utilize the deduction to offset A's salary income of 16,667*u* leaving A with zero taxable income at the time of the original investment.

This immediate deduction of 16,667*u* gives A an immediate tax savings of 6667*u* (16,667*u* multiplied by 40 percent).[10] The tax saved of 6667*u* will be deferred until the asset is sold after ten years (again assuming it is sold for 16,667*u* or more).[11] Professor Surrey states that one can say that "the Government has made a loan of [6667*u*] to A without asking for interest, collateral, or a definite time of payment of the loan, since it will wait until A decides to sell the asset. The higher A's tax bracket, the larger the interest-free loan."[12] If, for example, A were in the 50 percent tax bracket, then the amount of the "loan" from the Government would be 8333*u* (16,667*u* multiplied by 50 percent).

How much of a tax benefit does A receive from the 6667*u* "loan" from the Government? If a bank were to charge A 10 percent interest annually on a 6667*u* loan, then A saves 667*u* in interest payments less the benefit of the tax savings from the 667*u* interest deduction (667*u* multiplied by assumed 40 percent tax rate), for a total net savings each year of 400*u*. Over 10 years, this results in a total savings of 4000*u*. Using an after-tax discount rate of six percent (if A can borrow at a 10 percent pre-tax rate from a bank), the present value of the total savings of 4000*u* is 3120.68*u*.[13] This amount represents the savings to A from

---

10 *Id.* at 120. 11 *Id.* 12 *Id.*

13 The first 400*u* net savings is not discounted because it is assumed to have immediately taken place, giving A an immediate 400*u* net savings. The remaining nine payments are discounted back to present day at a six percent after-tax rate of return.

deducting the cost of the investment in the first year instead of in the tenth year, where it would normally be deducted as a reduction in the amount of gain on the sale.[14] In other words, A would be willing to pay 3120.68*u* to get this interest-free loan so that she could make the 10 percent pre-tax rate of return on her investment.[15]

C. Percentage Exclusion Analogy

Professor Surrey has also analogized deferral of tax on income to excluding a percentage of that income.[16] This second interpretation of tax deferral, is also not a demonstration of the Cary Brown model. But it is an excellent second step (after the first step of non-interest bearing, non-recourse loan analogy) in understanding the Cary Brown model. It begins to demonstrate the linkage between deferral of income and exclusion of income, which is one of the keys to understanding the Cary Brown model.

The percentage of exclusion depends on the taxpayer's marginal tax rate, the expected rate of return on investments, and the length of deferral.[17] Assume Investor A's marginal tax rate is 40 percent and the pre-tax expected rate of return on investments is 10 percent. If A has 16,667*u* of income, then deferring the tax on that income for 10 years is equivalent to excluding approximately 44 percent of the 16,667*u* of income. The exclusion percentage is calculated as follows: the tax on 16,667*u* of income at a 40 percent marginal tax rate is 6667*u*. If this amount of tax can be deferred for 10 years, then A will only need to set aside an amount today that will grow to 6667*u* in 10 years to fund the tax liability. If A sets aside 3723*u* today, it will grow to 6667*u* in 10 years at an after-tax rate of return of six percent. In other words, 3723*u* is the present value of 6667*u* discounted at six percent for 10 years.

By only having to set aside 3723*u* today, A is saving 2944*u* in taxes (6667*u* minus 3723*u*). This is equivalent to excluding an amount of income that saves 2944*u* in taxes. The amount of the exclusion of income is 7360*u* (2944*u* in taxes saved divided by the marginal tax rate of 40 percent). The excluded amount of 7360*u* represents 44 percent of the 16,667*u* of income (7360*u* divided by 16,667*u*).

If the length of deferral were for 20 years, then the exclusion percentage rises to 69 percent. In other words, A would be indifferent between a proposal deferring the tax on 16,667*u* of income for twenty years and a proposal excluding 69 percent of the 16,667*u* of income.[18]

---

[14] See Surrey Pathways, *supra* note 2, at 120–21. If the investment in the bond were capitalized and not deducted, A would have a basis in the bond of 16,667*u*. I.R.C. sections 1011(a), 1012. When A sells the bond for 16,667*u* in year ten, A would have no gain and therefore no tax liability to the Government. The basis, in essence, is equivalent to a deduction in year ten, the time of disposition.

[15] See *id.* at 120–21. [16] *Id.* at 121. [17] *Id.* [18] *Id.*

D. After-tax Rate of Profit on Remainder/Before-tax Rate of Profit on Entire Amount

Under this third alternative, Professor Surrey writes "the *after-tax* rate of profit on what is *left at risk* under the tax expenditure of immediate deduction and deferral of tax is equal to the *before-tax* rate of profit *on the entire investment* as counted under financial accounting."[19] Assume investor A sells the bond (she originally bought for 16,667*u*) at the end of 10 years for 25,000*u*. If A originally capitalized the cost of the bond, A will have a profit or gain of 8333.33*u* on the sale, giving A a 50 percent before-tax profit (8333.33*u* divided by 16,667*u*). She would then owe 3333.33*u* in taxes to the Government on the sale (8333.33*u* gain multiplied by 40 percent). A would therefore have an after-tax profit of 5000*u* (25,000*u* sales proceeds less 3333.33*u* in taxes less 16,667*u* investment) on a 16,667*u* investment, resulting in an after-tax profit of 30 percent.

If the Government permitted A to immediately deduct the 16,667*u* investment, then A will have 25,000*u* of gain on disposition in year ten, resulting in taxes of 10,000*u* (25,000*u* gain multiplied by 40 percent). A will be left with 15,000*u*. A, however, in essence, only invested 10,000*u* in year one because the Government, by permitting her to immediately deduct the entire investment, contributed 6667*u* towards the investment. Therefore, A has profited 5000*u* (25,000*u* sales proceeds less 10,000*u* of taxes less 10,000*u* initial investment) on a 10,000*u* investment, or an after-tax profit of 50 percent. As a result, A's after-tax profit on the 10,000*u* investment is equal to the before-tax profit on the entire 16,667*u* overall investment.[20]

Another way of viewing A in the above example, is to consider the Government a partner with A in the overall investment of 16,667*u*. A has contributed 10,000*u* towards the investment and the Government has contributed 6667*u* by allowing A to immediately deduct the cost of the overall investment of 16,667*u*. When the investment is sold for 25,000*u* in year ten, A receives 60 percent or 15,000*u* because A is a 60 percent partner. The Government receives 40 percent of 10,000*u* because it is a 40 percent partner. A has made a profit of 5000*u*, resulting in an after-tax rate of profit of 50 percent on A's investment of 10,000*u*.[21] This rate is equal to the 50 percent before-tax rate of profit on the entire overall investment of 16,667*u*.

As with Professor Surrey's first two interpretations of tax deferral, this third interpretation is technically not the Cary Brown model (at least it is not interpreted as such). But, as with the first two interpretations, it is an excellent additional step in

[19] *Id.* at 121.

[20] If the gain on the sale is subject to preferential tax treatment (i.e., capital gain), then the combination of expensing and capital gain tax preference can result in the investor having an after-tax rate of profit on what is left at risk under the tax expenditure of immediate deduction and deferral of tax greater than his before-tax rate of profit on the entire investment. For example, if the gain on sale of the bond were capital gain and subject to a 50 percent capital gains preference (i.e., only 50 percent of the gain were taxable), then the before-tax rate of profit on the entire investment of 16,667*u* would remain at 50 percent. But the after-tax rate of profit would increase from 30 percent to 40 percent. The after-tax rate of profit on the 10,000*u* that A, in essence, invested, would increase from 50 percent to 100 percent. *Id.* at 323.

[21] *Id.* at 323.

understanding the model. This third interpretation introduces the linkage between before-tax rates of return and after-tax rates of return, which is crucial in understanding the Cary Brown model.

E. Yield Exemption Analogy[22]

Under this interpretation, which is the generally accepted interpretation of the Cary Brown model,[23] Professor Surrey writes "that the immediate expensing of an investment is the equivalent of allowing the investor a tax-free return of the income yield from what he has left at risk in the venture – his initial investment less the tax benefit of its write-off through the immediate deduction."[24]

The yield exemption analogy has previously been thoroughly demonstrated in Chapter 2 and will only briefly be repeated. Assume investor A has received 16,667*u* in salary income. A is subject to tax at a 40 percent tax rate and any tax liability is due immediately. A has three investment options. First, she can invest in a tax-free municipal bond paying ten percent interest annually. Second, she can invest in a regular bond paying 10 percent interest annually. Finally, A can invest in a regular bond paying 10 percent interest annually, and the cost of the bond is immediately deductible, i.e., expensed.

Under the first option, investing in a tax-free municipal bond, A will only have 10,000*u* to invest because she has to pay 6667*u* (40 percent multiplied by 16,667*u*) in taxes on her salary income of 16,667*u*. Using a rate of return of 10 percent annually, A will earn 1000*u* of tax-free interest income each year until maturity. At maturity, A will not recognize gain or loss because her basis in the bond is 10,000*u*.

Under the second option, investing in a regular bond, A again will only have 10,000*u* to invest because she must pay 6667*u* in taxes on her salary income of 16,667*u*. A will earn 1000*u* of interest income each year until maturity. At a 40 percent tax rate, A will pay 400*u* in taxes on the 1000*u* of interest income leaving A with 600*u* in cash. At maturity, A will not recognize gain or loss because her basis in the bond is 10,000*u*.

Under the third option, investing in a regular bond in which the investment is deductible, A will have 16,667*u* to invest because the amount is fully deductible. By investing 16,667*u* in a deductible bond, A can utilize the deduction to offset A's salary income of 16,667*u* leaving A with zero taxable income at the time of the original investment. A will earn 1667*u* in interest income each year until maturity (10 percent multiplied by 16,667*u*). At a 40 percent tax rate, A will pay 667*u* in taxes on the 1667*u* of interest income leaving A with 1000*u* in cash. By immediately deducting the cost of the bond, A will receive 1000*u* after-tax each year – the exact same position A would be in by investing in a tax-free municipal bond. When A

---

22 See discussion at chapter two, which describes in greater detail what Professor Surrey refers to as the yield exemption analogy.

23 Professor Surrey seemed to agree that this interpretation is the Cary Brown model as he cites for authority Professor Shoup who in turn cites Professor Brown's article. *Id.* at 122–23.

24 *Id.* at 122.

collects 16,667*u* on the bond's maturity, A will have gain of 16,667*u*. At this time, A will owe taxes of 6667*u* (40 percent multiplied by 16,667*u*).

In the example, under option three (the deductible bond), A receives an after-tax rate of return of 10 percent each year (1000*u* divided by 10,000*u*) based on the 10,000*u* that A actually contributed towards the investment (the remaining 6667*u* is treated as being contributed by the Government). As a result, A's after-tax rate of return is the same percentage rate of return as if (1) no income tax was imposed and (2) A had financed the entire 16,667*u* investment itself keeping the entire cash flow.[25] In other words, A's after-tax rate of return of 10 percent on the 10,000*u* investment is the same as A's before-tax rate of return of 10 percent on the entire investment of 16,667*u*.

F. Exempting the Income from the Asset from Taxation

In 1970, the Treasury Department in its study on tax depreciation policy stated that "permitting the capital cost of an asset to be expensed has the effect of exempting the income from ownership of the asset from taxation."[26] The Treasury Department's description is almost identical to the previous interpretation, a fact Professor Surrey recognizes.[27] The Treasury Department gives the following example and explanation:

> An intuitive explanation of this somewhat surprising result takes the following form: a $1,000 asset will generate some stream of revenue over its life; if the cost is expensed and the tax rate is 48 percent, the net cost of the asset to the owner (ignoring the slight discount of the deduction as above) is only $520, after tax. However, in the future, each $1 of revenue will be taxed fully, with no allowance for depreciation, leaving $0.52 of net return on the $520 investment, the same ratio as $1 to $1,000 as if there were no tax.
>
> Incidentally, in those cases, as in minerals taxation, where the total *present value* of expensing and depletion deductions may actually exceed the cost of the investment, the effective tax rate is negative. That is, in some instances the tax rate equivalent of an investment tax incentive is a tax rate less than zero.[28]

G. Reinvesting Tax Savings

Professor Surrey writes that "if a person reinvests the total tax savings from immediately deducting the cost of an asset, then this will be equivalent to *full exemption* of the entire income from the original investment."[29] The reinvestment of tax savings analogy has previously been thoroughly demonstrated in Chapter 2 and will not be

[25] *Id.* at 122; Shoup, *supra* note 1, at 302.

[26] See Surrey, Pathways, *supra* note 2, at 123 (citing to the 1970 Treasury Department Study on Tax Depreciation Policy).

[27] *Id.* at 124–25. [28] *Id.* at 123. [29] *Id.* at 123.

discussed in detail again. Very briefly, by expensing the cost of the investment, the investor can increase the investment to $I/(1-t)$, where I is the amount of income to be invested and t is the tax rate. In the above example involving investor A and the three options in buying a bond, A would only have 10,000*u* to invest if the investment in the bond were not deductible (because A would owe taxes of 6667*u* on the income of 16,667*u*). By being allowed to immediately deduct the cost of the investment (bond), A would have 16,667*u* to invest (10,000*u*/(1 − 0.40)).[30] In other words, the investor can increase the amount to be invested by the tax savings generated by expensing the cost of the investment.

Professor Surrey writes that "assuming A can reinvest his repayments of cost [tax savings from the expensings], with similar expensing of the reinvestments, A is indifferent to whether he is offered (1) *full exemption* from income tax on his initial investment or (2) a *deferral of tax* on a total sum invested (an immediate expensing of that sum) that would leave him with an amount of *his* money at risk equal to that initial investment."[31]

III. Some Additional Interpretations of Tax Deferral and the Cary Brown Model

A. *Professor William Andrews*

In 1974, in one of the finest articles ever written in the American tax law literature, Harvard law professor William Andrews discussed adoption of a consumption-type or cash flow personal income tax.[32] In the article, he discussed the value of tax deferral and wrote that "sometimes it has been thought that mere deferral of income was not of great importance so long as every element of accretion was eventually accounted for."[33] But he then states that in more recent times, "[s]ophisticated taxpayers and their counsel, however, have realized that deferral is often of immense importance, and recent writings on matters of tax policy have come to reflect that realization."[34] Professor Andrews further notes that "[s]ome appreciation of the value of deferral is essential for an understanding of the argument in this Article [focusing on implementing a cash flow personal income tax] because the difference between accretion and consumption ideals is essentially one of deferral, and because the defects in present law that make it an unacceptable hybrid arise from inconsistencies in matters of timing."[35]

[30] An alternative way of looking at this is to have A pay 6667*u* of taxes on his income of 16,667*u*, leaving A with 10,000*u* to invest. If this investment is deductible, A will save 4000*u* in taxes which he can reinvest in the same type of deductible investment. This will save A another 1600*u* in taxes which he can reinvest again in the same type of deductible investment. This will save A another 640*u* in taxes and so on. This will continue and ultimately A will have invested a total of 16,667*u*. *Id.* at 123–24.

[31] *Id.* at 124.

[32] See William D. Andrews, "A Consumption-Type or Cash Flow Personal Income Tax," 87 *Harv. L. Rev.* 1113 (1974).

[33] *Id.* at 1123. [34] *Id.* [35] *Id.* at 1123–24.

Professor Andrews discusses the importance of tax deferral even if tax rates remain constant and tax exemption never takes place: "mere deferral can be immensely important. Deferral reduces the burden of a tax because of the time value of money; it requires less than a dollar put aside today to meet a dollar of tax liability in the future."[36]

Professor Andrews gives four examples of the value of tax deferral. In the first example, he discusses a fruit farmer who grows fruit on 100 trees. The farmer is subject to tax on the trees and a tax on the fruit. A 30 percent tax on the 100 trees, when they reach maturity, would leave the fruit farmer with 70 trees. A 30 percent tax on the fruit of those trees would leave the farmer with fruit from 49 trees. If, however, the fruit farmer could defer paying the 30 percent tax on the trees until the trees were disposed of at some point in the future then only the 30 percent tax on the fruit would apply to the fruit of 100 trees leaving the farmer with the fruit of 70 trees. This second result is the same result as taxing the fruit farmer on the 100 trees when they reach maturity but not taxing the fruit. In that case, the farmer would have the fruit of 70 trees.

In the second example, Professor Andrews describes the effect of one dollar set aside for retirement. At 9 percent compound interest, one dollar will grow to $8 in 24 years. If a 33 percent accretion-type tax is imposed on the one dollar and on the return on the one dollar, then only 67 cents is left to invest. At 6 percent compound interest for 24 years, it will grow to $2.67. If the tax were deferred until the end of 24 years, then the one dollar would grow to $8 and then be subject to a 33 percent tax, leaving $5.33 to spend. This second result of $5.33 is the same result as taxing the one dollar initially, leaving 67 cents, but exempting the return on the 67 cents.

In the third example, Professor Andrews analyses dividends on securities. Assume that securities have doubled in value and the taxpayer lives on the dividend income from the securities. At a 60 percent tax rate, the taxpayer will be left with 40 cents out of each dollar of pretax dividend income. This is assuming that the tax on the appreciation is deferred. If, however, the appreciation is immediately taxed at 60 percent, then 30 percent of the taxpayer's capital would be used to pay the tax. The amount of dividends would then be 70 percent of the original pretax dividend amount. A tax of 60 percent on the remaining dividend income would leave 28 cents for each dollar of original yield before the imposition of any taxes. Therefore, "[d]eferral of tax on the gain is the equivalent of exempting dividends on the gain which would have been left had the tax been imposed initially."[37]

The fourth example is when Professor Andrews refers to the Cary Brown model even though the previous three examples are also presumably applications of the model. Assume a taxpayer invests $100 so that revenues will be increased by $400 in a later year, leaving a pre-tax profit of 300 percent. If the investment is not deductible, there will be income of $300 in the later year ($400 revenue minus $100 investment). At a 40 percent tax rate, the taxes will be $120 reducing the proceeds to $280. The profit rate is reduced from 300 percent (pre-tax) to 180 percent (after-tax).

---

[36] *Id.* at 1124.

[37] *Id.* at 1125–26.

If the investment is deductible when made, then there will be $400 of income in the later year ($400 revenues minus zero investment). At a 40 percent tax rate, the taxes will be $160 leaving the taxpayer with $240. Because the investment was deductible when made, it really represented an after-tax expenditure of only $60, not $100. An after-tax return of $240 on an after-tax investment of $60 still represents $180 of profit. But $180 of profit on a $60 after-tax investment is a 300 percent profit, just as if no taxes had been in effect.

Professor Andrews states that "[a] study of these examples will reveal a simple but accurate relation: *where rates are constant, deferring the tax is the equivalent of imposing the tax initially, but exempting any subsequent profit due to continued investment of what is left after payment of the tax* (emphasis added)." This is his interpretation of the Cary Brown model.

Professor Andrews concludes that "[i]f only part of the original investment is deductible, the taxpayer's rate of return will be reduced by the tax but by less than the nominal rate of tax. On the other hand, if the taxpayer is able to deduct more than the amount of his original investment, even though it is all taken back into taxable income on liquidation, the effect will be that his rate of return on net investment will be *more* than it is in the absence of tax. This is essentially what is involved in leveraged tax shelter investments where a taxpayer is permitted to deduct capital expenditures paid for by lenders as well as himself."[38]

B. Blueprints for Basic Tax Reform

In 1977, the U.S. Treasury Department published a comprehensive study of the United States tax system and made a number of recommendations for a complete overhaul of the system. The small paperback book was titled *Blueprints for Basic Tax Reform*, and it remains one of the great books published on the U.S. tax system.

The U.S. Treasury Department discussed the Cary Brown model without actually mentioning it in its discussion of unrealized appreciation on property.[39] Treasury was concerned about the tax deferral that occurred with respect to unrealized appreciation on capital assets. The gain would not be triggered until a realization event, such as a sale, took place. This is an application of the Cary Brown model, which provides that immediately deducting the cost of an asset or initially excluding the gain in an asset is equivalent to exempting from gross income the future annual return on the asset or on the appreciation.[40] Treasury discussed the obvious solution of accrual taxation but recognized many of the problems associated with it.[41] As a result, Treasury proposed a fairly new concept: charging interest on the tax deferred

[38] *Id.* at 1127–28.

[39] See David F. Bradford and the U.S. Treasury Tax Policy Staff, *Blueprints for Basic Tax Reform* (2d ed., 1984) at 69, 74.

[40] In the next chapter, unrealized appreciation will be discussed in great detail. It will be demonstrated that unrealized appreciation is equivalent to having funds set aside in a qualified plan. It will be an example of what is referred to as the Super Cary Brown model.

[41] See Blueprints, *supra* note 39, at 73–74.

because of the realization requirement. The Treasury wrote:

> An alternative method that attempts to achieve the same economic effect as accrual taxation is taxation of capital gains at realization with an interest charge for deferral. But, in addition to the present complex rules defining realizations that would not be avoided in the model tax plan, rules would be required for the computation of interest on the deferred taxes. An appropriate rate of interest would have to be determined and some assumption made about the "typical" pattern of accruals. In order to eliminate economic inefficiency, the interest rate on the deferral should be the individual taxpayer's rate of return on his investments. However, because it is impossible to administer a program based on each investor's marginal rate of return, the government would have to charge a single rate of interest. The single interest rate would itself tend to move alternatives away from neutrality. Moreover, for simplicity, it would have to be assumed that the gain occurred equally over the period or that the asset's value changed at a constant rate. This assumption would be particularly inappropriate in those cases where basis was changed frequently by inflation adjustments, depreciation allowances, capital improvements, etc. Because a simple time pattern of value change would reflect reality in very few cases, the deferral charge would introduce additional investment distortions. To the extent that gains occur early in the holding period, capital gains would be undertaxed; when gains occur late in the period, capital gains would be overtaxed.[42]

C. The Meade Committee Report

In 1978, a committee established by the Institute of Fiscal Studies published a comprehensive study of the United Kingdom tax system and made a number of recommendations for a complete overhaul of the system. This large hardback book was titled *The Structure and Reform of Direct Taxation* and it remains one of the great books published on tax laws, not just the U.K. tax system. It is generally referred to as the Meade Committee Report, the committee having been chaired by Professor J.E. Meade.

The Meade Committee discusses the Cary Brown model without actually mentioning the model by name. The Committee discusses the model in its comparison of an income tax and an expenditure (or consumption) tax. It writes that "[a] basic difference between an income tax base and a consumption expenditure base for personal taxation is to be found in their effects upon the return to the taxpayer's savings."[43] The Committee illustrates this with an example using an individual named coincidentally (?) Mr. Brown. The Committee writes:

> Assume Mr. Brown has earned £150 and that there is a tax either (i) on his income, or (ii) on his expenditure on consumption. We illustrate this with tax at a (tax-inclusive) rate of 33 1/3 percent... and at a (tax-inclusive) rate of

---

[42] See *id.* at 74.

[43] See Institute for Fiscal Studies, *The Structure and Reform of Direct Taxation: Report of a Committee Chaired by Professor J.E. Meade* (1978) at 35.

> 50 percent.... We assume that Mr. Brown can invest any savings which he makes in machinery or some other form of physical investment which produces a return of 10 percent on the investment. [W]ith a 33 1/3 percent tax rate, under the income tax (IT) regime Mr. Brown has the choice of spending on consumption either a single lump sum of £100 or £6 2/3 a year thereafter, and under the expenditure tax (ET) regime a choice of spending on consumption either a single lump sum of £100 or £10 a year thereafter. Thus if Mr. Brown decides to save rather than to spend, he will obtain a return of only 6 2/3 percent on his postponed consumption under the income tax regime but a full 10 percent on his postponed consumption under an expenditure tax regime.[44]

The Committee notes that if the tax rate is increased to 50 percent, then Mr. Brown can only obtain a five percent rate of return on his postponed consumption under an income tax regime. Under the expenditure tax regime, he can still obtain the full 10 percent rate of return. As a result, the higher tax rate results in a lower level of consumption under an expenditure tax but the rate of return on postponed consumption remains at 10 percent. Under the income tax, however, the higher rate of tax results in a lower level of consumption *and* a lower rate of return on any postponed consumption.

The Committee concludes:

> It is indeed the characteristic feature of an expenditure tax as contrasted with an income tax that, at any given constant rate of tax, the former will make the rate of return to the saver on his reduced consumption equal to the rate of return which can be earned on the investment which his savings finances, whereas the income tax will reduce the rate of return to the saver below the rate of return which the investment will yield.[45]

D. Treasury I

In his 1984 State of the Union Address, President Ronald Reagan directed the U.S. Treasury Department to study the U.S. tax system and make recommendation for a complete overhaul of the system. Similar in some respects to the Shoup Mission, some of the top American tax scholars were assembled by Treasury Secretary Donald T. Regan to design a sweeping and comprehensive reform of the U.S. income tax system. The Treasury Department released its report, titled *Tax Reform for Fairness, Simplicity, and Economic Growth*, in November 1984. This report is commonly referred to as *Treasury I.*

In Treasury I, the Treasury Department described tax deferral as the "Federal Government effectively provid[ing] to the taxpayer an interest-free loan equal to the deferred tax liability. The value of tax deferral is greater, the longer the deferral and the higher the taxpayer's marginal tax rate."[46] The Treasury then provided the

[44] See *id.* at 35–37. [45] *Id.* at 37.

[46] See United States Department of the Treasury, *Tax Reform for Fairness, Simplicity and Economic Growth* (November 1984) at 126.

following chart showing the effective tax rate per dollar of income deferred by a taxpayer in the 50 percent marginal tax bracket.[47]

Interest rate (percent)	Deferral period (in years)					
	1	3	5	10	20	30
4	48.1	44.4	41.1	33.8	22.8	15.4
6	47.2	41.0	37.4	27.9	15.6	8.7
8	46.3	39.7	34.0	23.2	10.7	5.0
10	45.4	37.6	31.0	19.3	7.4	2.9
12	44.6	35.6	28.4	16.1	5.2	1.7

As the chart demonstrates, at a six percent interest rate, a 10 year deferral period effectively reduces a 50 percent marginal tax rate to only 27.9 percent. If the interest rate is 12 percent and the deferral period is 30 years, then a 50 percent marginal tax rate is effectively reduced to 1.7 percent, almost complete exclusion.

In its report, Treasury discussed tax deferral in a number of areas in the U.S. income tax system. One area related to installment sales. Treasury wrote: "Charging interest on the amount of the deferred tax liability for taxpayers electing the installment method would make the tax law neutral as to the financing of property sales and would end use of installment sales as a vehicle for tax deferral."[48] But Treasury went on to conclude that it "does not propose charging interest on installment sales, however, because of the increased complexity and taxpayer perception problems that such an approach would create. Most taxpayers would not readily comprehend why they should pay interest on the deferred taxes when the taxes are only paid as installment payments are received."[49]

E. Professor Daniel Halperin

In 1986, in a landmark article possibly equal in importance to Professor Andrews' 1974 Harvard Law Review article, Harvard law professor Daniel Halperin discussed the Cary Brown model as "deferral [being] equivalent to exemption of investment income."[50] He acknowledges Professor Andrews' article as leading toward the analysis in his article.[51]

Professor Halperin believes that in analysing transactions dealing with the time value of money aspect of tax deferral, it is important to tax the investment income

47 See *id.* at 127. 48 See *id.* at 129. 49 *Id.*

50 See Daniel I. Halperin, "Interest in Disguise: Taxing the 'Time Value of Money,' " 95 *Yale L. J.* 506, 519 (1986). Professor Halperin also wrote another brilliant article on tax deferral in 1984, that was a preview of his Yale Law Journal article. See Daniel I. Halperin, "The Time Value of Money – 1984," 23 *Tax Notes* 751 (14 May 1984).

51 See Halperin, *supra* note 50, at 519, n. 47.

from these transactions, which are, in essence, disguised loans. He states that there are three methods to achieve this result: (1) direct taxation in which the investment income is taxed directly by taxing the imputed interest on the loans; (2) indirect taxation in which the beneficiary is taxed indirectly by denying an otherwise allowable deduction; and (3) substitute taxation in which another party to the transaction (not the beneficiary) is denied a deduction for interest.[52]

Professor Halperin gives the following example of a disguised loan. Assume a buyer pays a seller $100 on 31 December 1984, in exchange for services worth $110 to be rendered on 31 December 1985. Professor Halperin argues that a loan has, in essence, taken place. The loan is from the buyer to the seller for $100 at 10 percent for one year. The loan does not need to be repaid in cash because of the obligation of the seller to deliver $110 worth of services to the buyer on 31 December 1985.

Professor Halperin discusses three ways to tax this transaction, emphasizing the need to focus on the investment income of $10. Under the first approach of direct (or accrual) taxation, the buyer would accrue $10 of interest income in 1985 and the seller would have a $10 interest deduction in 1985. Also, in 1985, the buyer would receive a $110 business deduction and the seller would have $110 of compensation for services income. The net result is that the buyer has a $100 deduction in 1985 and the seller has $100 of income in 1985.

Under the indirect taxation approach, the buyer simply has a $100 deduction and the seller simply has $100 of income in 1985. This result is reached by accounting for the transaction in 1985, which is when the economic performance actually took place, but using the amount that was paid in 1984. As a result, each party is indirectly taxed the correct amount. As Professor Halperin has written "[u]nderstating the amount actually paid for the services exactly offsets the effects of ignoring implicit interest. The buyer-lender fails to report $10 of interest income, but she also loses a $10 deduction. The seller-borrower loses a $10 deduction, but her sales income is lowered by the same amount."[53]

Under the substitute taxation approach, the seller is immediately taxed upon receiving payment in 1984. If the tax rate is 40 percent, the buyer would pay seller $103.77 ($110 discounted at the six percent after-tax rate) not $100 ($110 discounted at the 10 percent pre-tax rate). The seller would include $103.77 in income upon receipt in 1984 leaving the seller with $62.26 after-taxes. If the seller invests this amount for one year at a six percent after-tax rate of return, the seller will have $66 at the end of 1985. This is the exact same result if payment had not been accelerated and the seller received $110 in 1985. In other words, taxing the seller $103.77 upon receipt in 1984 is equivalent to taxing the seller $110 in 1985 when economic performance occurs. Similar results take place for the buyer. The buyer receives a deduction of $103.77 in 1984, resulting in a tax savings of $41.51. If the tax savings

[52] See *id.* at 508.

[53] *Id.* at 517 (it should be noted that "[i]f the payment is not deductible by the buyer, however, understating the amount paid has no tax effect. Although the seller is properly taxed, the buyer avoids $10 of interest income.").

is invested for one year at the six percent after-tax rate of return, the buyer will have $44 at the end of 1985, the exact same result as a $110 deduction in 1985.

Professor Halperin gives another example of tax deferral, this time involving a deferred payment for services, and focuses on the Cary Brown model:

> Assume that an employee performs services on December 31, 1984, for which the employer would pay her $100 at once. If the interest rate were 10% and taxes were not a consideration, the parties would be indifferent among payments of $100 in 1984, $110 in 1985, or $121 in 1986. Taxes, of course, will make a difference. If the tax rate were 40%, an employee who received $100 on December 31, 1984 would accumulate $67.42 by December 31, 1986 ($100 \times .6 \times (1.06)^2$). Suppose, however, they agreed on deferral until 1986. If the transaction were taxed in accordance with its form, the employee who receives $121 on December 31, 1986 would retain $72.60 after tax, exactly the same amount that would be accumulated if payment were made on December 31, 1984 and the net amount after tax ($60) were invested at the pre-tax rate of return of 10% ($60 \times (1.10)^2$). Thus deferral of $121 would be equivalent to exemption of investment income.[54]

Professor Halperin discusses eliminating the benefits of the Cary Brown model with respect to deferred compensation in the above example by accrual taxation, which is an example of direct taxation of the investment income (method one): "current imputation of both the compensation earned and the interest thereon to the employee."[55] The disguised loan is treated as running from the employee to the employer in the above example. As a result, the employee will include $100 of service income on 31 December 1984, and also include $10 of interest income in 1985 and $11 of interest income in 1986. The employer will receive a $100 business deduction on 31 December 1984, and also $10 of interest deduction in 1985 and $11 of interest deduction in 1986. Professor Halperin concludes that accrual taxation would be complex and also would require tax payment(s) by the employee before cash is received.[56]

He therefore suggests other methods of eliminating the benefits of the Cary Brown model through indirect taxation of the employee on the interest income (method two) or substitute taxation of the employer as a surrogate for the employee (method three).[57] The response to tax avoidance in this area has been to utilize substitute taxation of the employer (method three) by imposing a matching requirement, which denies the employer a deduction until the employee includes the deferred amount in income.[58] But Professor Halperin notes that matching is not necessary because the employee's tax advantage arises from the treatment of investment income.[59] If tax rates on investment income are the same, tax avoidance can be prevented by substitute taxation of the employer without matching the deduction and income.[60]

---

54 *Id.* at 519. 55 *Id.* at 519–20. 56 *Id.* at 520. 57 *Id.* 58 *Id.* 59 *Id.*
60 *Id.*

As a result, in the area of nonqualified deferred compensation, Professor Halperin suggests imposing a special tax on the investment income earned by the nonqualified plan.[61] If this special tax on investment income were enacted, it would eliminate the need to tax the employee on an accrual basis prior to receipt and would also preserve the tax advantages of qualified plans relative to nonqualified plans.

Professor Halperin's article was probably the first article to apply the Cary Brown model to a wide number of provisions in the tax law. As he acknowledged Professor Andrews' article as leading toward the analysis in his article, Professor Halperin's article has led to the analysis in this book. The following chapter will take Professor Halperin's analysis and attempt to modify and extend it.

---

[61] *Id.* at 539–50.

Chapter 4

A New Way of Looking at an Old Model

I. Introduction

The Cary Brown model generally holds that immediately deducting the cost of an asset is equivalent to excluding from gross income the future annual return of the asset. Although a number of leading commentators have expressed the model in slightly different words,[1] the focus and confusion has always been on the concept of

---

[1] See, e.g., William D. Andrews, "A Consumption-Type or Cash Flow Personal Income Tax," 87 *Harv. L. Rev.* 1113, 1126 (1974) ("[W]here rates are constant, deferring the tax is the equivalent of imposing the tax initially, but exempting any subsequent profit due to continued investment of what is left after payment of the tax."); Martin D. Ginsburg, "Teaching Tax Law After Tax Reform," 65 *Wash. L. Rev.* 595, 604 (1990) ("Assuming stability of tax rates and investment yields, deduction at initiation of the cost of an investment is the equivalent of excluding from gross income the taxpayer's future annual return on her investment."); Michael J. Graetz and Deborah H. Schenk, *Federal Income Taxation: Principles and Policies* 304 (3rd ed. 1995) ("The tax savings that occur when the cost of an investment is immediately deductible, under certain conditions, can be described as equivalent to disallowing the deduction initially but exempting from tax the income from the investment."); Jane C. Gravelle, "The Economics of Taxing Capital Income" in *Tax Conversations: A Guide to the Key Issues in the Tax Reform Debate*, 223, 241 (1997) ("Early on, it was recognized, for example, that deducting the cost of an investment when purchased eliminated any tax on the investment."); Daniel I. Halperin, "The Time Value of Money – 1984," 23 *Tax Notes* 751, 752 (14 May 1984) ("The concept that deferral is equivalent to immediate taxation accompanied by the avoidance of tax on the continued investment of the after-tax earnings. ... "); Calvin H. Johnson, "Soft Money Investing Under the Income Tax," 1989 *Ill. L. Rev.* 1019, 1022 ("Under the Cary Brown thesis, the ability to make an investment with untaxed soft money is usually as valuable as exempting subsequent investment income from tax."); Richard A. Musgrave, "Clarifying Tax Reform," 70 *Tax Notes* 731, 735 (5 February 1996) ("By allowing immediate deduction of the investment cost against other income, the government in effect renders an interest-free loan to the investor. In the course of continuous reinvestment, this loan will generate an income stream the present value of which, after tax, equals the tax on the normal return on the initial investment."); Carl S. Shoup, *Public Finance* 302 n. 20 (1969) ("The fact that completely accelerated depreciation, when coupled with complete loss offset, is equivalent to exemption of net return from the asset, under an income tax, was discovered by E. Cary Brown."); C. Eugene Steuerle, "Zero Tax Rates on Returns to New Investment & Learning," 72 *Tax Notes* 1311 (2 September 1996) ("If tax rates are constant throughout time – admittedly a strong assumption – pure *ex ante* and pure *ex post* taxes leave the taxpayer in exactly the same position when all is said and done."); Alvin C. Warren, Jr., "Accelerated Capital Recovery, Debt, and Tax Arbitrage," 38 *Tax Law.* 549, 551 (1985) ("An immediate deduction for the cost of a capital asset, which is often called expensing, can produce the same results as exempting the income produced by the asset under certain conditions ... ").

excluding the future annual return (or future investment income) of the asset from gross income. I believe that one aspect of Professor Brown's discussion of his model has been almost completely ignored in the tax literature. He discusses the "partnership" that takes place between the taxpayer and the government in a tax deferral situation.[2] Understanding this partnership analogy removes much of the mystery surrounding tax deferral, and as a result, will be referred to numerous times in this chapter. Equally important, the partnership analogy clearly demonstrates the idea of excluding the future annual return of the asset from gross income, which as previously stated, has created a tremendous amount of confusion over the years. In fact, it is difficult to see how one can understand the concept of expensing being equivalent to exclusion without fully understanding the partnership analogy of the Cary Brown model.

The Cary Brown model will be discussed in five different situations. The first situation demonstrates the Cary Brown model in its most basic form – that of an immediate deduction, often referred to as expensing. The next three situations demonstrate further applications of the model in situations unfamiliar to many people, focusing on the income side, as opposed to the deduction side, and demonstrating the wide-ranging applicability of the model. The last situation, involving unrealized appreciation, is a variation on the basic model and yields some interesting results. It should be noted that the focus is solely on tax deferral, meaning either deferral of income or acceleration of a deduction. So, for example, unrealized appreciation in property will be discussed in detail while unrealized depreciation in property will not be discussed at all.

II. Immediate Deduction

A. Introduction

Assume an individual T has 10,000*u* of income, which could be salary, interest, dividends, or rent. But it is income and the individual must pay taxes on it. Unless otherwise stated (which will occur later), we will always assume a tax rate of 40 percent, taxes are due immediately (so ignore withholding and estimated tax payments), and the taxpayer's pre-tax rate of return on investments and borrowings is 10 percent.[3]

---

[2] The partnership analogy has been touched on by several leading commentators but has not been explored in great detail. See, e.g., William D. Andrews, *Basic Federal Income Taxation*, 260–62 (4th ed. 1991); Noel B. Cunningham, "The Taxation of Capital Income and the Choice of Tax Base," 52 *Tax L. Rev*. 17, 25 (1996); Mary Louise Fellows, "A Comprehensive Attack on Tax Deferral," 88 *Mich. L. Rev*. 722, 749 n. 63 (1990); Johnson, *supra* note 1, at 1027–30; Stephen B.Land, "Defeating Deferral: A Proposal for Retrospective Taxation," 52 *Tax L. Rev*. 45, 83–84; Charles E. McLure, Jr. and George R. Zodrow, "The Economic Case for Foreign Tax Credits for Cash Flow Taxes," 51 *Nat'l Tax J*. 1, 5–6 (1998); Myron S. Scholes and Mark A. Wolfson, *Taxes and Business Strategy: A Planning Approach*, Ch. 3, (1992); Stanley S. Surrey, *Pathways to Tax Reform* 124, 323 n. 5, 324 n. 7 (1973).

[3] See Graetz and Schenk, *supra* note 1, at 306–07 (describing in detail the conditions that must exist when applying the Cary Brown model; these include: (1) constant tax rates, (2),constant interest rates , (3) expensing produces an immediate tax savings equal to the taxpayer's marginal rate multiplied by the expensed amount, (4) taxpayers are concerned only with their after-tax position, (5) the ratio of borrowing to after-tax investment were the same under a yield exemption and an immediate deduction, and (6) the system is closed); Michael J. Graetz, "Implementing a Progressive Consumption Tax," 92 *Harv. L.*

Assume that individual T has three investment options with the money. Under the first option, T can invest in a tax-exempt bond (when T receives the interest on the bond, the interest is not included in income). The second option is to invest in a regular taxable bond (the interest received on the bond is included in T's income). The third option is a little different. Under this option, the cost of the bond is immediately deductible but the interest is fully taxable.

Table 1 demonstrates the results under each of the three options. Under the first two options, T must pay 4000*u* in taxes immediately to the government, thereby having only 6000*u* to invest. Under the third option, T must pay 4000*u* in taxes when the bond matures, thereby having 10,000*u* to invest at the outset.

Table 1

	Tax-exempt bond	Taxable bond	Deductible taxable bond
Gross income	10,000*u*	10,000*u*	10,000*u*
Deductions	0	0	10,000*u*
Taxes (40 percent)	4000*u*	4000*u*	0
Cash to invest	6000*u*	6000*u*	10,000*u*
Return at 10 percent	600*u*	600*u*	1000*u*
Taxes (40 percent)	Exempt	240*u*	400*u*
Net return	600*u*	360*u*	600*u*

Now compare options one and three in Table 1. The bottom-line results are identical each year. Immediately deducting the cost of an asset and taxing the return on the asset (option three) is equivalent to allowing no immediate deduction but exempting from gross income the future annual return on the asset (option one). This is probably the clearest demonstration of the Cary Brown model. The equivalence between options one and three has been recognized by, for example, the Kemp Commission in 1996, in trying to decide whether to allow an immediate deduction of an asset or exemption of the gross income from the asset.[4]

Rev. 1575 (1979); Johnson, *supra* note 1, at 1031–36; Richard A. Musgrave, *The Theory of Public Finance* 262–67 (1959); Shoup, *supra* note 1, at 266–69; Warren, *supra* note 1, at 552 n. 12.

[4] See The National Commission on Economic Growth and Tax Reform, "Unleashing America's Potential," reproduced in 70 *Tax Notes* 413 (22 January 1996) at 425. ("In order to end these biases [against work, saving, and investment] the tax system must either *let savers deduct their savings or exclude the returns on the savings from their taxable income. It must end double-taxation of business and their owners and permit expensing of investment outlays.*")

See also John S. Nolan, "Erwin N. Griswold Lecture: The Merit of an Income Tax Versus a Consumption Tax," 12 *Amer. J. Tax Policy* 207, 208 (1995) ("The key to understanding the basic equivalence of these two systems [the Nunn-Domenici USA Tax and the Armey flat tax] as being solely taxes on consumption is that the *economic effect* of not taxing an amount received, but taxing the investment returns on that amount, as in the USA Tax, is exactly the same as taxing the amount received but not taxing the investment returns, as in the Armey flat tax."); Martin D. Ginsburg, "Taxing the Components of Income: A U.S. Perspective," 86 *Geo. L. J.* 123, 132 (1997) (questioning whether the legislative sponsors of the USA Tax and the Armey flat tax understand the equivalence described by the Cary Brown model).

This example can be generalized algebraically. In the case of option one, no deduction for the cost of the bond and the interest on the bond is tax-exempt, an amount A of income is reduced by tax t such that $A(1-t)$ may be invested. At an annual rate of return r, $A(1-t)$ invested will earn $rA(1-t)$ per year, which will not be subject to tax. The taxpayer's net annual after-tax position each year will be:

$$rA(1-t).$$

In the case of option two, no deduction for the cost of the bond and the interest on the bond is taxable, an amount A of income is reduced by tax t such that $A(1-t)$ may be invested. At an annual rate of return r, $A(1-t)$ invested will earn $rA(1-t)$ per year, which will be subject to tax at rate t equaling tax each year of $trA(1-t)$. The taxpayer's net annual after-tax position each year will be:

$$rA(1-t)-trA(1-t) \text{ which equals } rA(1-t)(1-t).$$

In the case of option three, an immediate deduction for the cost of the bond and the interest on the bond is taxable, an amount A of income is not reduced by tax t such that A may be invested. At an annual rate of return r, A invested will earn rA per year, which will be subject to tax at rate t equaling tax each year of trA. The taxpayer's net annual after-tax position each year will be:

$$rA-trA \text{ which equals } rA(1-t).$$

This is equal to the taxpayer's net annual after-tax position when no deduction is allowed for the cost of the bond but the interest on the bond is exempt from tax.[5]

B. Partnership Analogy

How would Cary Brown describe option three? He would say that by immediately deducting the cost of an asset that will generate future income, the government is, in essence, entering into a partnership with the taxpayer.[6] In other words, by allowing the taxpayer to immediately deduct the cost of the bond, which will generate income

---

As to the flat tax and the USA Tax, see Robert E. Hall and Alvin Rabushka, *The Flat Tax* (2d ed. 1995) reprinted in 68 *Tax Notes* 1 (Special Supp.) (4 August 1995) and *USA Tax System: Description and Explanation of the Unlimited Savings Allowance Income Tax System, 66 Tax Notes* 1483 (10 March 1995).

[5] Of course, the interest on the tax-exempt bond will, in all likelihood, be lower than the interest received from a regular taxable bond.

[6] Professor Brown described the partnership as follows:

> By paying the entrepreneur the tax on the asset's cost, the Government would literally be a partner in the firm. It would make a capital contribution on new investments at the same rate at which it shared in the future net receipts of the enterprise. The contribution would be made at the same time the investment was undertaken.

E. Cary Brown, "Business Income Taxation and Investment Incentives," in *Income, Employment and Public Policy: Essays in Honor of Alvin H. Hansen*, 300, 309–10 (1948).

in the future, the government is, in essence, contributing 4000*u* towards the purchase of the bond. The taxpayer is contributing 6000*u* towards the purchase of the bond. They are, in a sense, a "partnership." During the first year after purchase, the bond generates 1000*u* of interest income (it will do this each year until maturity). Of the 1000*u* of interest income, 400*u* in taxes is paid to the government and the taxpayer keeps 600*u*. Is this 1000*u* of interest income taxed though? The obvious answer seems to be "yes" as the government receives 400*u* of it. But the 1000*u* of interest income really is not taxed at all. The government put up 40 percent of the cost of the bond. Now it is simply receiving its 40 percent share of the return on the bond (or 400*u*) each year. The taxpayer put up 60 percent of the cost of the bond and is getting his 60 percent share of the return on the bond (or 600*u*) each year. If this is the final result, then in essence, the taxpayer is not being taxed on the interest income. Therefore, immediate deduction is equivalent to excluding the return on the asset from gross income.

Table 2

	Contributions to the partnership	Income of the partnership
Taxpayer	6000*u*	**600*u***
Government	4000*u*	400*u*
Total	10,000*u*	1000*u*

The taxpayer should be taxed by the government on his 60 percent share or 600*u* of interest income (highlighted in Table 2), otherwise the income really is excluded from gross income according to the Cary Brown model. The key is for the government to tax the taxpayer's 600*u* share of interest income if the government wants to prevent the time value of money benefit of tax deferral from taking place in this hypothetical situation. If the taxpayer's 600*u* share of interest income is taxed at 40 percent, then the taxpayer will pay 240*u* in taxes, leaving the taxpayer with 360*u* after taxes. This is equivalent to option two (the nondeductible taxable bond). The tax deferral benefit has been eliminated.[7] It looks like the government is double-taxing the taxpayer, but in substance, it is not.

Under option three, when the bond matures, the taxpayer receives 10,000*u* and has 10,000*u* of gross income because the taxpayer's basis in the bond is zero.[8] At a 40 percent tax rate, the taxpayer will owe the government 4000*u* at maturity. This is, in essence, merely returning the portion the government originally invested with the taxpayer as a partnership. In other words, the partnership is terminated, the taxpayer receives his original contribution of 6000*u*, and the government is returned its original contribution of 4000*u*. (Table 3)

[7] Of course, the government could have eliminated the tax deferral benefit by simply disallowing the initial expensing of the bond. But for purposes of this example, we are assuming that the cost of the bond can be expensed.

[8] The basis is zero because the taxpayer initially deducted the entire cost of the bond.

Table 3

	Contributions to the partnership	Income of the partnership each year	Termination of the partnership (return of contributions)
Taxpayer	6000*u*	600*u*	6000*u*
Government	4000*u*	400*u*	4000*u*
Total	10,000*u*	1000*u*	10,000*u*

C. Key Steps in the Partnership Analogy

A number of steps and conclusions can be drawn from Professor Brown's partnership analogy with respect to the above example:

1. The partnership is formed between the taxpayer and the government at the time tax deferral is taking place, whether deferring income or accelerating a deduction. In the above example, tax deferral takes place at the time the bond is expensed.[9] The taxpayer contributes to the partnership the amount expensed less the taxes saved by expensing. In the above example, the taxpayer's contribution to the partnership was 10,000*u* (expensed amount) less 4000*u* (taxes saved by expensing) or 6000*u*. The government contributes to the partnership the taxes saved by expensing. In the above example, it was 10,000*u* (expensed amount) multiplied by 40 percent (tax rate) or 4000*u*.
2. The profits of the partnership are allocated between the taxpayer and the government based on the tax rate in effect on the investment income generated by the partnership. Assuming a 40 percent tax rate, the profits of the partnership will be allocated 60 percent to the taxpayer and 40 percent to the government. This allocation ratio will not change from year to year (unless the tax rate on the investment income changes, in which the case the allocation ratio will also change). Assuming constant tax rates, the allocation of profits is formally a tax; in essence, it is not. It is merely allocating the profits of the partnership between the two partners – the taxpayer and the government.
3. The government should collect its share of the profits (allocated under Step 2) at least annually to prevent an additional (or continuing) tax deferral situation from taking place.
4. The taxpayer should be allocated his share of the profits annually but does not need to collect it annually. If the taxpayer collects his share of the profits of the partnership annually, the government should tax the profits at that time. If the

[9] In actuality, tax deferral takes place when the taxes are owed to the government. This distinction becomes important, for example, when dealing with the interest charge rule with respect to certain large installment sales. See *infra* Part III (discussing installment sales).

taxpayer leaves his share of the profits in the partnership, then the government can wait to tax the profits.[10]

5. When the tax deferral period ends, the partnership is terminated and both the taxpayer and the government should have their original contributions returned. In addition, the taxpayer should collect any profits of the partnership he has not previously collected (see Step 4) and the government should tax those profits. (see Table 4)

Table 4

	Partnership contribution (Step 1)	Allocation of income of the partnership (Steps 2–4)	Partnership termination (Step 5)
Taxpayer	Deferred income less taxes deferred ($A-At$) equaling $A(1-t)$	Income times one minus the tax rate ($Ar-Art$) equaling $rA(1-t)$	Return of contribution plus any remaining share of the partnership Income not previously collected
Government	Taxes deferred (At)	Income times tax rate (Art)	Return of contributions
Total	Deferred income (A)	Income for the Year (Ar)	Contributions plus any remaining income of the partnership

III. Installment Sales

A. *Introduction*

The second situation is a very specific application of the Cary Brown model and it also suggests various solutions to eliminating tax deferral that are not mark-to-market. Assume an individual owns land with a negligible basis and a fair market value of 10,000*u*. The individual has two options on selling the land. First is an all-cash sale of the land for 10,000*u*. The second option is to sell it to a buyer who will pay the sales price in two years – an installment sale. The buyer will also pay the seller 10 percent interest each year until the sales price is paid off.

Under option one (the all-cash sale), the seller will pay 4000*u* in taxes at the time of sale, leaving the seller with 6000*u*. The seller can invest this amount at a 10 percent pre-tax rate of return. At the end of one year, the seller will have 6000*u* plus 600*u* return less 240*u* in taxes totaling 6360*u* (6000*u* times 1.06). At the end of two years, the seller will have 6741.60*u* (6000*u* times $(1.06)^2$).

If an individual makes an installment sale and reports the gain on the installment method, then the seller does not include the gain in gross income at the time

[10] We will see later that this fourth step is the key to the principle credited to Professors Daniel Halperin and Alvin Warren that, under certain conditions, there is no advantage to tax deferral if the deferred amount increases by the after-tax rate of return. See *infra* Part V.A.

of sale.[11] The gain is deferred because the buyer has not paid anything yet. At the end of the first year, the seller will receive 1000*u* of interest from the buyer (10,000*u* multiplied by 10 percent). The seller will pay 400*u* in taxes, leaving the seller with 600*u*. At the end of year two, the seller will receive another 1000*u* in interest from the buyer plus 10,000*u* of the sales price. The seller will also have invested the 600*u* from year one. The seller will have, at the end of year two, 7236*u*. Again, this is consistent with the Cary Brown model. Deferring the gain in an asset under the installment method is equivalent to exempting from gross income the future annual return on the recognized gain. What makes an installment sale interesting with respect to the Cary Brown model is that a realization event has taken place (the sale) between the time of appreciation in the property and the recognition of the appreciation as gain.

This example can be generalized algebraically. In the case of a cash sale in which tax is immediately imposed, an amount A of gain is reduced by tax t such that $A(1-t)$ may be invested. At an annual rate of return r, $A(1-t)$ invested will earn $rA(1-t)$ per year, which will be subject to tax at rate t equaling tax each year of $trA(1-t)$. The seller's net annual after-tax position each year will be:

$$rA(1-t)-trA(1-t) \text{ which equals } rA(1-t)(1-t).$$

In the case of an installment sale, the amount A of gain is not reduced by tax t. At an annual rate of return r, A invested will earn rA per year, which will be subject to tax at rate t equaling tax each year of trA. The seller's net annual after-tax position will be:

$$rA-trA \text{ which equals } rA(1-t).$$

This is higher than the seller's net annual after-tax position when a cash sale is made and tax is immediately imposed. It is equal to the seller's net annual after-tax position when an all-cash sale is made, tax is immediately imposed, and the return of $rA(1-t)$ is exempt from tax.

B. *Attacking Tax Deferral*

In the mid-1980s, the U.S. government recognized the tax deferral that was taking place in an installment sale and decided to do something about it.[12] Let's focus on

[11] I.R.C. § 453(a).

[12] In 1984, the U.S. Treasury Department recognized the tax deferral benefit that sellers received using the installment method but concluded, at that time, not to eliminate the benefit. United States Department of the Treasury, *Report to the President, Tax Reform for Fairness, Simplicity, and Economic Growth* 129 (November 1984). Treasury did not propose charging interest on the taxes being deferred through use of the installment method because "of the increased complexity and taxpayer perception problems that such an approach would create." *Id.* The report stated that "[m]ost taxpayers would not readily comprehend why they should pay interest on the deferred taxes when the taxes are only paid as installment payments are received." *Id.* One leading commentator was quoted as saying that Treasury's reasoning in not charging interest on the deferred taxes "makes no sense." See Lee A. Sheppard, "Ginsburg Discusses Taxing the Privilege of Tax Deferral in Installment Sales," *27 Tax Notes* 457, 458 (29 April 1985). The U.S. Congress, in the Tax Reform Act of 1986 and the Revenue Reconciliation Act of 1987, imposed an interest charge regime on certain sellers of property that use the installment method.

the first year after the sale. During that first year, the buyer pays 1000*u* of interest to the seller. By deferring the taxes on the gain of 10,000*u*, Cary Brown would describe the government as being in partnership with the seller – the government contributing 4000*u* and the seller contributing 6000*u* (Step 1). Of the 1000*u* in interest paid from buyer to seller the first year, 400*u* of taxes is owed to the government. In essence, the partnership generates 1000*u* of interest income, which is allocated 600*u* to the seller and 400*u* to the government (Step 2). The government should collect this 400*u* to prevent additional tax deferral from taking place (Step 3). In essence, the 1000*u* of interest income is not taxed. (see Table 5)

Table 5

	Contributions to the partnership	Income of the partnership
Taxpayer	6000*u*	600*u*
Government	4000*u*	400*u*
Total	10,000*u*	1000*u*

The seller's portion of the 1000*u* is 600*u*, which is the seller's return from the partnership (Step 2). The government should collect tax of 40 percent on the seller's share if it wants to eliminate the time value of money benefit of tax deferral in an installment sale (Step 4). Consequently, the government should collect 240*u* in taxes from the seller (40 percent multiplied by 600*u*). Therefore, the government should collect a total of 640*u* (400*u* plus 240*u*) from the seller the first year after sale. It looks like the 1000*u* of interest income is being double-taxed but it really is not. The 400*u* the government collects on the 1000*u* of interest income is really the government's share of the profits of the partnership it has entered into with the taxpayer. The 240*u* the government collects from the taxpayer is a tax on the taxpayer's share of the profits of the partnership. This procedure should be done again in year two. If so, at the end of year two, the seller will have 6741.60*u*, the exact same result as if the seller made an all-cash sale.

What the U.S. government does is to charge interest on the taxes that are deferred by the installment method.[13] The interest charge rules represent a congressional judgment that the seller can reasonably be thought of as owing the tax on the gain from the time of the installment sale and that the deferral of recognition is only a matter of legislative grace. In the case of the installment sale, at the end of the first year, the seller has deferred 4000*u* in taxes. Therefore, the U.S. government requires the seller to pay interest to the government – assuming a 10% interest rate, 400*u* in

[13] I.R.C. § 453A(c). Under the interest charge method, the government is viewing tax deferral not as a partnership between the taxpayer and the government but rather as a non-interest bearing loan from the government to the taxpayer. See, e.g., Musgrave, *supra* note 1 (viewing tax deferral as an interest-free loan from the government to the investor); Surrey, *Pathways*, *supra* note 2, at 120–25 (discussing both the partnership and the loan views of tax deferral).

interest is owed to the government (4000*u* deferred taxes multiplied by 10 percent interest rate).[14] If the seller can deduct the interest, then this is really an out-of-pocket payment of only 240*u* (400*u* interest payment minus 160*u* tax savings), leaving the seller with 360*u*. This is the exact same result as taxing the seller on 600*u* of the interest income, which results in 240*u* in additional taxes, again leaving the seller with 360*u*. For individuals, however, the U.S. government maintains that the interest payment is not deductible, which actually makes the installment sale worse than an all-cash sale.[15] The seller will be left with 200*u* (600*u* minus 400*u*), which is an incorrect result.

Even though the U.S. government utilizes an interest charge method, Professor Brown's partnership analogy in describing tax deferral demonstrates the correct result and the impropriety of denying the seller's interest deduction. The purpose of the interest charge is to achieve parity, not to penalize. But apparently as a partial consolation, the U.S. interest charge rule only applies to installment sales over $5 million. Or alternatively the $5 million de minimis rule may be simply to confine the interest charge rule to large installment sales.

The interest charge method can be generalized algebraically. In the case of an installment sale in which the interest charge rule applies, the amount A of gain is not reduced by tax t. At an annual rate of return r, A invested will earn rA per year, which will be subject to tax at rate t equaling tax each year of trA. If interest r is charged on the deferred tax liability of tA, then the interest on deferred tax liability is rtA. The deduction of the interest on deferred tax liability will be $trAt$, leaving the seller with an interest burden of $rAt - trAt$ which equals $rAt(1-t)$. The seller's net annual after-tax position will be:

$$rA(1-t) - rAt(1-t) \text{ which equals } rA(1-t)(1-t).$$

This is equal to the seller's net annual after-tax position when a cash sale is made and tax is immediately imposed.

If the seller cannot deduct the interest on deferred tax liability, then the seller's net annual after-tax position is $rA(1-t) - rAt$. The seller is worse off by the amount of tax that would be saved by the deduction of the interest on the deferred tax liability.

The partnership analogy also demonstrates when the interest paid by the seller should be deducted. It should first be paid beginning in the year after sale and deducted in that year. The U.S. government, however, charges the interest at the end of the year of sale (and each subsequent year until the installment obligation is no

[14] There is a $5 million de minimis rule in the United States, which is ignored for purposes of this example. I.R.C. § 453A(c)(4). In addition, the interest rate on deferred tax liability used by the U.S. government is the federal short-term rate plus three percentage points. I.R.C. § 453A(c)(2)(B).

[15] I.R.C. § 163(h)(1) (personal interest is not deductible); Temp. Reg. § 1.163-9T(b)(2)(i) (interest on deferred tax liability is treated as interest on a tax deficiency which is treated as personal interest).

See, e.g., *Miller v. United States*, 65 F.3d 687, 691 (8th Cir. 1995) (regulation § 1.163-9T is valid as a permissible construction of the statute); *Redlark v. Commissioner*, 141 F.3d 936 (9th Cir. 1997), *rev'g*, 106 T.C. 31 (1996) (regulation § 1.163-9T is valid); *Stecher v. United States*, 1998 U.S. Dist. LEXIS 10173 (D. Colo. 1998); *Allen v. United States*, 1999 U.S. App. LEXIS 7591 (4th Cir. 1999). But see, e.g., *Kikalos v. Commissioner*, T.C. Memo. 1998–92 (1998) (regulation § 1.163-9T is invalid).

longer outstanding). As a result, the interest is really an advance charge imposed by the U.S. government to prevent the time value of money benefit of tax deferral.[16] This is why no interest is charged in the year that the installment obligation is completely paid off and why the interest is not prorated for the year of sale.[17]

C. Varying Tax Rates

1. Known Capital Gains Tax Rate

What if the tax rate on the gain deferred by the installment method is different than the tax rate on the interest income generated by the installment obligation? Does the partnership analogy still hold? The answer formally is "yes" although substantively this is different than the Cary Brown model because the assumption of constant tax rates is changed. Assume the 10,000*u* of gain that is deferred will be subject to a 28 percent capital gains tax rate when it is recognized in a later year.[18] The pre-tax rate of return is still 10 percent but the tax rate on the interest income is 40 percent, i.e., the seller is in the 40 percent tax bracket each year.

Let's focus on the first year after the sale. During that first year, the buyer pays 1000*u* of interest to the seller. By deferring the taxes on the gain of 10,000*u*, Cary Brown would describe the government as being in partnership with the seller – the government contributes 2800*u* and the seller contributes 7200*u* (Step 1). Of the 1000*u* in interest paid from buyer to seller the first year, 400*u* of taxes is owed to the government. The 400*u* of taxes collected by the government is its share of the profits of the partnership that it entered into with the seller (Steps 2 and 3). The tax rate is in essence 28 percent (not 40 percent) on the entire transaction. The 40 percent tax rate on the interest income is the allocation percentage for the profits of the partnership (Step 2). (see Table 6)

Table 6

	Contributions to the partnership	Income of the partnership each year	Termination of the partnership (return of contributions)
Taxpayer	7200*u*	600*u*	7200*u*
Government	2800*u*	400*u*	2800*u*
Total	10,000*u*	1000*u*	10,000*u*

[16] See Christopher H. Hanna and Samuel Olchyk, "Interest Under Section 453A(c): Is It or Isn't It?," 56 *Tax Notes* 1345, 1350 (7 September 1992) ("The interest on deferred tax liability [under section 453A(c)] computed at the close of the year of sale should be deductible in the following year, not in the year of sale. The reason is that the interest on deferred tax liability relates to the delay in paying tax on the gain through use of the installment method.").

[17] *Id.*

[18] See *Mostowy v. United States*, 24 Cl. Ct. 193, 91-2 U.S.T.C. 50,469 (1991), *aff'd*, 966 F.2d 669 (Fed. Cir. 1992) (the taxpayers made a contract in 1985 but collected the payment in 1988; the tax rate in 1988 was used to determine the tax owed to the government even though the rate in 1985, the year of contract, was lower).

The seller's portion of the 1000*u* is 600*u*, which is the seller's portion of the profits from the partnership (Step 2). The government should collect tax of 28 percent on the seller's share if it wants to eliminate the time value of money benefit of tax deferral in an installment sale (Step 4). Again, the tax rate on the entire transaction is 28 percent. Consequently, the government should collect 168*u* in taxes from the seller (600*u* multiplied by 28 percent) (Step 4). Therefore, the government should collect a total of 568*u* (400*u* plus 168*u*) from the seller in year one, leaving the seller with 432*u* (1000*u* minus 568*u*). The 400*u* the government collects on the 1000*u* of interest income is the government's share of the profits of the partnership it has entered into with the taxpayer. The 168*u* the government collects from the taxpayer is a tax on the taxpayer's share of the profits of the partnership. This procedure should be done again in year two. If so, at the end of year two, the seller will have 8089.92*u*, the exact same result as if the seller made an all-cash sale and the capital gains tax rate at the time of sale was 28 percent.

The U.S. government uses an interest charge method with respect to certain large installment sales.[19] In the case of the installment sale, at the end of the first year, the seller has deferred 2800*u* in taxes. Therefore, the U.S. government requires the seller to pay interest to the government – assuming a 10 percent interest rate, 280*u* in interest is owed the government (2800*u* deferred taxes multiplied by 10 percent interest rate).[20] If the seller can deduct the interest, then this is really an out-of-pocket payment of only 168*u* (280*u* interest payment minus 112*u* tax savings). This is the exact same result as taxing the seller on 600*u* of the interest income, which resulted in 168*u* in additional taxes. As stated previously though, the interest represents an advance charge by the U.S. government for the seller's deferral of taxes through use of the installment method.

2. Unknown Capital Gains Tax Rate

What if the tax rate on the capital gain that is deferred by the installment method is not known? In other words, the rate in the year of sale is, for example, 20 percent, but may change in two years when the seller collects the sales price.[21] The government could simply use the appropriate capital gains rate in effect each year that the installment obligation is outstanding, as the United States currently does under Section 453A(c). Alternatively, the government could wait until the end of the deferral period to eliminate the tax deferral benefit. The partnership analogy, slightly modified, still works in this latter case.

Let's focus on the first year after the sale. By deferring the taxes on the gain of 10,000*u*, Cary Brown would describe the government as being in partnership with the seller. The government contributes some unknown amount because the tax rate on the deferred capital gain is not known and the seller contributes 10,000*u* less the government's amount (Step 1). The contributions to the partnership still total 10,000*u*.

Of the 1000*u* in interest paid from buyer to seller the first year, 400*u* of taxes is owed to the government. The 400*u* of taxes collected by the government is its share of the

[19] I.R.C. § 453A(c).

[20] There is a $5 million de minimis rule in the United States, which is ignored for purposes of this example. I.R.C. § 453A(c)(4). In addition, the interest rate on deferred tax liability used by the U.S. government is the federal short-term rate plus three percentage points. I.R.C. § 7453A(c)(2)(B).

[21] See *supra* note 18.

profits of the partnership that it entered into with the seller (Steps 2 and 3). The tax rate is some unknown percentage on the entire transaction. The 40 percent tax rate on the interest income is the allocation percentage for the profits of the partnership (Step 2).

The seller's portion of the 1000*u* is 600*u*, which is the seller's portion of the profits from the partnership (Step 2). The government should collect tax of an unknown percentage on the seller's share (600*u*) if it wants to eliminate the time value of money benefit of tax deferral in an installment sale (Step 4). The government can collect it at the end of the deferral period (Step 5) by *treating* the seller's share of the profits as staying in the partnership (Step 4).

In year two, the partnership generates 1060*u*, which is allocated 60 percent to the seller and 40 percent to the government because that is the tax rate in effect on the investment income (Step 2).[22] The government collects 424*u* (1060*u* multiplied by 40 percent) (Step 3). At the end of year two, the seller collects the 10,000*u* owed by the buyer. Let's assume that the tax rate in effect at the end of year two is 28 percent on the seller's capital gain. The government should tax the seller's share of the profits of the partnership, which is 1236*u* (600*u* from year one plus 636*u* from year two). At a 28 percent tax rate, the tax owed to the government is 346.08*u* (1236*u* multiplied by 28 percent). The government will also receive its contribution to the partnership, which was originally unknown and now is determined to be 2800*u* (10,000*u* multiplied by 28 percent). The seller will have 1236*u* (share of the profits of the partnership) less 346.08*u* (taxes on those profits) plus 7200*u* (share of its contribution to the partnership). The seller will have 8089.92*u*, the exact same result as if the seller made an all-cash sale (subject to a 28 percent capital gains tax rate). In this case, it does not matter if the government taxes the taxpayer's share of the profits of the partnership annually (Step 4) or at the end of the deferral period (Step 5).

IV. Deferral of Prepaid Income[23]

The interest charge rules are used in many situations today in the United States.[24] It appears to be the U.S. government's preferred method for eliminating tax deferral.

[22] This 1060*u* would actually be derived by the 1000*u* of interest income paid by the buyer to the seller in year two and the 60u of interest income earned by the seller from the 600*u* retained from the previous year.

[23] In the United States, the literature on the taxation of prepaid income is quite voluminous. See, e.g., Jeffrey P. Cantrell, et al., "Notice 89–21 Crashes the Interest Rate Swap Party," 45 *Tax Notes* 337 (16 October 1989); Alan Gunn, "Matching of Costs and Revenues as a Goal of Tax Accounting," 4 *Va. Tax Rev.* 1 (1984); Laurie L. Malman, "Treatment of Prepaid Income – Clear Reflection of Income or Muddied Waters," 37 *Tax L. Rev.* 103 (1981); Robert H. Scarborough, "Payments in Advance of Performance," 69 *Taxes* 798 (1991).

Generally, the commentators are split on whether prepaid service income should be taxed on receipt by an accrual method taxpayer or whether the income should be deferred and included in income over the period of time in which the services will be rendered. See, e.g., Calvin H. Johnson, "The Illegitimate "Earned" Requirement in Tax and Nontax Accounting," 50 *Tax L. Rev.* 373 (1995) (arguing that prepaid service income should be included in income upon receipt); W. Eugene Seago and Debra Callihan, "Toward a Sound (Neutral) Tax Policy for Prepaid Income from Services," 74 *Tax Notes* 359 (20 January 1997) (criticizing Professor Johnson and arguing that prepaid service income should be included in income over the life of the contract); Letter from Calvin H. Johnson, "The Roads Not Traveled: Professor Johnson Responds," 74 *Tax Notes* 367 (20 January 1997) (responding to Seago and Callihan's article).

But it is only one of several methods.[25] Another method is to impute income and tax the imputed income.[26] Under the imputation of income method, the U.S. government, in a tax deferral situation involving prepaid service income of an accrual method taxpayer, currently imputes income at a pre-tax rate of return, which appears to be inaccurate.[27] The income should be imputed at an after-tax rate of return.[28]

Assume on 1 January 1998, an accrual method automobile dealer receives 1000*u* for a service warranty contract that carries a term of two years. The automobile dealer pays to an unrelated third party 1000*u* to insure its obligations under the two-year service warranty contract. The U.S. government maintains that the automobile dealer cannot simply offset these amounts against each other. The automobile dealer must immediately include 1000*u* in income in year one and then is permitted to deduct only 500*u* in year one and 500*u* in year two. The reason that the deductions are spread over two years is that when the automobile dealer paid the unrelated third party to insure its obligations, this created an asset with a useful life of two years.

The automobile dealers argued that this created a cash flow problem for them because they may not have the cash to pay the taxes on 500*u* of net income in year one (1000*u* income minus 500*u* of deductions). As a result, the U.S. government issued a revenue procedure providing relief for automobile dealers. The automobile dealers could defer the inclusion of income but with an interest component added on. Assume the automobile dealer elects to use the service warranty income method of accounting for its qualified payment amounts on service warranty contracts as prescribed by the U.S. government in Revenue Procedure 97–38.[29] Under the

---

For purposes of this discussion, I assume that Revenue Procedure 97–38, 1997–2 C.B. 479, is valid in forcing inclusion of the prepayment in income and merely question whether the applicable federal rate (AFR) used by the U.S. government is accurate.

[24] See, e.g., sections 167(g) (income forecast method for depreciation), 367 (outbound transfers of property), 453(l) (installment sales of timeshare and residential lots), 453A (large installment sales), 460 (long-term contracts), 668 (foreign trusts), 995(f) (domestic international sales corporations), and 1291 (passive foreign investment companies).

[25] See Christopher H. Hanna, "The Virtual Reality of Eliminating Tax Deferral," 12 *Amer. J. of Tax Pol'y* 449, 460–507 (1995) (describing five different methods of eliminating tax deferral: interest charge method, imputed income method, immediate inclusion in income method, deposit method, and double inclusion in income method).

[26] See *id.* at 481–90.

[27] See, e.g., Daniel I. Halperin, "Assumption of Contingent Liabilities on Sale of a Business," 2 *Fla. Tax Rev.* 673, 695 n. 59 (1996) (questioning the use of a pre-tax rate of return but acknowledging there is precedent for its use in Section 468); Hanna, *supra* note 25, at 481–89 (questioning whether a pre-tax rate of return is appropriate).

[28] See Halperin, *supra* note 27, at 695 no. 59; Hanna, *supra* note 25, at 483–89.

[29] 1997-2 C.B. 479. The U.S. government issued the revenue procedure in response to the outcry from automobile dealers with respect to the issuance of Technical Advice Memorandum 92-18-004 (23 January 1992). See Lee A. Sheppard, "The Goldberg Variations, or Giving Away the Store," 58 *Tax Notes* 530 (1 February 1993). A number of commentators wrote letters with respect to the technical advice memorandum and revenue procedure. See, e.g., Letter from James P. Holden, "Lee Sheppard's Grumpy Attack," 58 *Tax Notes* 1130 (22 February 1993); Letter from Sheldon S. Cohen, "In Defense of Lee Sheppard," 58 *Tax Notes* 1386 (8 March 1993); Letter from Milton Cerny, "Sheppard Variations," 58 *Tax Notes* 981

revenue procedure and using an interest rate (applicable federal rate (AFR)) of 10 percent, the automobile dealer would include 523.80*u* in income for the year of receipt and 523.80*u* in the year following the year of receipt.[30] If the AFR is converted to an after-tax rate of return by multiplying the AFR by the automobile dealer's assumed tax rate of 40 percent, then 6 percent should be the rate at which the U.S. government imputes income to the automobile dealer. Under the revenue procedure, this would result in the automobile dealer including 514.60*u* in income for the year of receipt and 514.60*u* in the year following the year of receipt. Which of these rates is accurate? The partnership analogy should easily resolve this issue. (see Table 7)

Table 7

	Contributions to the partnership	Income for the year after receipt	Termination of the partnership
Taxpayer	300*u*	30*u*	300*u*
Government	200*u*	20*u*	200*u*
Total	500*u*	50*u*	500*u*

In the year of receipt, the automobile dealer must include half (500*u*) of the prepaid amount in income pursuant to the revenue procedure.[31] Therefore, the remaining half of 500*u* is deferred to the next year. This deferral of 500*u* of income creates the partnership between the taxpayer and the government, with the taxpayer contributing 300*u* to the partnership and the government contributing 200*u* (Step 1). In the year after receipt, the partnership generates 50*u* of income. The government taxes this at a 40 percent tax rate leaving 30*u* for the taxpayer, which is, in substance, the allocation of the profits of the partnership (Steps 2 and 3). The 30*u* allocated to the taxpayer should be taxed to prevent the time value of money benefit of tax deferral (Steps 4 and 5). Requiring the taxpayer to include 30*u* in income in year two is equivalent to requiring the automobile dealer to include 14.60*u* in year one (the year of receipt) and 14.60*u* in year two, which are the imputed amounts using an *after-tax* rate of return of 6 percent.

(15 February 1993); Letter from James P. Fuller, "In Defense of Fred Goldberg," 58 *Tax Notes* 1259 (1 March 1993); Letter from George K. Yin, "The Tax Administrator's Duty to Take Pro-Government Positions," 58 *Tax Notes* 1387 (8 March 1993).

[30] These amounts are determined pursuant to a table provided in Revenue Procedure 97–38. Rev. Proc. 97–38, 1997-2 C.B. 479. If the term of the service warranty contract is longer, then obviously the income inclusion each year would also change. For example, if the term is five years, then the amount that the automobile dealer would include in income each year would be 239.80*u* using an applicable federal rate of 10 percent and 224*u* using an applicable federal rate of 6 percent.

[31] 1997-2 C.B. 479. See Johnson, *supra* note 23, at 383 n. 39 (1995) (criticizing the Revenue Procedure in allowing deferral of prepaid income and forcing the government to be a creditor of the taxpayer).

If the pre-tax rate of return of 10 percent is used, then the automobile dealer must include imputed income of 23.80*u* in year one and 23.80*u* in year two. This is equivalent to having the automobile dealer include 50*u* in year two. As Table 7 demonstrates, this is too much. Fifty dollars represents the return for the entire partnership, including the government's portion of 20*u*, which the government already takes as its share by being a partner in the partnership. Formally, the government takes its 20*u* as a tax on the entire 50*u*. If the government were to then impute 50*u* of income, it would be overtaxing the automobile dealer.

The imputed income method can be demonstrated algebraically. Focusing solely on the income side of the automobile dealer, the above example can be generalized algebraically using the following additional assumptions: (1) the deductions to the automobile dealer are disregarded, and (2) the option is to either include the prepaid service income on receipt or defer it until the end of the contract. In the case of *immediate recognition of income*, an amount A of income is reduced by tax t such that $A(1-t)$ may be invested. At an annual rate of return r, $A(1-t)$ invested will earn $rA(1-t)$ per year, which will be subject to tax at rate t equaling tax each year of $trA(1-t)$. The automobile dealer's net annual after-tax position each year will be:

$$rA(1-t)-trA(1-t) \text{ which equals } rA(1-t)(1-t).$$

In the case of imputing interest income in which prepaid service income is recognized *at the end of the contract* (not over the life of the contract), an amount A of prepaid service income is not reduced by tax t at the time of receipt. At an annual rate of return r, A invested will earn rA per year, which will be subject to tax at rate t equaling tax each year of trA. In addition, interest income is imputed each year in the amount of $rA(1-t)$, which is an after-tax rate of return. This is subject to tax at rate t equaling tax each year of $trA(1-t)$. The automobile dealer's net annual after-tax position will be:

$$rA(1-t)-trA(1-t) \text{ which equals } rA(1-t)(1-t).$$

This is equal to the automobile dealer's net annual after-tax position when immediate recognition of income is required and tax is immediately imposed.

If a pre-tax rate of return is used in imputing interest income in which prepaid service income is recognized at the end of the contract, the amount A of prepaid service income is not reduced by tax t at the time of receipt. At an annual rate of return r, A invested will earn rA per year, which will be subject to tax at rate t equaling tax each year of trA. In addition, interest income is imputed each year in the amount of rA, which is a pre-tax rate of return. This is subject to tax at rate t equaling tax each year of trA. The automobile dealer's net annual after-tax position will be $rA(1-\mathrm{t})-rAt$. The automobile dealer is worse off by the amount of tax that would be saved by only including imputed interest income at an after-tax rate of return.

Focusing on tax deferral through Professor Brown's partnership analogy demonstrates how to achieve the proper result in eliminating tax deferral, regardless of what method is used. If the interest charge method is used, the interest paid to the government should be deductible (unless the interest rate used is an after-tax rate of return). If the imputed income method is used, the proper rate in imputing income is an after-tax rate of return.[32]

V. Deferred Compensation

A. *Introduction*

It is important to demonstrate another very crucial principle with respect to tax deferral, which is credited to Professor Daniel Halperin[33] and advanced by Professor Alvin Warren.[34] Assume that T has entered into a nonqualified deferred compensation arrangement with her employer. T has deferred 10,000*u* of compensation that will be paid out in its entirety at the end of three years. As a result of the deferred compensation plan, T has deferred paying 4000*u* in taxes (40 percent multiplied by 10,000*u* income). If the deferred income amount of 10,000*u* increases by the after-tax rate of return of 6 percent, then there is no time value of money advantage to deferral. Assume that the employer is subject to tax on its earnings at a 40% tax rate (and T is also in the 40% tax bracket). As a result, T's deferred income amount will increase in value by a 6% after-tax rate of return each year. At the end of three years, T's deferred amount is 11,910.16*u*. If T receives the entire amount at the end of three years, T's income would be 11,910.16*u*, and T will owe taxes of 4764.06*u*, leaving T with 7146.10*u*.

Another way of viewing the above example is that if T currently receives the compensation of 10,000*u*, T would have 6000*u* after taxes (10,000*u* income less 4000*u* taxes paid). T could then invest the money and earn an after-tax rate of return of 6 percent annually. At the end of three years, T would have 7146.10*u*. This is exactly same amount as if T deferred the compensation for three years, and the deferred amount increased by a 6 percent after-tax rate of return each year. T has achieved no tax deferral benefit by deferring taxes on the original compensation of 10,000*u*. As a result, the example demonstrates that "deferral of income (or deductions) is not

---

[32] See Halperin, *supra* note 27, at 695 (noting that although an after-tax rate of return is the proper result, converting the AFR into the taxpayer's after-tax rate of return may be too low because a taxpayer cannot borrow at the AFR).

[33] See Daniel I. Halperin, "Interest in Disguise: Taxing the 'Time Value of Money,' 95 *Yale L.J.* 506 (1986). This article is probably the leading article on tax deferral and time value of money. Professor Halperin writes that, with respect to nonqualified deferred compensation, "it is not essential to allow a deduction or require inclusion at any particular time. The timing can be flexible as long as the amount of the item is adjusted to achieve an equivalence in the present discounted value of the income or deduction." *Id.* at 523–24.

[34] See Alvin C. Warren, Jr., The Timing of Taxes, 39 *Nat'l Tax J.* 499, 499 (1987) ("The present value to a taxpayer of a consistently defined tax will be the same whether the tax is deferred or accelerated, as long as the tax rate remains constant and the base of a deferred tax increases over time by the rate of return generally applicable to investment of proceeds available after payment of an accelerated tax.").

advantageous (or disadvantageous) to taxpayers if the deferred amount is increased by the after-income-tax rate of return" during the deferral period.[35]

Can the Cary Brown model and partnership analogy illustrate this principle of tax deferral? The answer again is "yes." Because of the deferral that takes place as a result of the deferred compensation arrangement, Professor Brown would describe the government as being a partner with the taxpayer (Step 1). The government should be allocated (Step 2) and collect its share of the profits of the partnership each year (Step 3). Plus, either annually (Step 4) *or at the end of the deferral period* (Step 5), the government should tax the taxpayer's profits from the partnership to eliminate the time value of money benefit of tax deferral. In other words, when the deferral period is terminated, the taxpayer needs to end up with his contribution plus an *after-tax rate of return on his contribution* to the partnership (the government taxing the return). This is consistent with the five-step partnership analogy used throughout this chapter. Professors Halperin and Klein have written that Professor Warren's advancement "may perhaps best be described as a 'mathematical trick.'"[36] While that may be true, Professor Warren's advancement is consistent with the partnership application of the Cary Brown model.[37]

B. Employer in the Same Tax Bracket as Employee

Under the partnership analogy, because T has deferred 10,000*u* of income, T is treated as contributing 6000*u* to the partnership, and the government is treated as contributing 4000*u* (Step 1). If the 10 percent pre-tax rate of return on the deferred compensation is taxed each year to the employer, then the 1000*u* of earnings in the first year, although actually taxed to the employer, is really earnings of the partnership between T and the government. T (and not the employer) is the one deferring income. As a result, T's share of the earnings is 60 percent, or 600*u* in this case (Step 2). The government's share is 40 percent, or 400*u* in this case (Step 2). The government collects its 400*u* from the employer at the end of year one (step 3). This is not really a tax but the government's share of profits from the partnership. The government generally does not care whom it collects its share of the profits from as long as the share is collected. In year two, the investment now of 10,600*u* will generate 1060*u* of earnings to the employer, which can again be described as earnings of the partnership between T and the government. T's share of the earnings is 636*u*, and the government's share is 424*u* (step 2). The government collects its 424*u* from the employer at the end of year two (step 3). Again, the 424*u* is not really a tax, but rather it is the government's share of profits from the partnership.

In year three, the investment now of 11,236*u* will generate 1123.60*u* of earnings to the employer, which can again be described as earnings of the partnership

35 *Id.* at 501; see also Halperin, *supra* note 33, at 523–24.

36 Letter from Daniel I. Halperin and William A. Klein, "Accounting for Future Obligations – Once More," 39 *Tax Notes* 266 (11 April 1988).

37 See David G. Hartman, "Tax Policy and Foreign Direct Investment in the United States," 37 *Nat'l Tax J.* 475 (1984) (applying the principle that, under certain conditions, there is no time value of money advantage to tax deferral if the deferred amount increases at the after-tax rate of return, in the international tax context).

between T and the government. T's share of the earnings is 674.16*u*, and the government's share is 449.44*u* (Step 2). The government collects its 449.44*u* from the employer at the end of year three (Step 3).

Also at the end of year three, T receives her deferred income of 11,910.16*u*, for which the employer is entitled to a deduction.[38] The deferred amount can be treated as 1910.16*u* of profits and 10,000*u* return of contribution (Step 5). As to the 1910.16*u* of profits, it is all allocated to T, as the government has already been allocated its share of the profits on its contribution to the partnership (from the employer). T is taxable on her profit of 1910.16*u* (Step 5). Therefore, the government collects 764.06*u* of T's share of the profits (1910.16*u* of income multiplied by 40 percent). T is left with 1146.10*u*. As to the return of the contributions, 6000*u* is returned to T and 4000*u* is returned to the government. Consequently, T receives a total of 7146.10*u*, and the government 4764.06*u* of the total 11,910.16*u*.

T has received no time value of money benefit by deferring taxes on the compensation of 10,000*u*. The government is allocated (Step 2) and collects its share of the profits each year (Step 3) and taxes T's share of the profits when the partnership terminates at the end of three years (Step 5).[39] In other words, all five steps of the partnership analogy eliminate the time value of money benefit of tax deferral.[40]

---

[38] I.R.C. § 404(a)(5). The employer's deduction of 11,910.16*u* at the time of payment does not appear to be relevant as to the employer for purposes of the partnership aspect of the Cary Brown model. It is the employee, T, who is deferring income. The employer has neither deferred income nor accelerated a deduction. The employer merely receives a deduction upon parting with cash of 11,910.16*u*.

[39] One reviewer of this chapter suggests an alternative way of viewing the partnership aspect of the Cary Brown model in this example. At the end of the first year, the government should collect tax on T's share of the earnings of the partnership. The amount of tax should be 240*u* (600*u* multiplied by 40 percent). Because the government does not collect this amount at the end of year one, the amount is treated as credited to the government's interest in the partnership. Consequently, the government's interest is increased to 4240*u*.

During year two, the partnership generates 1060*u* of income, of which the government's share is 424*u* (1060*u* multiplied by 40 percent), which is 10 percent of its interest of 4240*u*. In year two, the government should collect tax on T's share of the earnings of the partnership. The amount of tax should be 254.40u. Because the government does not collect this amount at the end of year two, the amount is treated as credited to the government's interest in the partnership. As a result, the government's interest is increased to 4494.40*u*.

During year three, the partnership generates 1123.60*u* of income, of which the government's share is 449.44*u* (1123.60*u* multiplied by 40 percent), which is 10 percent of its interest of 4494.40*u*. In year three, the government should collect tax on T's share of the earnings of the partnership. The amount of tax should be 269.66*u*. When the partnership terminates at the end of year three, the government receives 4,494.40*u* plus 269.66*u* totaling 4764.06*u*. The taxpayer receives 7146.10*u* (6000*u* plus 600*u*, minus 240*u*, plus 636*u*, minus 254.40*u*, plus 674.16*u*, minus 269.66*u*).

Under this alternative view, there is no advantage to tax deferral because the deferred tax is credited to the government's interest in the partnership at the end of each year. As a result, the government earns the return on the deferred tax, not the taxpayer.

The methodology in the text achieves the same numerical result as this alternative. The purpose of the methodology in the text is to demonstrate that it does not matter *when* the government taxes the taxpayer's share of profits, either annually or at the end of the deferral period when the partnership terminates, because the time value of money benefit of tax deferral is eliminated in either case.

[40] Steps four and five are, in essence, interchangeable. As demonstrated in this chapter, the government can tax the taxpayer's share of the profits annually or at the end of the deferral period.

C. Employer in a Different Tax Bracket from Employee

Can the partnership analogy be used if the employer and employee are in different tax brackets? Again, the answer is formally "yes," but substantively this is different than the Cary Brown model because the assumption of constant tax rates is changed. Assume the employer is in the 20 percent tax bracket and earns a 10 percent pre-tax rate of return each year. The employee, T, is in the 40 percent tax bracket and earns a 10 percent pre-tax rate of return each year. If the 10 percent pre-tax rate of return on the deferred compensation is taxed each year to the employer, then the 1000*u* of earnings in the first year, although actually taxed to the employer, is really earnings of the partnership between T and the government. Again, it is T who is deferring income, not the employer. But this time, T and the government will share the earnings of the partnership each year on an 80 percent to 20 percent profit sharing ratio (Step 2). This is clearly advantageous to T because T has originally contributed 60 percent of the capital of the partnership but is allocated 80 percent of the earnings each year – clearly one reason why T would want to enter into this deferred compensation arrangement.[41] As a result, T's share of the earnings is 80 percent, or 800*u* in this case (Step 2). The government's share is 20 percent, or 200*u* in this case (Step 2). The government collects its 200*u* from the employer at the end of year one (Step 3). This is the government's share of profits from the partnership. As long as the government collects its share of the profits, it does not care much from whom the share is collected.[42]

In year two, the investment now of 10,800*u* will generate 1080*u* of earnings to the employer, which can again be described as earnings of the partnership between T and the government. T's share of the earnings is 864*u*, and the government's share is 216*u* (Step 2). The government collects its 216*u* from the employer at the end of year two (Step 3). The 216*u* is the government's share of profits from the partnership.

In year three, the investment now of 11,664*u* will generate 1166.40*u* of earnings to the employer. T's share of the "partnership" earnings is 933.12*u*, and the government's share is 233.28*u* (Step 2). The government collects its 233.28*u* from the employer at the end of year three (Step 3).

Also at the end of year three, T receives her deferred income of 12,597.12*u*, for which the employer is entitled to a deduction.[43] The deferred amount can be treated

[41] In other words, assuming equal pre-tax returns, T will earn a higher after-tax rate of return by entering into this deferred compensation plan with her employer than if she immediately received the compensation and invested the after-tax proceeds on her own behalf.

[42] In this example, the government would have preferred to collect its share of the profits from the employee if the employee's tax rate were used to determine the profit sharing ratio. But that is not the case in a nonqualified, unfunded deferred compensation plan.

[43] I.R.C. § 404(a)(5). As stated previously, the employer's deduction does not appear relevant with respect to the employer as to the partnership aspect of the Cary Brown model. It is the employee T who is deferring income. The employer has not deferred income and also has not accelerated a deduction. The employer is merely receiving a deduction upon parting with cash of 12,597.12*u*. See *supra* note 38.

as 2597.12*u* of profits and 10,000*u* return of contribution (Step 5). As to the 2597.12*u* of profits, it is all allocated to T because the government has already been allocated its share of the profits on its contribution to the partnership (from the employer). T is taxable on her profit of 2597.12*u* (Step 5). Therefore, the government collects tax of 1038.85*u* on T's share of the profits (2597.12*u* of income multiplied by 40 percent). T is left with 1558.27*u*. As to the return of the contributions, 6000*u* is returned to T, and 4000*u* is returned to the government. Consequently, T receives a total of 7558.27*u*, and the government 5038.85*u* of the total 12,597.12*u*.

It appears that T has received a time value of money benefit by deferring taxes on the compensation of 10,000*u* even though T earned an after-tax rate of return on her contribution to the partnership. This is true even though all five steps of the partnership analogy have taken place. T's advantage is that she is able to earn a higher after-tax rate of return on her contribution to the partnership because the partnership generates a higher after-tax rate of return than T can earn individually.[44] T's situation becomes closer to that of an employee participating in a qualified plan.[45] In fact, if the earnings of the partnership each year are allocated entirely to T, perhaps because the employer is tax-exempt[46] or has a net operating loss carry forward to eliminate any tax on the investment income, then T's situation becomes almost identical to that of a participant in a qualified plan.[47]

D. Comparison of Nonqualified Plans to Qualified Plans

Professor Halperin has written on a number of occasions that the sole advantage of qualified plans relative to nonqualified plans from a tax deferral standpoint is that qualified plans provide exemption of the investment income and nonqualified plans do not.[48] As even Professor Halperin has acknowledged, there still seems to be a lot of confusion in the tax community regarding this concept.[49] Perhaps the partnership analogy can clear up the lack of understanding. Assume that T, in the 40% tax

---

[44] See Halperin, *supra* note 33, at 523 (noting that while an employee will also benefit from deferral if the employer can earn a higher pre-tax return than the employee, this is not a tax policy concern).

[45] See Letter from Daniel I. Halperin, "More on Deferred Compensation from Prof. Halperin," 64 *Tax Notes* 1485 (12 September 1994) ("[T]he advantage of qualified plans can be described solely as *tax exemption for investment income*." In the case of nonqualified plans, the amounts contributed are taxed at the employer's tax rate. "In the case of a tax-exempt institution, the rate would be zero, the same as it is under a qualified plan. In the case of a taxable employer, however, at least one that does not have tax losses, the rate would be positive and fairly consistent with the employee's own rate.").

[46] See I.R.C. § 457 (deferred compensation plans of state and local governments and tax-exempt organizations).

[47] See Halperin, *supra* note 33, at 539–550.

[48] See *id.*; see also Halperin, *supra* note 45, at 1485.

[49] See Halperin, *supra* note 45, at 1485 (questioning whether some tax advisors really understand the tax deferral advantage of qualified plans versus nonqualified plans).

bracket, has entered into a deferred compensation arrangement with her employer that is part of a *qualified plan*. T has deferred 10,000*u* of compensation that will be paid out in its entirety at the end of three years. As a result of the deferred compensation plan, T has deferred paying 4000*u* in taxes (40 percent multiplied by 10,000*u* income). The employer receives a 10,000*u* deduction upon contributing the money to the plan.[50] T, the employee, will not have income until the money is withdrawn (let us assume at the end of three years with no penalty).[51] T's deferred income will increase in value by a 10 percent pre-tax rate of return each year.[52] At the end of three years, the deferred amount is 13,310*u*. If T receives the entire amount at the end of three years, T's income is 13,310*u*. After taxes of 5324*u*, T is left with 7986*u*.

Under the partnership analogy, because T has deferred 10,000*u* of income, T is treated as contributing 6000*u* to the partnership and the government is treated as contributing 4000*u* (Step 1). During the first year, the partnership earns 1000*u*. Because this is a qualified plan, these earnings are not currently taxed.[53] Using the partnership analogy, all of the profits are allocated to T during the first year, and none are allocated to the government (Step 2). Because the government is not allocated any of the profits, it has nothing to collect from the partnership during the first year (Step 3). The government does nothing to prevent tax deferral during the first year. In other words, step 1 has taken place, creating the partnership between T and the government, Steps 2 and 3 take place but the profit sharing ratio of taxpayer to government is 100 percent to 0%. In addition, Steps 4 and 5 do not take place because T does not collect her share of the profits for the government to tax (step 4) and the partnership does not terminate (step 5).

During the second year, the partnership earns 1100*u*. Because this is a qualified plan, these earnings are not currently taxed. All of the profits are allocated to T during the second year, and none are allocated to the government (Step 2). Thus the government has nothing to collect from the partnership during the second year (Step 3). The government does nothing to prevent tax deferral during the second year. As in the first year, step 1 takes place, creating the partnership between T and the government, Steps 2 and 3 take place, but the profit-sharing ratio is again 100 percent to 0 percent, and Steps 4 and 5 do not take place.

During the third year, the partnership earns 1210*u*, and the funds are distributed to T at the end of year three. Of the 1210*u* earned during year three, the government collects 40 percent of it, or 484*u*; this is not due to steps 2 and 3, because all the year's profits are still allocated to T, but rather due to steps 4 and 5. The partnership also returns the accumulated profits from the earlier years plus the capital contributions made by T and the government. T receives 2100*u* of accumulated profits, plus

---

[50] See I.R.C. § 404(a). As stated previously with respect to nonqualified plans, the employer's deduction does not appear relevant as to the partnership aspect of the Cary Brown model. See *supra* note 38. The employer is neither deferring income nor accelerating a deduction. The employer has actually parted with cash of 10,000*u* that it will not receive back.

[51] See I.R.C. § 402(a). [52] See I.R.C. § 501(a). [53] See *id.*

6000*u* of capital contributions (step 5). The accumulated profits of 2100*u* are taxed by the government (step 5). At a 40 percent tax rate, T owes 840*u*. T will be left with 726*u* (1210*u* less 484*u*), plus 1260*u* (2100*u* less 840*u*), plus T's capital contributions of 6000*u*, which total 7986*u*. The government receives 484*u*, plus 840*u* of taxes on T's accumulated profits, plus 4000*u* of capital contributions. This totals 5324*u*. The partnership analogy works again to describe the tax consequences of a qualified plan (see Table 8).

Table 8

	Contributions to the partnership	Income of the partnership each year	Termination of the partnership after three years (return of contributions plus current profits less taxes plus accumulated profits less taxes)
Taxpayer	6000*u*	1000*u* (year one); 1100*u* (year two); 1210*u* (year three)	7986*u* (6000*u* plus 1210*u* less 484*u* taxes owed plus 2100*u* less 840*u* of taxes)
Government	4000*u*	0*u* (each year)	5324*u* (4,000*u* plus 484*u* plus 840*u* of taxes)
Total	10,000*u*	3310*u*	13,310*u*

The partnership analogy shows the difference between a qualified plan and a nonqualified plan. In a qualified plan, the government is not allocated any of the profits of the partnership. All of the profits are allocated to the taxpayer. The taxpayer leaves the profits in the partnership until termination of the partnership. At termination, the government finally taxes the taxpayer's profits of the partnership. In the nonqualified plan, the government collects it share of the profits each year. The taxpayer leaves his share of the profits in the partnership until termination of the partnership. The government taxes the taxpayer's profits of the partnership at termination.

The qualified plan example is also different than the previous situations that demonstrated the application of the Cary Brown model. For example, in the case of the immediate deduction of the taxable bond or an installment sale (with no interest charge), the government is allocated (Step 2) and collects its share of the profits of the partnership each year (Step 3). But the taxpayer is never taxed on his share of the partnership income (Steps 4 and 5 never take place). As a result, immediately deducting the cost of an asset (or deferring the gain on an installment sale) is equivalent to excluding the future annual return of *the asset* from gross income as described by the Cary Brown model. In the case of the deductible taxable bond, the asset is the bond and the income exclusion is the taxpayer's portion of the interest income received each year on the bond.[54] In the case of an installment sale of property with a zero basis, the asset is the installment obligation and the income exclusion is the taxpayer's portion of the interest income received each year on the installment obligation.

In the qualified plan example, the government is not allocated any of the profits of the partnership each year (Step 2) and consequently does not collect its share of the profits of the partnership each year (Step 3). As a result, Steps 2 and 3 take place, but the profit sharing ratio for the taxpayer to government is 100 percent to 0 percent. Steps 4 and 5 take place upon termination of the partnership, which does not happen in the Cary Brown model.

As a result, the qualified plan example is a demonstration that is equivalent to the Cary Brown model as to the original contribution to the plan and the return on the original contribution for the first year only. If the partnership is terminated immediately after one year, the government will, in substance, collect its share of the profits of the partnership, not through Steps 2 and 3, but rather through Steps 4 and 5. Under the Cary Brown model, the government collects its share of the profits of the partnership under Steps 2 and 3. If the time frame involved is only one year, then collecting taxes under Steps 4 and 5 yields equivalent results to collecting taxes under Steps 2 and 3 (assuming constant tax rates). But after the first year, when the government does not collect its tax because the partnership does not terminate, a different type of tax deferral situation takes place, as illustrated by the qualified plan example.

Under the qualified plan example, it is possible to analyze the allocation of 100 percent of the profits of the partnership to the taxpayer as creating an additional tax deferral situation. In other words, an additional Step 1 of the partnership analogy takes place once a year is completed. All of the profits of the partnership of the completed year are allocated to the taxpayer, and the profits are left in the partnership. This situation is referred to as the Super Cary Brown model and is demonstrated in Tables 9–11.

Table 9

	Contributions to the partnership	Income of the partnership	Termination of the partnership after one year (return of contributions plus accumulated profits)
Taxpayer	6000*u*	1000*u*	6600*u* (6000*u* plus 1000*u* less 400*u* of taxes)
Government	4000*u*	0*u*	4400*u* (4000*u* plus 400*u* of taxes)
Total	10,000*u*	1000*u*	11,000*u*

54 See, e.g., Surrey, Pathways, *supra* note 2, at 323 n. 6.

Table 9 demonstrates the equivalent Cary Brown model as to the *original* contribution of 10,000*u* to the qualified plan. But as stated earlier, an additional equivalent Cary Brown type of situation takes place each year when the government does not tax and collect the profits of the partnership through Steps 4 and 5. During the first year, the partnership generates 1000*u* in profits, which is all allocated to the taxpayer (Step 2). The government collects no share of the profits (Step 3). The government does not collect its 400*u* tax on the 1000*u* of profits from the first year because it is not allocated any of the profits of the partnership (Steps 2 and 3), the taxpayer does not collect its share of the profits (Step 4 does not take place), and the partnership does not terminate at the end of the first year (Step 5 does not take place). By not collecting the tax on the profits, this is, in essence, an additional capital contribution to the partnership (or alternatively, the creation of a second partnership at the beginning of year two). Therefore, Table 9 is not accurate *after the first year* is completed and the second year has commenced.

Table 10

	Contributions to the partnership at the beginning of year two	Income of the partnership	Termination of the partnership after two years (return of contributions plus accumulated profits)
Taxpayer	6600*u*	1100*u*	7260*u* (6600*u* plus 1100*u* less taxes owed of 440*u*)
Government	4400*u*	0*u*	4840*u* (4400u plus 440*u*)
Total	11,000*u*	1100*u*	12,100*u*

Table 10 demonstrates the equivalent Cary Brown model as to the 11,000*u* in the qualified plan. Again, an additional equivalent Cary Brown type of situation takes place each year when the government does not tax and collect the profits of the partnership through Steps 4 and 5. The partnership generates 1100*u* in profits during the second year, which is all allocated to the taxpayer (Step 2). The government collects no share of the profits (Step 3). The government does not collect its 440*u* tax on the 1100*u* of profits from the second year because it is not allocated any of the profits of the partnership (Steps 2 and 3), the taxpayer does not collect his share of the profits (Step 4 does not take place), and the partnership did not terminate immediately after the second year (Step 5 does not take place). Essentially, by not collecting the tax on the profits, an additional capital contribution to the partnership is made (or, alternatively, the creation of an additional partnership at the beginning of year three). Therefore, Table 10 is not accurate *after the second year* is completed and the third year has commenced.

Table 11

	Contributions to the partnership at the beginning of year three	Income of the partnership each year	Termination of the partnership after three years (return of contributions plus accumulated profits)
Taxpayer	7260*u*	1210*u*	7986*u* (7260*u* plus 1210*u* less 484*u*)
Government	4840*u*	0*u*	5324*u* (4840*u* plus 484*u*)
Total	12,100*u*	1210*u*	13,310*u*

Table 11 accurately demonstrates the results of a qualified plan if the distribution to T is made at the end of year three, which is the assumption in this example. The equivalent Cary Brown model applies to the 12,100*u* that is in the qualified plan at the beginning of year three. At the end of year three, the government collects its tax on the profits of the partnership (484*u*) and also collects its contribution to the partnership because the partnership is terminating (Steps 4 and 5). The taxpayer is allocated his share of the profits for year three of 1210*u* and must pay taxes of 484*u* on these profits; contributions of 7260*u* are also returned to the taxpayer. After taxes, the taxpayer is left with a total of 7986*u*. Year three, in isolation, is an equivalent example of the Cary Brown model because the government collects its tax under Steps 4 and 5, which is equivalent to collecting its tax under Steps 2 and 3 of the Cary Brown model. In essence, the taxpayer's share of the profits of the partnership in year three is never taxed, similar to an installment sale or expensing of an asset. Looking at all three years together is an example of the Super Cary Brown model.

VI. Unrealized Appreciation

A. Realization Doctrine – Introduction

A complicated example of the Cary Brown model involves the realization doctrine. Many people may not realize the specific tax deferral that takes place, at least from a time value of money standpoint, with respect to unrealized appreciation in property. Assume an individual has 10,000*u* of after-tax cash to invest. The individual has two investment options. The first is to invest in an undeveloped vacant piece of land costing 10,000*u* (Option 1). The land is expected to and does increase in value each year by 10 percent. The second option is to invest in a fully developed piece of land that can be rented at 10 percent of its value each year – 1000*u* rent each year paid to the owner by the tenant (Option 2). It is assumed that the land in the second option will not increase in value. Assume under either option that the taxpayer will sell the land at the end of three years.

Under option one, at the end of three years, the land will be worth 13,310*u* (end of year one – 11,000*u*; end of year two – 12,100*u*). If the land is sold at the end of three years, the gain is 3310*u* (13,310*u* less 10,000*u*). The tax at 40 percent is 1324*u* (3310*u* multiplied by 40 percent). Therefore, the individual is left with 11,986*u* after-taxes at the end of three years.

Under option two, at the end of the first year, the taxpayer will still have land worth 10,000*u* plus rent of 1000*u*. The rent is gross income, so 400*u* of taxes must be paid at the end of year one. Therefore, the taxpayer has 10,600*u* at the end of year one. In year two, the taxpayer receives another 1000*u* of rent and has investment income of 60*u* from the rental income earned in year one. In year three, the taxpayer receives another 1000*u* of rent and has investment income of 123.60*u* from the rental income earned in years one and two. At the end of year three, the taxpayer sells the land for 10,000*u*, resulting in no gain or loss. This leaves the taxpayer with 11,910.16*u* after taxes. This is less than option one, even though the taxpayer is in the same economic position at the end of year three. Under both options, the taxpayer begins with 10,000*u* cash, earns a 10 percent pre-tax rate of return each year on his investment, is subject to a 40% tax rate, invests in land, and closes out the investment at the end of three years. The discrepancy in results between the two options is created by the realization doctrine, which defers taxation until a realization event takes place.[55]

B. Using the Partnership Analogy

Can Professor Brown's partnership analogy accurately demonstrate the realization doctrine in the above example? The answer is "yes," although the realization doctrine adds an additional layer of complexity to the partnership model that was not present in the previous situations. The reason is that additional tax deferral takes place as the property continues to appreciate in value each year. In other words, the equivalent Cary Brown model applies to the original unrealized appreciation for the first year and will continue to apply to it in an additional capacity as long as it remains and is untaxed. But the equivalent Cary Brown model will also apply in an additional capacity as the property continues to appreciate in value. This continuous additional application of the equivalent Cary Brown model will occur as the property increases in value from year to year.

Returning to the appreciated property example, at the end of the first year, the land has appreciated in value to 11,000*u*. At this point, tax deferral takes place. The

[55] See, e.g., David P. Hariton, "The Accrual of Interest on Derivative Investments: Where Do We Go From Here?," 74 *Taxes* 1011, 1012 (December 1996) ("[S]o long as we continue under a realization system of tax accounting, it is not possible to achieve an equivalent tax treatment of economically equivalent financial investments."); David S. Miller, "Taxpayers' Ability to Avoid Tax Ownership: Current Law and Future Prospects," 51 *Tax Law*. 279, 333 (1998) ("Some argue that deferral through nonownership is a natural consequence of our realization-based tax system, and entirely consistent with the indefinite deferral enjoyed by owners of appreciated real estate and stock of corporations that never declare a dividend, such as Microsoft."); Deborah H. Schenk, "Taxation of Equity Derivatives: A Partial Integration Proposal," 50 *Tax L. Rev*. 571, 631–35 (1995) (stating that once the realization principle is adopted, the tax burden is distributed unequally).

appreciation of 1000*u* in essence creates a partnership between the taxpayer and the government, with the taxpayer contributing 600*u* and the government contributing 400*u* (Step 1). During the second year, the partnership generates 100*u* of investment income (1000*u* of appreciation multiplied by 10 percent rate of return) which is allocated entirely to the taxpayer because, under the realization doctrine, the government does not tax mere appreciation in property (Step 2). The government does not collect its 40*u* tax on the 100*u* of profits from the second year because it is not allocated any of the profits of the partnership (Steps 2 and 3). Further, the taxpayer does not collect his share of the profits (Step 4 does not take place), and the partnership does not terminate immediately after the second year (Step 5 does not take place).

By not collecting the tax on the profits, the government has done nothing to prevent tax deferral in year two. Also, during the second year, the land appreciates another 1000*u*. This is, in essence, an additional contribution of 600*u* by the taxpayer to the partnership and an additional contribution of 400*u* by the government to the partnership (a new Step 1 takes place), bringing their total contributions to 1200*u* and 800*u*, respectively.

The taxpayer sells the property at the end of year three for 13,310*u*. During year three, the partnership generates 210*u* of investment income, which is allocated entirely to the taxpayer because the government does not tax mere appreciation in property (Step 2). The government collects its 124*u* tax on the 310*u* of profits from the second and third years even though it was not allocated any of the profits of the partnership (Steps 2 and 3) but rather because the partnership terminated at the end of the third year (Steps 4 and 5 take place). Also, during the third year, the land appreciates another 1000*u*. Again, this is, in essence, an additional contribution of 600*u* by the taxpayer to the partnership and an additional contribution of 400*u* by the government to the partnership (a new Step 1 takes place), bringing their total contributions to 1800*u* and 1200*u*, respectively.

Because the land is sold for 13,310*u* at the end of year three, the partnership is terminated, and the taxpayer receives 10,000*u* as a return of basis. The taxpayer also receives 1800*u* as a return of its contribution to the partnership, plus 310*u* as its share of the profits of the partnership, less the taxes of 124*u* owed to the government. The government receives 1200*u* as a return of its contribution to the partnership, plus 124*u* as its tax on the profits of the partnership. The taxpayer receives a total of 11,986*u*, and the government receives a total of 1324*u*.

C. Comparison of Unrealized Appreciation to Qualified Plans

It should be apparent that unrealized appreciation (when isolated from the after-tax investment in the underlying property) is an example of the Super Cary Brown model. As demonstrated, qualified plans are also an example of the Super Cary Brown model. *As a result, assuming stable tax rates with no preferential treatment for capital gains, no fair market value basis at death rules, and stable investment yields, unrealized appreciation is equivalent to having a corresponding amount set aside in a qualified plan.* In other words, from a tax deferral standpoint and using the assumptions previously stated, a taxpayer would be indifferent between having property with unrealized appreciation of, for example, 1000*u* and having 1000*u* set aside in a qualified plan.

An example will demonstrate the equivalence of unrealized appreciation and funds set aside in a qualified plan. Assume individual T receives 30,000*u* salary from her employer. T contributes 1000*u* to a qualified retirement plan. The 1000*u* contributed to the qualified plan should be either deducted from gross income or excluded from gross income. The end result is that T will only have 29,000*u* of taxable income for the year. In other words, the money in the qualified plan is comprised of pre-tax dollars. The 1000*u* in the qualified plan will grow to 1100*u* at the end of one year; 1210*u* at the end of two years; 1331*u* at the end of three years; and so on. It will continue to grow at a 10 percent pre-tax rate of return each year. At the end of x years, the fund will have $1000u(1+r)^x$. When the money is distributed to T from the qualified plan, T will receive 60 percent of the total funds, and the government will receive 40 percent based on the application of the partnership analogy to the Super Cary Brown model.

Assume individual A receives 29,000*u* in salary from his employer. A also owns undeveloped land. During the current year, the land has appreciated 1000*u* in value. A will only include 29,000*u* in gross income. The 1000*u* of appreciation is not taxed because of the realization doctrine.[56] In other words, *the portion of the property* that represents the unrealized appreciation can be likened to 1000*u* of pre-tax dollars. This is, in some sense, similar to A receiving a 30,000*u* salary but using 1000*u* of the salary to buy property for which the government allows an immediate deduction. If this were the case, A would have taxable income of 29,000*u* and own property with a value of 1000*u* and a basis of zero, in other words, unrealized appreciation of 1000*u*. This unrealized appreciation will increase to 1100*u* at the end of one year; 1210*u* at the end of two years; 1331*u* at the end of three years; and so on. It will continue to grow at a 10 percent pre-tax rate of return each year. At the end of x years, the amount of unrealized appreciation will be $1000u(1+r)^x$. When A receives the money from this unrealized appreciation (by selling or otherwise disposing of the property in a taxable event), A will receive 60 percent of the total funds and the government will receive 40 percent based on the application of the partnership analogy to the Super Cary Brown model. Unrealized appreciation of 1000*u* is equivalent to 1000*u* set aside in a qualified plan.

Of course, the funding of qualified plans and unrealized appreciation is completely different. A qualified plan is almost always funded with pre-tax dollars, whereas unrealized appreciation in property is, in almost all cases, achieved by using after-tax dollars.[57] But once the unrealized appreciation is generated, whether expected or not, then it is equivalent to funds set aside in a qualified plan.

[56] I.R.C. § 1001(a).

[57] It is possible that unrealized appreciation in property could be generated by pre-tax dollars. For example, Section 179 allows an immediate deduction for certain types of personal depreciable property purchased for use in a trade or business. I.R.C. § 179. But this type of property almost always depreciates in value and is purchased for the increased income stream it will generate for the business.

In fact, it may be appropriate to isolate unrealized appreciation from the after-tax dollars used to purchase the underlying property for several reasons. When property is bought using after-tax dollars, tax deferral has not yet taken place. Once the property appreciates in value, then tax deferral has taken place. In other words, the partnership between the taxpayer and the government is created once appreciation occurs. It is at this point (when appreciation occurs) that an analysis of the tax deferral benefit should be made and appropriate action, if any, should be taken to prevent deferral.

In addition, in terms of attacking tax deferral, the after-tax dollars invested in the appreciated property, in certain instances, may not be particularly relevant. For example, probably the most discussed method for eliminating deferral with respect to unrealized appreciation is a mark-to-market approach. Under a mark-to-market approach, the after-tax investment in the property is ignored except for determining the beginning and ending bases of the property. Assume a taxpayer owns land that has appreciated 1000*u* during the year. Under a mark-to-market approach, the 1000*u* would be included in the taxpayer's gross income. It does not matter whether the taxpayer paid 10,000*u* or 1,000,000*u* for the land. The end result is that 1000*u* is included in the taxpayer's gross income, and the basis in the property (whatever it may be) is increased by 1000*u*.

It seems particularly appropriate to focus solely on the unrealized appreciation and ignore the after-tax dollars used to purchase the underlying property if the unrealized appreciation was due to labor or luck and not to a predictable rate of return.[58] For example, assume T owns land long thought essentially worthless, which has a negligible basis. A valuable mineral deposit is found nearby, immediately causing the value of T's land to rise to 10,000*u*. The appreciation of the land to 10,000*u* is equivalent to having 10,000*u* set aside in a qualified plan. They are both examples of the Super Cary Brown model. Assume the land's value continues to rise by 10 percent annually for three years. At the end of three years, T sells the land (still undeveloped) for 13,310*u*, resulting in 13,310*u* of gain. T will have 7986*u* remaining after-taxes, just as if T had set aside 10,000*u* in a qualified plan for three years. If T receives preferential capital gains treatment on sale of the land,[59] or dies and the property's basis is stepped up to fair market value,[60] the benefit of the unrealized appreciation can become greater than having a corresponding amount set aside in a qualified plan.[61]

---

[58] See, e.g., William M. Gentry and Glenn R. Hubbard, "Distributional Implications of Introducing a Broad-Based Consumption Tax," 11 *Tax Policy and the Econ.* 1, 2–6 (James M. Poterba, ed. 1997 (inframarginal returns are returns associated with rents to ideas, managerial skill, or market power); Alvin C. Warren, Jr., "How Much Capital Income Taxed Under an Income Tax is Exempt Under a Cash Flow Tax?, 52 *Tax L. Rev.* 1, 6 (1996) (distinguishing increased wealth arising from brilliance, hard work, and luck from above-normal return to capital investment); Cunningham, *supra* note 2, at 23 (arguing much of what is thought of as a return to capital is really a return to labor, luck, or ingenuity).

[59] I.R.C. §§ 1221, 1222, and 1(h).

[60] I.R.C. § 1014.

[61] See, e.g., Eric M. Engen and William G. Gale, "The Effects of Fundamental Tax Reform on Saving" in *Economic Effects of Fundamental Tax Reform* 83, 87, (Henry J. Aaron and William G. Gale eds. 1996), (discussing the fact that assets that result in capital gains can sometimes provide more favorable tax advantages than assets held in retirement plans due to preferential tax treatment for capital gains and fair market value basis at death rules for capital assets).

D. Attacking Tax Deferral on Unrealized Appreciation

One of the most discussed methods for eliminating tax deferral with respect to unrealized appreciation is the mark-to-market approach.[62] Under mark-to-market, [63] no partnership is ever created between the taxpayer and the government. In other words, Step 1 of the partnership analogy never takes place. This is due to the fact that at the time the partnership would be created, the basis of the property is marked to fair market value, eliminating any gain in the property and thereby also eliminating any tax deferral.[64]

A mark-to-market regime has been discussed by a number of commentators.[65] Most agree that it is a theoretically correct approach in an ideal income tax system.

---

[62] There are other methods of eliminating tax deferral created by the realization doctrine. See, e.g., Alan J. Auerbach, "Retrospective Capital Gains Taxation," 81 *Amer. Econ. Rev*. 167 (1991) (discussing a proposal to charge interest on the tax deferred at the risk-free rate of return and to treat each asset as appreciating at the risk-free rate); David F. Bradford, "Fixing Realization Accounting: Symmetry, Consistency and Correctness in the Taxation of Financial Instruments, 50 *Tax L. Rev*. 731 (1995) (proposing a risk-free rate of return on property but also establishing a gain reference date at the time the investment is made and using that date to compute any interest charge); Noel B. Cunningham and Deborah H. Schenk, "Taxation Without Realization: A "Revolutionary" Approach to Ownership," 47 *Tax L. Rev*. 725 (1992) (proposing a guide-line rate of return using the risk-free rate of return to the taxpayer's basis in the property interest); Mary L. Fellows, "A Comprehensive Attack on Tax Deferral," 88 *Mich. L. Rev*. 722 (1990) (proposing an interest charge for the period that the tax on appreciation is deferred, generally referred to as retrospective taxation); Mark P. Gergen, "The Effects of Price Volatility and Strategic Trading Under Realization, Expected Return and Retrospective Taxation," 49 *Tax L. Rev*. 209 (1994) (discussing mark-to-market, retrospective taxation, and expected return taxation).

In part to avoid the problems created by the realization doctrine, Professor Andrews has favored a consumption-based tax. See Andrews, *supra* note 1. See also William D. Andrews, "Fairness and the Choice Between a Consumption-Type and an Accretion-Type Personal Income Tax: A Reply to Professor Warren," 88 *Harv. L. Rev*. 947 (1975); Barbara H. Fried, "Fairness and the Consumption Tax," 44 *Stan. L. Rev*. 961 (1992); Graetz, *supra* note 3; Alvin C. Warren, "Fairness and a Consumption-Type or Cash Flow Personal Income Tax," 88 *Harv. L. Rev*. 931 (1975); Alvin C. Warren, "Would a Consumption Tax Be Fairer Than an Income Tax?," 89 *Yale L. J*. 1081 (1980).

[63] The term "mark-to-market" is used interchangeably with the terms "accrual taxation" and "accretion taxation."

[64] The assumption being made here is that the property will be marked-to-market on the last day of the taxpayer's taxable year and that any increase or decrease during the course of the year is ignored until the last day. As a result, the assumption is that no tax deferral takes place during the course of the year even though the property may have appreciated in value. Tax deferral is treated as taking place on the last day of the year when the amount of appreciation (if any) is calculated. See, e.g., Jeff Strnad, "Periodicity and Accretion Taxation: Norms and Implementation," 99 *Yale L. J*. 1817 (1990) (discussing continuous accretion taxation); Land, *supra* note 2, at 73–75 (suggesting tax deferral created by the realization requirement should be addressed by continuous accretion taxation).

[65] The recent literature on mark-to-market, accrual taxation, and accretion taxation is quite voluminous. See, e.g., Fred B. Brown, "'Complete' Accrual Taxation," 33 *San Diego L. Rev*. 1559 (1996); Cunningham and Schenk, *supra* note 62; Joseph M. Dodge, "A Combined Mark-to-Market and Pass-Through Corporate-Shareholder Integration Proposal, 50 *Tax L. Rev*. 265 (1994); Thomas L. Evans, "The Evolution of Federal Income Tax Accounting – A Growing Trend Towards Mark-to-Market, 67 *Taxes* 824 (1989); Fellows, *supra* note 62; Gergen, *supra* note 62; Daniel I. Halperin, "Saving the Income Tax: An Agenda for Research," 77 *Tax Notes* 967 (1997); Edward D. Kleinbard and Thomas L. Evans, "The Role of Mark-to-Market Accounting in a Realization-Based Tax System," 75 *Taxes* 788 (1997); David J. Shakow, "Taxation Without Realization: A Proposal for Accrual Taxation," 134 *U. Pa. L. Rev*. 1111

In other words, it implements the Haig–Simons definition of income, which is considered the ideal definition of income by most tax theorists.[66] Under the Haig–Simons definition, income is defined as the "algebraic sum of (1) the market value of rights exercised in consumption and (2) the change in the value of the store of property rights between the beginning and the end of the period in question."[67] As many commentators have noted, however, eliminating the realization requirement and adopting a mark-to-market approach for unrealized appreciation in property could lead to numerous problems.[68] These problems include liquidity in paying the resulting income tax, the administrative difficulty of determining the changes in fair market value of the taxpayer's assets (particularly those not traded on a publicly-traded exchange), and possible constitutional (or political) problems.[69] However, because unrealized appreciation is equivalent to having a corresponding amount of funds set aside in a qualified plan, it appears that a strong argument can be made to partially or completely repeal the realization doctrine, at least as to publicly-traded property where problems of liquidity and valuation generally are not present.[70]

E. Another View of the Realization Doctrine

1. Introduction

Rather than focusing solely on the unrealized appreciation component of property, it is possible to focus on the entire piece of property and analyse it under tax deferral principles. Assume T has 10,000*u* of salary that T includes in gross income. T invests

---

(1986); Theodore S. Sims, "Long-Term Debt, the Term Structure of Interest and the Case for Accrual Taxation," 47 *Tax L. Rev*. 313 (1992); Jeff Strnad, "The Taxation of Bonds: the Tax Trading Dimension," 81 *Va. L. Rev*. 47 (1995); Strnad, *supra* note 64, at 1817; Patricia D. White, "Realization, Recognition, Reconciliation, Rationality and the Structure of the Federal Income Tax System," 88 *Mich. L. Rev.* 2034 (1990); Edward A. Zelinsky, "For Realization: Income Taxation, Sectoral Accretionism, and the Virtue of Attainable Values," 19 Cardozo *L. Rev.* 861 (1997).

66 See Robert M. Haig, "The Concept of Income – Economic and Legal Aspects," in *The Federal Income Tax* 1, 7, (Robert M. Haig ed., 1921) reprinted in American Economic Assn., *Readings in the Economics of Taxation* 54, 55 (Richard A. Musgrave and Carl S. Shoup eds., 1959); Henry C. Simons, *Personal Income Taxation* 50 (1938).

67 Simons, *supra* note 66, at 50.

68 See, e.g., David F. Bradford and the Treasury Dept. Tax Policy Staff, *Blueprints for Basic Tax Reform*, (2nd ed. 1984); George F. Break and Joseph A. Pechman, *Federal Tax Reform: The Impossible Dream?* (1975); Boris I. Bittker, " 'Comprehensive Tax Base' as a Goal of Income Tax Reform," 80 *Harv. L. Rev*. 925 (1967); Boris I. Bittker, "Tax Reform and Tax Simplification," 29 *U. Miami L. Rev*. 1 (1974).

69 See Alvin C. Warren, Jr., "Financial Contract Innovation and Income Tax Policy," 107 *Harv. L. Rev.* 460, 462 (1993); Cunningham and Schenk, *supra* note 62, at 741 (arguing that constitutionality should not be a problem in adopting a mark-to-market regime, based in part on the Ninth Circuit's decision in *Murphy v. United States*, 992 F.2d 929 (9th Cir. 1993)).

The U.S. Congress has adopted mark-to-market in several areas of the Internal Revenue Code. See, e.g., I.R.C. 475 (dealers and traders in securities and commodities); 817 and 817A (certain life insurance contracts); 1256 (regulated futures contracts); 1296 (marketable stock in a passive foreign investment company).

70 See Halperin, supra note 65, at 971 (arguing that mark-to-market should be adopted for all publicly-traded instruments and contractual arrangements on which the payments are dependent on the value of publicly-traded instruments).

the after-tax proceeds of 6000*u* in property that will appreciate in value by 10 percent each year. Assume at the end of three years, T dies and the property receives a fair market value basis at death equaling 7986*u* (6000*u* times $(1.10)^3$). The recipient of T's property can dispose it for its fair market value of 7986*u* with no income tax liability. This is in many ways an equivalent result to investing the entire salary in a qualified plan for three years.[71] As shown earlier, the qualified plan is an example of the Super Cary Brown model. Property with unrealized appreciation (focusing on the entire property, including the after-tax dollars used to purchase the property as well as the unrealized appreciation), in which the fair market value basis at death rule *is* utilized, is really an application of the Super Cary Brown model, or more specifically, kind of a reverse Super Cary Brown.

The reverse Super Cary Brown is a situation where no partnership is created, but the investment income is excluded from gross income. In addition, the investment income generated by the previous year's investment income is also excluded from gross income. As shown above, an example would be appreciated property in which the fair market value basis at death rule applies.

In the United States, two types of retirement plans can be contrasted to demonstrate the Super Cary Brown model and the reverse Super Cary Brown. Under a traditional IRA, the taxpayer is permitted a deduction for an amount contributed to the retirement account.[72] The earnings on the contributions are not taxed;[73] however, when the taxpayer receives the money in the account on retirement, it is included in income and therefore subject to tax.[74] Assuming a 40 percent tax bracket, the taxpayer keeps 60 percent of the money received on retirement, and the government collects 40 percent. As a result, the traditional IRA is an example of the Super Cary Brown model.

In 1997, as part of the Taxpayer Relief Act of 1997,[75] the United States enacted the Roth IRA, named after Senator William Roth of Delaware, who is the chair of the United States Senate Finance Committee. Under a Roth IRA, the taxpayer is not permitted a deduction for an amount contributed to the retirement account.[76] The earnings on the contribution are not taxed;[77] however, when the taxpayer receives the money in the account on retirement, it is not included in income and therefore not subject to tax.[78] The Roth IRA is an example of the reverse Super Cary Brown because no partnership is created between the taxpayer and the government. The Roth IRA is funded with after-tax dollars. Each year the investment income is solely that of the taxpayer and not the government. When the Roth IRA is terminated, the taxpayer collects the entire amount, as it is free of income taxes.

2. *Combining the Two Views on Realization*

It is possible to combine the views of focusing solely on unrealized appreciation (ignoring the actual investment) under the Super Cary Brown model and also

[71] Of course, T has to die to get this equivalent result.
[72] See I.R.C. § 219.
[73] See I.R.C. § 408(e)(1).
[74] See I.R.C. § 408(d)(1).
[75] Pub. L. No. 105–34, Section 302(a) (1997).
[76] See I.R.C. § 408A(c)(1).
[77] See I.R.C. §§ 408A(a), 408(e)(1).
[78] See I.R.C. § 408A(d)(1).

focusing on the entire appreciated property (including the actual investment) under a reverse Super Cary Brown analysis. Assume a brilliant inventor, who is also an entrepreneur, makes an important technological discovery that is marketed by the inventor's own company.[79] The inventor established the company 10 years ago by contributing 5000*u* for all of the stock of the company. As a result of the brilliant discovery, the inventor's stock is now worth 1,000,000*u*. Assume also that comparable investments during this 10-year time frame yielded an annual rate of return of 10 percent.[80]

At a 10 percent rate of return, 5000*u* invested for 10 years will grow to 12,968.71*u*.[81] It may make sense to bifurcate the value of the stock – focus on the investment growing from 5000*u* to nearly 13,000*u* by looking at the entire investment and treat the remaining value of the stock (987,000*u*) under the Super Cary Brown analysis, in which 987,000*u* is likened to a corresponding amount set aside in a qualified plan.[82] In other words, the 5000*u* investment is treated as creating an asset now worth 13,000*u*. The remaining 987,000*u* is treated separately as it was arguably created by brilliance, hard work, and luck, not by the 5000*u* investment.[83]

Under this bifurcated view, it may make sense to allow 8000*u* of the gain (13,000*u* minus 5000*u*) to potentially escape tax under the fair market value basis at death rule when the investor dies because that would be no better than having

---

[79] See Warren, *supra* note 58, at 4–5; Cunningham, *supra* note 2, at 23–24.

[80] Using a rate of return based on what similar investments have generated is obviously subject to interpretation in terms of what are similar investments. But the idea is to break the unrealized appreciation into four components: (1) risk-free rate of return on the after-tax investment, (2) risk premium on the after-tax investment, (3) inflation premium on the after-tax investment, and (4) inframarginal return. See, e.g., Cunningham, *supra* note 2, at 23 (describing capital income as composed of three components: the risk-free rate of return, the risk premium, and the inframarginal return, but not the inflation premium in a normative income tax and noting that inframarginal return may not be a return on capital but rather a return to labor or an investor's luck or ingenuity); Warren, *supra* note 58, at 4–5 ("[S]ome gains that at first might appear to be inframarginal returns to capital are actually returns to labor, or more particularly, to entrepreneurship"). The first three components would be subject to the reverse Super Cary Brown approach on the entire property, and the fourth component would be isolated from the underlying property and analyzed under the Super Cary Brown model.

[81] 5000*u* multiplied by $(1+0.10)^{10}$.

[82] Bifurcation in the case of financial instruments (dividing a financial instrument into a collection of component instruments and taxing each according to its economic substance), has been suggested as one possible solution in taxing the wide array of financial instruments. See Prop. Treas. Reg. § 1.1275-4(g), 56 Fed. Reg. 8303 (1991)(withdrawn); see also David P. Hariton, "New Rules Bifurcating Contingent Debt – A Mistake," 51 *Tax Notes* 235 (opposing bifurcation because of its inability to account for contingent payment obligations); Lawrence Lokken, "New Rules Bifurcating Contingent Debt – A Good Start," 51 *Tax Notes* 495 (supporting bifurcation but admitting that it is not a perfect approach); David A. Weisbach, "Tax Responses to Financial Contract Innovation," 50 *Tax L. Rev*. 491 (1995) (bifurcation is the best approach to taxing financial instruments); Jeff Strnad, "Commentary, Taxing New Financial Products in a Second Best World: Bifurcation and Integration," 50 *Tax L. Rev*. 545 (1995).

[83] See Warren, *supra* note 58, at 5–6; see also Gentry and Hubbard, *supra* note 58, at 2–6; Cunningham, *supra* note 2, at 23.

5000*u* set aside initially in a qualified plan, such as a Roth IRA, earning an annual 10 percent rate of return. But, under this bifurcated view of the property, it appears to be overly beneficial to allow the 987,000*u* to escape tax under the fair market value basis at death rule. It may also be overly beneficial to give preferential tax treatment to the 987,000*u* in the form of capital gains if the investor sells the stock. As stated earlier, the unrealized appreciation of 987,000*u* can be likened to having a corresponding amount set aside in a qualified plan, which is already a tremendous tax benefit, one that usually requires that a number of very rigid requirements be met.

F. Extension of the Realization Doctrine

The realization doctrine can be utilized in an almost infinite number of similar situations. For example, compare the difference between investing in stock of a growth company that pays no dividends versus investing in stock of a mature company that pays out all earnings by way of dividends. The investment of stock in a growth company will not be taxed until a realization event takes place, such as a sale. The dividends from ownership of stock in a mature company will be taxed each year as the dividends are received.

The realization doctrine also creates tremendous problems in taxing financial instruments and derivatives. A leading commentator on derivatives has written that because of the realization doctrine, it is not possible to achieve an equivalent tax treatment of economically equivalent financial investments.[84] This is because of the tax deferral that results from the realization doctrine. Professor Andrews wrote a number of years ago that the realization doctrine is the "Achilles' heel of the income tax" – referring, in large part, to the tax deferral that takes place.[85] The benefit of the tax deferral is explained by the Super Cary Brown model. The tax deferral benefit of unrealized appreciation is equivalent to a corresponding amount set aside in a qualified plan. As a result, the taxation of financial instruments and derivatives involve issues of tax deferral, which I believe Professor Brown identified 50 years ago.

---

[84] See Hariton, *supra* note 55, at 1012 ("[S]o long as we continue under a realization system of tax accounting, it is not possible to achieve an equivalent tax treatment of economically equivalent financial investments."); see also Reed Shuldiner, "A General Approach to the Taxation of Financial Instruments," 71 *Tex. L. Rev*. 243, 246 (1992) ("Most, if not all, of these problems [shortcomings in the present tax treatment of financial instruments] could be solved by abandoning our current realization system and adopting mark-to-market accounting for financial instruments."); Peter C. Canellos, "Commentary, 50 *Tax L. Rev*. 829 (1995) ("It is impossible to erect a sound structure on the flawed foundation represented by the realization requirement, which, as has been noted so often, has little to do with the proper measurement of economic income.").

[85] See William D. Andrews, "The Achilles' Heel of the Comprehensive Income Tax," in *New Directions in Federal Tax Policy for the 1980s*, 278, 280 (Charls E. Walker and Mark A. Bloomfield eds., 1983) ("But unrealized appreciation has proved, in fact, to be the Achilles' heel of the whole comprehensive income tax ideal.").

VII. Final Thoughts on Cary Brown Model and Super Cary Brown Model

The Cary Brown model and the Super Cary Brown model can easily be described by the five-step partnership analogy used throughout this article. Under the Cary Brown model, Steps 1–3 have taken place but Steps 4 and 5 have not. Under the Super Cary Brown model, Steps 1, 4 and 5 take place. To eliminate tax deferral, Steps 4 and 5 must be analyzed in the Cary Brown situation and Steps 2 and 3 must be analyzed in the Super Cary Brown situation.

As a result, one can easily see that in eliminating tax deferral, first it is important to determine whether the Cary Brown model or the Super Cary Brown model is applicable. Once this determination is made, appropriate measures can be taken to combat deferral. For example, assume an installment sale has taken place. As demonstrated earlier, installment sales are an example of the Cary Brown model. As a result, Steps 1–3 of the partnership analogy have taken place. The government needs to focus on Steps 4 and 5 to eliminate tax deferral. It generally does not matter what method is adopted to eliminate deferral, as long as it is consistent with Steps 4 and 5.

Assume instead that the government wants to take a serious look at eliminating the tax deferral benefit of unrealized appreciation. As demonstrated earlier, unrealized appreciation is an example of the Super Cary Brown model. As a result, Step 1 of the partnership analogy takes place. The government needs to focus on Steps 2 and 3 to eliminate tax deferral. Again, it generally does not matter what method is adopted to eliminate deferral as long as it is consistent with Steps 2 and 3.

Table 12 summarizes this:

Table 12

	Steps in the partnership analogy that have taken place	Steps in the partnership analogy that are lacking	Examples
Cary Brown Model	1 (Deferral is taking place); 2 (Allocate the profits of the partnership based on the tax rate on investment income); 3 (The government collects its share of the profits)	4 (Government taxes the taxpayer's share of the profits either at the time of allocation or on collection); 5 (When tax deferral period ends, government taxes the taxpayer's share of profits that were not previously taxed in Step 4)	Expensing, installment sales (with no interest charge)

Table 12 *Continued*

	Steps in the partnership analogy that have taken place	Steps in the partnership analogy that are lacking	Examples
Super Cary Brown Model	1 (Deferral is taking place); 4 (Government taxes the taxpayer's share of the profits either annually or at the end of the deferral period); 5 (When tax deferral period ends, government taxes the taxpayer's share of profits that were not previously taxed in Step 4)	2 (Allocate the profits of the partnership based on the tax rate on investment income); 3 (The government collects its share of the profits)	Qualified plans, unrealized appreciation in property

Chapter 5

Various Deferral Scenarios

I. Introduction

The Cary Brown model's application to expensing and accelerated depreciation is well established and has been discussed by a number of commentators. The Cary Brown model, however, can also be applied to a number of other situations in the tax laws, many of which are overlooked by academics and practitioners. For example, it also applies to sales of property under the installment method. The U.S. Congress apparently discovered the application of the Cary Brown model to installment sales of property in the early 1980s even though the installment sales rules were enacted in the U.S. Internal Revenue Code more than 60 years ago. It partially addressed the issue as part of the Revenue Act of 1987 and the Technical and Miscellaneous Revenue Act of 1988.

In this chapter, the Cary Brown model will be applied to eleven different fact patterns, including expensing, installment sales, and prepaid service income, as well as to some other less obvious situations. If the Cary Brown model is applicable to a given fact pattern, the taxpayer is, in essence, excluding the future annual return of the asset from income. The different areas of the tax laws selected in this chapter for analysis under the Cary Brown model have not been selected at random. Some traditional areas have been selected. But other areas have been selected because they seem to have caused a lot of confusion among tax commentators, some of whom are even familiar with the original Cary Brown model. The Cary Brown model can be applied not only to the deduction side, which is where it has traditionally been applied, but also to the income side, for example, to unrealized appreciation.

It should be emphasized that the various scenarios discussed in this chapter are by no means an exclusive list of tax deferral scenarios. Any academic or practitioner with some familiarity with U.S. and Japanese income taxation realizes that there are an inconceivable number of fact patterns that result in tax deferral. Japan, in particular, has numerous tax incentives as part of its Special Taxation Measures Law that result in tax deferral. This chapter, however, will provide enough scenarios and explanation and analysis of these scenarios so that the concepts and principles of tax deferral can be applied to any fact pattern that may arise.

In this chapter, the various fact patterns presented will include a discussion of U.S. and Japanese income tax laws. This will, of course, be helpful to those readers interested in both taxation systems. It will also be a nice lead-in to the following chapter, which will discuss how the United States has eliminated the tax deferral problems raised by the fact patterns in this chapter and offer insights on how Japan might resolve the same issues.

II. Various Deferral Scenarios under the United States Internal Revenue Code and Japanese Income Tax Law, Corporation Tax Law, and Special Taxation Measures Law

A. *Expensing*

1. United States

Expensing is the classic situation to which the Cary Brown model has been applied and discussed. The Cary Brown model, as it applies to expensing, has been discussed in some detail in the previous three chapters. To illustrate application of the model in the context of the current U.S. income tax system, assume a taxpayer purchases $10,000 of equipment to be used exclusively in the taxpayer's trade or business. Under I.R.C. Section 179, a taxpayer is permitted to immediately deduct up to $17,500 of depreciable business assets assuming that several other requirements are also met.[1] If the taxpayer meets the requirements of I.R.C. Section 179, it can immediately deduct the $10,000 cost of the equipment. At a 40 percent tax rate, the taxpayer would save an immediate $4000 in taxes. The taxpayer could take these immediate tax savings and invest it. If this additional $4000 capital investment could also be deducted, the taxpayer would save another $1600 in taxes, which could be invested in another deductible capital investment. By expensing the cost of the investment, the taxpayer can increase the investment to $I/(1-t)$, where I is the amount of income to be invested and t is the tax rate. In this case, it would be $10,000/(1 – 0.40) equaling $16,667.

This stimulus to investment, of course, is a result that the U.S. Congress intended when it originally enacted I.R.C. Section 179 in 1958 allowing a taxpayer to expense up to $2000 (or $4000 if married filing jointly).[2] Congress subsequently increased the amount that could be deducted culminating in the amount of $17,500 as part of the Omnibus Budget Reconciliation Act of 1993.[3] However, in the Small Business Job Protection Act of 1996,[4] the U.S. Congress raised the expensing amounts under I.R.C. Section 179 beginning in 1997. For tax years beginning in

---

[1] I.R.C. §§ 179(a) and (b)(1). Generally, the asset must be acquired by purchase and used in an active trade or business. I.R.C. § 179(d)(1). The dollar limitation of $17,500 is also phased out dollar by dollar by the amount by which the cost of Section 179 property placed in service during the year exceeds $200,000. I.R.C. § 179(b)(2). Finally, the Section 179 deduction cannot exceed the aggregate amount of taxable income for the year that is derived from the active conduct of any trade or business during the year. I.R.C. § 179(b)(3)(A). Any excess can be carried forward to future years. I.R.C. § 179(b)(3)(B).

[2] Pub. L. No. 85-866, Section 204(a) (1958).

[3] Pub. L. No. 103-66, Section 13116(a) (1993).

[4] Pub. L. No. 104-188, Section 1111(a) (1996).

1997, the maximum amount eligible for expensing is increased to $18,000. In 1998, the maximum amount is increased to $18,500; in 1999 to $19,000; in 2000 to $20,000; in 2001 to $24,000; and finally in 2003 and all subsequent years, it is increased to $25,000.

Through enactment of I.R.C. Section 179, the U.S. Congress was trying to stimulate the economy by encouraging small businesses to increase their investment in depreciable assets. Obviously, in enacting and enhancing I.R.C. Section 179, the U.S. Congress was not trying to eliminate any tax deferral privilege because that is what it intended under I.R.C. Section 179. If the U.S. Congress feels that it is too generous, it can reduce the dollar limitation of I.R.C. Section 179 or simply repeal it.

The U.S. Congress has provided for expensing in a number of areas of the income tax laws. These areas include:

I.R.C. Section 173 – circulation expenditures
I.R.C. Section 174 – research and experimentation expenditures
I.R.C. Section 175 – soil and water conservation expenditures
I.R.C. Section 179A – clean fuel vehicles and certain refueling property
I.R.C. Section 180 – expenditures by farmers for fertilizers
I.R.C. Section 190 – expenditures to remove architectural and transportation barriers to the handicapped and elderly
I.R.C. Section 198 – expensing of environmental remediation costs

2. *Japan*

The Japanese income tax system also allows for expensing of equipment similar to Section 179 of the U.S. Internal Revenue Code. Under the Japanese system, however, the limitation on expensing is based on a percentage of the acquisition cost of the asset rather than based on a fixed yen amount.[5] This percentage expensing is generally referred to as "special initial depreciation."[6] For example, a corporation that acquires new machinery and equipment used for the prevention of environmental pollution, such as air or water pollution, is eligible for an immediate depreciation deduction of 18 percent of the acquisition cost of the asset during the first accounting period the asset is used.[7] In other words, the corporation can immediately

[5] The Japanese income tax system does allow for expensing of minor assets. These include: (1) assets with a useful life of less than one year or (2) assets with an acquisition cost of less than ¥100,000. CTL Enf. Order 133 (1998) (applicable for the period beginning 1 April 1998). See Yuji Gomi, *Guide to Japanese Taxes 1998–99* (1998) at ¶ 6-265.

[6] See Gomi, *supra* note 5, at ¶ 6-310; Tax Bureau of the Ministry of Finance, *An Outline of Japanese Taxes* 1997 (1997) at 91.

There are a number of requirements that must be met for a corporation to qualify for special initial depreciation. Generally, these include: (1) the corporation must file a blue return; (2) it is available for only a limited period; (3) it is available for only new items; (4) the items cannot be purchased with loan proceeds; and (5) the depreciation schedule must be attached with the blue return.

[7] Special Taxation Measures Law 43-1(1) (1998) (applicable for the period from 1 April 1996 to 31 March 2000).

expense 18 percent of the cost of the asset during the first accounting period of use. This special initial depreciation is in addition to the ordinary depreciation deductions allowed for the property.[8] Other examples of special initial depreciation include: (1) new machinery and equipment used for recycling which contributes to the promotion of efficient use of resources – 14 percent of the acquisition cost;[9] (2) new machinery and equipment acquired by small or medium-sized enterprises or agricultural cooperative associations which have a cost of ¥2.3 million or more – 30 percent of the acquisition cost;[10] and (3) new assets acquired for use in earthquake disaster prevention – 13 percent of the acquisition cost (six percent of the cost of reinforcing buildings against earthquakes).[11]

The tax deferral analysis of special initial depreciation is practically identical to that discussed with respect to expensing under Section 179 of the U.S. Internal Revenue Code. The difference is in the percentage amount of expensing. For example, assume a Japanese corporation acquires equipment for ¥1 million eligible for 18 percent special initial depreciation. It can immediately deduct 18 percent of the cost of the equipment or ¥180,000. At a 34.5 percent corporate tax rate, the corporation would save an immediate ¥62,100 in taxes (¥180,000 multiplied by 34.5 percent corporate tax rate). The corporation could take these immediate tax savings and reinvest it. If 18 percent of this additional ¥62,100 capital investment could also be immediately deducted, the corporation would save another ¥3,856 in taxes (¥62,100 multiplied by 18 percent multiplied by 34.5 percent corporate tax rate), which could be reinvested in another deductible capital investment. By expensing the cost of the initial investment, the corporation can increase the investment to $I/(1-(t \times e))$, where I is the amount of income to be invested, t is the tax rate, and e is the percentage expensed.[12] In this case, it would be ¥1,000,000/$(1-(0.345 \times 0.18))$ equaling ¥1,066,212. The greater the expensing percentage, the greater the amount of the overall investment. Conversely, the lower the expensing percentage, the lower the amount of the overall investment.

Special initial depreciation is part of the Special Taxation Measures Laws, which contains special tax measures or incentives to promote particular economic goals.[13] It is separate from the ordinary income tax laws. Special Taxation Measures Laws containing incentives for depreciation were used quite often in the 1950s and proliferated in the 1960s and early 1970s.[14] For example, special initial depreciation for

---

[8] The corporation is not also entitled to additional depreciation. Additional depreciation will be discussed at part B.2.

[9] Special Taxation Measures Law 44-9(1) (1998) (applicable for the period from 1 April 1996 to 31 March 2000).

[10] Special Taxation Measures Law 42-12(1) (1998) (applicable for the period from 1 June 1998 to 31 May 1999). Prior to 1 June 1998, the percentage was 11 percent. Special Taxation Measures Law 45-2(1) (1997).

[11] Special Taxation Measures Law 44-1 (1998) (applicable for the period from 1 April 1987 to 31 March 1999).

[12] Under Section 179 of the U.S. Internal Revenue Code, e was 100 percent and therefore was ignored in expressing the formula for the increase in investment.

[13] MOF 1997, *supra* note 6, at 22.

[14] Hiromitsu Ishi, *The Japanese Tax System* (2d ed., 1993) at 199–201.

important industries, with a 50 percent expensing amount in the first year, was introduced from 1952 to 1961.[15] In 1973, however, Japan reduced special initial depreciation for important industries.[16] The criticism of special tax measures actually began in the mid-1960s and, in fact, since the late 1970s, Japanese tax policy has focused primarily on equity and neutrality rather than tax incentives.[17]

Similar to the U.S. system, Japan originally adopted the special initial depreciation to encourage the acquisition of assets eligible for the benefit thereby promoting business investment and stimulating the economy.[18] The MOF has written, "it is expected that the purchase of such depreciable assets will be encouraged by this measure [special initial depreciation]."[19] As a result, special initial depreciation is not an inadvertent tax benefit granted to Japanese businesses. Rather, it was part of Japan's industrial policy during the post-World War II period to promote economic growth through exports, private savings, investment, and innovation.[20] If the Japanese government determines that special initial depreciation is too generous, it can cut back on it or simply eliminate it.

Similar to the United States, Japan allows for expensing of a number of expenditures that would otherwise be capitalized and amortized over a designated period of time. These deferred assets that a corporation may elect to expense include:

disbursements in establishing a corporation;
disbursements in starting a business;
expenditures for research and experiments;
disbursements in developing a new market;
disbursements in issuing new shares of stock; and
disbursements in issuing bonds.[21]

3. *Tax Deferral Principle*

Expensing is the classic situation to which the Cary Brown model has been applied and discussed. As previously stated, expensing the cost of an asset is equivalent to excluding the future annual return of the asset from income. The Cary Brown model, as it applies to expensing, has been discussed in detail in the previous three chapters.

---

[15] See *id.* at 201. [16] *Id.*

[17] See Hiroshi Kaneko, "The Development of the Japanese Tax System After World War II," in *A Final Draft Report from FAIR (Foundation for Advanced Information and Research) to the World Bank on "Taxation and Economic Growth" (Asian Miracle Project)* 1, 19; Ishi, *supra* note 14, at 198; Eiji Tajika and Yuji Yui, "Public Policies and Capital Accumulation: Japan at the Dawn of Economic Growth", in *A Final Draft Report from FAIR (Foundation for Advanced Information and Research) to the World Bank on "Taxation and Economic Growth" (Asian Miracle Project)* 39, 50 (1993) ("By 1976, the number of measures listed in the Special Taxation Measures Law for fiscal incentives for corporations had reached ninety-eight, and it was only after 1976 that a substantial reduction of ad hoc measures for special purposes was begun.").

[18] See Ishi, *supra* note 14, at 201. [19] MOF 1997, *supra* note 6, at 90.

[20] See Ishi, *supra* note 14, at 198.

[21] CTL Enf. Order 14(1) (1998); Gomi, *supra* note 5, at ¶6-325.

4. The United States' solution to preventing tax deferral
Expensing is an affirmative action by the U.S. government to allow businesses to achieve a tax benefit in purchasing equipment. The obvious solution to eliminating the tax deferral benefits of expensing is to simply reduce it or eliminate it. The United States Congress has actually gone in the opposite direction by increasing the expensing limitation amount under section 179 as part of the Small Business Job Protection Act of 1996.

B. Accelerated depreciation and investment tax credit

1. United States
The Cary Brown model has also been applied to the combination of accelerated depreciation and investment tax credit ("ITC"). In fact, after passage of the Economic Recovery Tax Act of 1981 ("ERTA"),[22] President Ronald Reagan's first piece of major tax legislation, Congress actually made the combination of accelerated depreciation and investment tax credit more attractive than expensing. In other words, the combination, from a tax standpoint by looking through the lens of the Cary Brown model, was more attractive than exempting income of the asset from tax.

The following example demonstrates the combined effect of accelerated depreciation and investment tax credit after the passage of ERTA in 1981.[23] Assume investor has $10,000 to invest, with a 46 percent tax rate,[24] a 10 percent after-tax rate of return on investments, and a 10 percent ITC with no corresponding basis reduction. Assume the property purchased by investor has a five-year recovery period under the 1981 version of accelerated cost recovery system ("ACRS") and the basis is not reduced for ITC. The ITC for year one would be $1000 ($10,000 multiplied by 10 percent). The ACRS deductions for years one through five would be as follows:

Year	ACRS deduction ($)
1	10,000 multiplied by 15% = $1500
2	10,000 multiplied by 22% = $2200
3	10,000 multiplied by 21% = $2100
4	10,000 multiplied by 21% = $2100
5	10,000 multiplied by 21% = $2100

[22] Pub. L. No. 97-34 (1981).

[23] This example is adapted from Alvin C. Warren, Jr., "Accelerated Capital Recovery, Debt, and Tax Arbitrage," 38 *Tax Law*, 549, 553–55 (1985).

[24] The 46 percent tax rate was the highest marginal tax rate in the U.S. tax system for corporations from 1981 to 1986.

Using an after-tax discount rate of 10 percent, the present value of the tax savings from the ITC and ACRS deductions is as follows:

Year	ACRS deduction ($)	Present value ($)
1	1500	1500
2	2200	2000
3	2100	1735.54
4	2100	1577.76
5	2100	1434.33
Present value of the ACRS deductions		8247.63
Present value of the tax savings from the ACRS deductions (46% multiplied by $8247.63)		3793.91
Present value of the tax savings from the ITC		1000
Present value of the total tax savings from ACRS and ITC		4793.91

As the above example demonstrates, the present value of the tax savings from the ACRS deductions and ITC ($4793.91) is greater than the present value of the tax savings from expensing the cost of the investment ($4600). As a result, the combination of ACRS and ITC yielded a present value tax benefit greater than exempting the income of the investment from tax. This is sometimes referred to as a negative income tax and is easily seen when looked at through the Cary Brown model.

In the Tax Equity and Fiscal Responsibility Act of 1982 ("TEFRA"),[25] the U.S. Congress changed ACRS and ITC making it less generous to taxpayers. The Senate Finance Committee stated than the combination of ACRS and ITC under ERTA in 1981 generated tax benefits with a present value greater that the tax benefits generated by expensing the cost of the asset.[26] In other words, the combination of ACRS and ITC was better than exempting the future annual return of the asset from tax. The Senate Finance Committee further stated:

> In evaluating alternative ways to correct this distortion, the committee concluded that a basis adjustment for one-half of the amount of the regular investment credit allowed would make the combination of ACRS cost recovery deductions and the regular investment credit equivalent to expensing at a 10% after-tax discount rate. These benefits would provide investment incentives comparable to those in a system without an income tax, and thus would encourage the private sector to undertake the maximum amount of productive investment.[27]

[25] Pub. L. No. 97-248 (1982).

[26] S. Rep. No. 494, 97th Cong., 2d Sess. 122 (1982).

[27] See *id.* at 123. See also Staff of the Joint Committee on Taxation, *General Explanation of the Revenue Provisions of the Tax Equity and Fiscal Responsibility Act of 1982* (1982) at 35–40.

As a result, in 1982, Congress changed the combination of ACRS and ITC so that it would yield tax benefits with a present value *equal* to the tax benefits generated by expensing the cost of the investment at a 10 percent after-tax discount rate. The following example demonstrates this equivalence, using a basis of only $9500 (the original basis of $10,000 is reduced by one-half of the ITC of $1000 as required by TEFRA in 1982) for property with a five-year recovery period:

Year	ACRS deduction	Present value ($)
1	($)1425 (15% multiplied by $9500)	1425
2	($)2090 (22% multiplied by $9500)	1900
3	($)1995 (21% multiplied by $9500)	1649
4	($)1995 (21% multiplied by $9500)	1499
5	($)1995 (21% multiplied by $9500)	1363
Present value of the ACRS deductions		7836
Present value of the tax savings from the ACRS deductions (46% multiplied by $7836)		3600
Present value of the tax savings from the ITC		1000
Present value of the total tax savings from ACRS and ITC		4600

As the above example demonstrates, the present value of the tax savings from the ACRS deductions and ITC ($4600) is equal to the present value of the tax savings from expensing the cost of the investment ($4600). As a result, the combination of ACRS and ITC yielded a present value tax benefit equal to exempting the income of the investment from tax. If the after-tax discount rate were greater than 10 percent, the present value tax benefits of ACRS and ITC would be less than the tax benefits of expensing.[28] If the after-tax discount rate were less than 10 percent, then the present value tax benefits of ACRS and ITC would be greater than the tax benefits of expensing.[29]

As Professor Alvin Warren has pointed out, the ACRS deductions, the ITC, and adjusted basis can be changed in a number of ways so that the tax benefits yielded will equal, in present value terms, the tax benefits of expensing.[30] This is what the U.S. Congress did in 1982 as part of TEFRA, simply requiring the basis of the asset to be reduced by one-half of the ITC and thereby slightly changing the amount of depreciation each year during the recovery period. The U.S. Congress partially eliminated the combination of ACRS and ITC as part of the Tax Reform Act of 1986, when it repealed the ITC effective 31 December 1985. The U.S. Congress also modified the ACRS rules in 1986, making it slightly less generous. For example, automobiles had a three year recovery period under the 1981 legislation but had a five-year recovery period under the 1986 changes. Machinery and equipment had a five-year

[28] See Warren, *supra* note 23, at 555. [29] See *id.* [30] *Id.* at 553.

recovery period under the 1981 legislation but had a seven-year recovery period under the 1986 changes.

In recent years, the United States Republican Congress in its Contract with America has looked into manipulating accelerated depreciation and adjusted basis so that the tax benefits will equal, in present value terms, the benefits of expensing. The Republican Congress proposed that the basis of the asset be increased each year thereby generating larger depreciation deductions to equal the tax consequences of allowing an immediate deduction.[31] The Republicans' proposal, which was widely distributed in 1995 and 1996, has since been completely dropped.

2. *Japan*

The Japanese income tax system has, in essence, two types of accelerated depreciation. The first is the declining balance method ("*teiritsu ho*") under the general rules for depreciation in the Income Tax Law and Corporation Tax Law. The declining balance is one of a number of permissible methods of depreciation, which also include the straight-line method ("*teigaku ho*"), unit of production method ("*seisandaka hirei ho*"), replacement method ("*torikae ho*"), and physical or economic exhaustion method.[32] The second type of accelerated depreciation is generally referred to as additional depreciation ("*warimashi shokyaku*") and is provided under the Special Taxation Measures Law. It is an incentive-type of depreciation very limited in application. For example, additional depreciation on machinery and equipment equal to 24 percent (32 percent in the case of buildings) of the ordinary depreciation amount is allowed to a corporation in which at least 50 percent of its employees are physically or mentally challenged.[33] This provision is designed to encourage corporations to employ physically or mentally challenged individuals.[34]

Japan used accelerated depreciation quite often during the 1950s as a way of promoting business investment for corporations.[35] During the 1960s, Japan extended the use of accelerated depreciation.[36] For example, in 1963, small and medium-sized enterprises were allowed to use accelerated depreciation.[37] By the early 1970s, however, the trend towards expanding accelerated depreciation provisions began to slow down.[38] In fact, the trend in recent years has been to reduce many tax incentives, particularly accelerated depreciation provisions.[39]

Japan also allows for an investment tax credit that is, like additional depreciation, an incentive-type of measure very limited in application.[40] The amount of the credit is seven percent of the acquisition cost of the asset. In lieu of the credit, the corporation

[31] See generally Calvin H. Johnson, "Three Errors in the Neutral Cost Recovery System," 67 *Tax Notes* 1229 (1995).

[32] CTL Articles 31 and 32 (1998); CTL Enf. Orders 48, 49, and 50 (1998). See MOF 1997, *supra* note 6, at 86; Gomi, *supra* note 5, at ¶ 6-270.

[33] Special Taxation Measures Law Art. 46-2 (1998) (applicable for the period from 1 April 1973 to 31 March 1999).

[34] See MOF 1997, *supra* note 6, at 94.

[35] See Ishi, *supra* note 14, at 200–01.

[36] See *id.* at 201.

[37] *Id.*

[38] *Id.*

[39] *Id.*

[40] Special Taxation Measures Law 42-5 through 42-8 (1998).

may elect special initial depreciation of 30 percent of the acquisition cost of the asset. If the corporation utilizes the credit, the maximum amount of the credit allowed is 20 percent of the corporation's income tax liability for the taxable year. Examples of property qualifying for the investment tax credit include equipment that contributes toward the efficient use of energy and also equipment that contributes toward the utilization of solar power, wind power, and energy resources other than petroleum.[41] Japan has provided an investment tax credit for energy saving equipment since 1981.[42]

This part will focus on the application of the first type of accelerated depreciation under the Corporate Tax Law to machinery and equipment. This is the typical type of depreciation that applies today. Assume Tanaka Corporation purchases on 1 January 1996, a copying machine to be used in its business. Tanaka Corporation paid ¥400,000 for the copier. It will use the declining balance method of depreciation with respect to the copier.[43] The useful life of the copier and all other assets is provided by the Ministry of Finance in its Ministerial Ordinance Regarding the Useful Life of Depreciable Assets.[44] The copier's useful life is five years. The salvage value is treated as 10 percent of the acquisition cost of a tangible asset. The cumulative amount of depreciation that may be taken, however, is 95 percent of the acquisition cost so that the asset may be depreciated to five percent of its acquisition cost once it has been depreciated down to its salvage value.[45]

In computing the depreciation deduction each year, the Ministry of Finance has provided a table giving the multiplier to be used in making the computation.[46] The depreciation deduction each year is as follows:

Year	Depreciation deduction
1	¥147,600 (0.369 multiplied by 400,000)
2	¥93,135.60 (0.369 multiplied by 252,400)
3	¥58,768.56 (0.369 multiplied by 159,264.40)
4	¥37,082.96 (0.369 multiplied by 100,495.84)
5	¥23,399.35 (0.369 multiplied by 63,412.88)

41 Special Taxation Measures Law 42-5 (1998).

42 See Ishi, *supra* note 14, at 201.

43 If no method of depreciation is adopted by the corporation, the declining balance method will apply to most tangible assets. See John W. Darcy, *Japan-U.S. International Tax Transactions* (1994) at ¶ 635.30 (citing to CTL Art. 31(1) (1998) and CTL Enf. Order Art. 53(1)(i) (1998)); Gomi, *supra* note 5, at ¶ 6-275; MOF 1997, *supra* note 6, at 87.

44 See Darcy, *supra* note 43, at ¶ 635.20 (citing to Ministry of Finance Ordinance No. 15 (1965), most recently revised by Ministry of Finance Ordinance No. 50 (31 March 1998)); MOF 1997, *supra* note 6, at 89.

45 CTL Enf. Order Art. 61(1) (1998). See Darcy, *supra* note 43, at ¶ 635.40; MOF 1997, *supra* note 6, at 87–88.

46 See Darcy, *supra* note 43, at ¶ 635.40 (citing Table No. 10 to Ministry of Finance Ordinance No. 15 (1965), most recently revised by Ministry of Finance Ordinance No. 50 (31 March 1998)).

At the end of the fifth year, the copier's unrecovered basis is approximately ¥40,000, which is the copier's designated salvage value (10 percent multiplied by ¥400,000). Tanaka Corporation can take an additional ¥20,000 of depreciation after the fifth year, depreciating the copier to five percent of its acquisition cost.

3. Tax Deferral Principle

a. Cary Brown Model

Applying the Cary Brown model to accelerated depreciation is very similar to the analysis with respect to expensing. For example, assume T purchases equipment on 1 January 1996 for 10,000*u*. The equipment is expected to last five years at which time it is expected to have negligible value. Assume that T is entitled to 3000*u* of depreciation in 1996 and that the equipment declines in value during 1996 from 10,000*u* to 8000*u*. Ideally, T should only have a 2000*u* depreciation deduction in 1996 to reflect the actual decline in value of the equipment.

T's 3000*u* depreciation deduction can be bifurcated into two components: (1) 2000*u*, which reflects the actual decline in value of the property and (2) 1000*u*, which is an expensed amount relating to property that is still worth 1000*u*. The second component is equivalent to T purchasing equipment for 1000*u* and immediately deducting its cost, i.e., expensing the cost. In other words, by taking a 3000*u* depreciation deduction in 1996, which is 1000*u* too much, T has, in essence, expensed an asset with a cost of 1000*u*.

In 1997, assume T's depreciation deduction is again 3000*u* and the asset has declined in value from 8000*u* to 6000*u*. Ideally, T should only have a 2000*u* depreciation deduction in 1997 to reflect the actual decline in value of the equipment. T's 3000*u* depreciation deduction can again be bifurcated into two components: (1) 2000*u*, which reflects the actual decline in value of the property, and (2) 1000*u*, which is an expensed amount relating to property that is still worth 1000*u*. The second component is equivalent to T purchasing equipment for 1000*u* and immediately deducting its cost, i.e., expensing the cost. In other words, by taking a 3000*u* depreciation deduction in 1997, which is 1000*u* too much, T has, in essence, expensed an asset with a cost of 1000*u*.

In looking at the years 1996 and 1997 as a whole, the equipment has declined in value by 4000*u* and the taxpayer has deducted a total of 6000*u*. The taxpayer has, in essence, expensed 2000*u* of the equipment, 1000*u* in 1996 and 1000*u* in 1997. As previously stated, expensing an asset is the equivalent of excluding the future annual return of the asset from income.

b. Samuelson Depreciation

It is important to introduce another concept of tax policy, which is closely linked to the Cary Brown model. In a famous paper published in 1964, MIT economics professor Paul Samuelson introduced the concept of economic depreciation, many times referred to as Samuelson depreciation.[47] The concept has been most clearly

---

[47] Paul A. Samuelson, "Tax Deductibility of Economic Depreciation to Insure Invariant Valuations," 72 *J. of Pol. Econ.* 604 (1964).

described in the tax law literature by Columbia Professor Marvin Chirelstein, and it is his example that will be used here.[48]

Assume a taxpayer purchases equipment for 4000*u*. In theory, the ideal amount of depreciation deduction each year is equal to the decline in value of the equipment each year. This is consistent with the Haig–Simons definition of income in which income is defined as consumption plus (or minus) the change in the value of assets. Also, in theory, the taxpayer purchased the equipment for the income stream the equipment will generate for the taxpayer's business. Let's assume the equipment is expected to generate income of 1200*u* each year for five years. The pre-tax rate of return for the taxpayer's investment in the equipment is slightly greater than 15 percent, compounded annually. In other words, 1200*u* a year for five years discounted at a 15 percent rate of return, compounded annually, equals 4000*u*.

As a result, the present value of each payment is as follows:

Year	1	2	3	4	5	Total
Expected receipt	1200*u*	1200*u*	1200*u*	1200*u*	1200*u*	6000*u*
Present value	1045*u*	905*u*	790*u*	687*u*	573*u*	4000*u*

The total present value of all payments equals 4000*u*, which is the original cost of the equipment.

At the beginning of year one, the present value of the expected income stream is 4000*u*. At the end of year one, there are only four 1200*u* payments left to be received. When these four payments are discounted back to the end of year one at a 15 percent rate of return, compounded annually, the present value is 3427*u*. The loss in present value for year one is 573*u*. As Professor Chirelstein has written:

> As each year of useful life expires the expected stream of payments become shorter and the present value of the sum of all remaining payments necessarily declines. There is just that much less to anticipate in the way of future returns. The taxpayer's economic loss from the year's operations – his annual cost – is measured by the decline in the present value of anticipated receipts which takes place between the beginning and the end of the taxable year. In effect, the difference between the value of the future income stream on 1 January and its value on 1 January of the following year represents the cost of using the machine for the year in question. If the object of the depreciation allowance is to reduce gross income by the true cost of operations, then the annual allowance should be no more or less than that amount.[49]

---

[48] Marvin A. Chirelstein, *Federal Income Taxation* § 6.08 (8th ed., 1997).

[49] Chirelstein, *supra* note 48, at § 6.08.

The schedule of the annual decline in the present value of the income stream that represents the taxpayer's investment in the equipment is as follows:

	Present value of the investment	Present value of payment (1)	Present value of payment (2)	Present value of payment (3)	Present value of payment (4)	Present value of payment (5)	Annual loss in present value
Beginning of year 1	4000*u*	1045*u*	905*u*	790*u*	687*u*	573*u*	0*u*
End of Year 1	3427*u*	0*u*	1045*u*	905*u*	790*u*	687*u*	573*u*
End of Year 2	2740*u*	0*u*	0*u*	1045*u*	905*u*	790*u*	687*u*
End of Year 3	1950*u*	0*u*	0*u*	0*u*	1045*u*	905*u*	790*u*
End of Year 4	1045*u*	0*u*	0*u*	0*u*	0*u*	1045*u*	905*u*
End of Year 5	0*u*	0*u*	0*u*	0*u*	0*u*	0*u*	1045*u*
Total							4000*u*

From the above chart, the taxpayer's depreciation deduction each year should be: 573*u* in year one; 687*u* in year two; 790*u* in year three; 905*u* in year four; and 1045*u* in year five. As a result, the theoretically proper amount of depreciation *increases* each year (assuming a constant income stream) – the exact opposite of accelerated depreciation. It should be noted, however, that if the expected income stream is not level but rather decreases over time, then the theoretically proper amount of depreciation each year would be more level or may even decline over time.

It is generally conceded that it would be very difficult to adopt Samuelson depreciation. The primary reason is the difficulty in predicting the income stream that the equipment is expected to generate. This is in contrast to assets such as mortgages, leases, and zero coupon bonds, in which the future payments are generally fixed by contract and therefore can be easily determined. As shown, Samuelson depreciation "is simply a function of expected cash flows."[50] Despite the difficulty in applying Samuelson depreciation, however, it "is the only proper method of apportioning the taxpayer's capital investment in accordance with the economic cost of use."[51]

It should be noted, however, that the United States has adopted principles based on Samuelson depreciation in areas even where the future payments are not fixed. For example, the rules for contingent payment debt instruments require adoption of a rate

[50] Chirelstein, *supra* note 48, at § 6.08.

[51] See *id.*

of return even though the actual payments may vary from the projected payment schedule using the rate of return.[52] Any difference between the projected payments and the actual contingent payments is accounted for at a subsequent period in time when the actual contingent payments are made. The application of the principles of Samuelson depreciation to contingent payment debt instruments will be discussed in more detail in Chapter 6, which includes numerous methods of eliminating tax deferral.

4. United States' Solution to Preventing Tax Deferral

The United States repealed the ITC as part of the Tax Reform Act of 1986. It has retained accelerated depreciation and has not given serious thought to adopting Samuelson depreciation for tangible depreciable property.

C. Unrealized Appreciation

1. United States

The Cary Brown model can also be applied to property with unrealized appreciation. The realization doctrine is one of the cornerstones of the U.S. income tax system.[53] However, one leading commentator has described it as the "Achilles' heel" of the income tax system primarily because of the tax deferral it provides to taxpayers.[54] Generally, gain or loss is not included in a taxpayer's gross income until a realization event has taken place, which in many cases is a sale or exchange.[55] As a result, appreciation in property is generally not taxed until the property is sold or exchanged.[56] Several reasons have been given for not taxing unrealized appreciation. These include: (1) the administrative burden of annual reporting; (2) the hardship in determining asset values annually (particularly those not traded on a publicly traded exchange); (3) the potential hardship of obtaining the funds to pay taxes on accrued

---

[52] Treas. Reg. § 1.1275-4 (1996).

[53] Much has been written on the realization doctrine. See, e.g., Boris I. Bittker & Lawrence Lokken, *Federal Income Taxation of Income, Estates and Gifts* ¶ 40.1 (1990); Noel B. Cunningham & Deborah H. Schenk, "Taxation Without Realization: A "Revolutionary Approach to Ownership," 47 *Tax L. Rev.* 725 (1992); David J. Shakow, "Taxation Without Realization: A Proposal for Accrual Taxation," 134 *U. Pa. L. Rev.* 1111 (1986).

[54] William D. Andrews, "The Achilles' Heel of the Comprehensive Income Tax," in *New Directions in Federal Tax Policy for the 1980's*, at 278, 280 (Charls E. Walker and Mark A. Bloomfield eds., 1983).

[55] I.R.C. § 1001(a). The realization requirement in the U.S. income tax system has generally been attributed to the U.S. Supreme Court's decision in *Eisner v. Macomber*, 252 U.S. 189 (1920), in which the Court held that a stock dividend was not income under the 16th Amendment to the U.S. Constitution because there was no gain derived from capital, labor, or both.

[56] The United States has eliminated the realization requirement and adopted a mark to market method in a few limited situations. See, e.g., I.R.C. § 475 (mark to market method for dealers in securities); I.R.C. § 817 and 817A (mark to market method for variable contracts and modified guaranteed contracts); I.R.C. § 1256 (mark to market method for regulated futures, foreign currency, and certain other contracts); and I.R.C. § 1296 (mark to market method available for publicly traded passive foreign investment company (PFIC) stock).

but unrealized gains (liquidity problem); and (4) possible constitutional or political problems.[57]

A simple example will demonstrate the tax deferral that results from the realization doctrine. Assume an investor purchased stock in Microsoft Corporation for $5000 a number of years ago. The stock is now worth $250,000. The $245,000 of appreciation is not taxed until a realization event takes place, for example, the investor selling the stock. The investor, by holding onto the stock, defers paying tax on the appreciation because of the realization doctrine.

2. Japan

The Japanese income tax system has also adopted the realization doctrine. Generally, under the Japanese income tax system, gain or loss is not included in a taxpayer's gross income until a realization event has taken place, which in many cases is a sale or exchange. As a result, appreciation in property is generally not taxed until the property is sold or exchanged.[58] One commentator has stated that the realization requirement is derived from the word "transaction" that is found in the tax statutes.[59] The word "transaction" is interpreted to exclude mere appreciation in value from being included in income.[60]

The National Tax Administration has issued rulings detailing the timing of the realization event.[61] In the case of a transfer of a fixed asset, the realization event is the delivery of the asset.[62] As a result, the gain or loss is determined on the date of delivery. The date of delivery rule also applies to the sale of inventory[63] and the sale of securities.[64] In the case of a transfer of real property, such as land or buildings,

---

[57] See, e.g., David M. Bradford and the U.S. Treasury Tax Policy Staff, *Blueprints for Basic Tax Reform* (2d ed. 1984) at 73; Alvin C. Warren, "Financial Contract Innovation and Income Tax Policy," 107 *Harv. L. Rev.* 460, 462 (1993).

[58] Japan does provide for a mark to market method with respect to foreign exchange licensed banks as to trading activities in currency futures and options. See Shigeki Fujitani, Tax Aspects of Derivative Financial Instruments: Japan, reprinted in 80b *Cahiers De Droit Fiscal International* [*Studies on International Fiscal Law*] 327, 332–335 (International Fiscal Association ed., 1995); Charles T. Plambeck, H. David Rosenbloom, and Diane M. Ring, Tax Aspects of Derivative Financial Instruments: General Report, reprinted in 80b *Cahiers De Droit Fiscal International* [*Studies on International Fiscal Law*] 653, 682 n. 61 (International Fiscal Association ed., 1995).

[59] See Kitagawa, Corporation Tax, in *Doing Business in Japan*, § 2.03 (1989) citing to CTL Art. 22(2) which provides:

> "In computing the amount of taxable income of a domestic corporation for each business year, the amount to be included in gross income shall, unless otherwise provided, be the amount of revenue in the business year resulting from sale of assets, transfer of assets or rendering of services with or without counter-value, acquisition of assets without counter-value, and other transactions excluding capital transaction."

[60] See *id.*

[61] See Yuji Gomi, *Japan Corporation Tax Law 1996*, at 41–45 (summarizing the rulings).

[62] See generally Darcy, *supra* note 43, at ¶ 900.10 (citing to CTL Basic Circular 2-1-14); Kitagawa, *supra* note 59, at § 2.05 (also citing to CTL Basic Circular 2-1-14 and adding that, at the taxpayer's option, the income can be included in the business year of the effective date of the applicable contract).

[63] See Kitagawa, *supra* note 59, at § 2.05 (citing to CTL Basic Circulars 2-1-1 and 2-1-2).

[64] See Masatami Otsuka and Kenju Watanabe, *Butterworths International Taxation of Financial Instruments and Transactions: Japan* (2d ed., 1994) at 41 (citing CTL Basic Circular Art. 2-1-22 but

however, the realization event can be the effective date of the contract, which is generally the date the contract is entered into, as opposed to the delivery date.[65] As a result of Japan's adoption of the realization requirement in its income tax system, the taxation of gains is delayed until realization.

3. Tax Deferral Principle

The following two examples will demonstrate the Cary Brown model (actually the Super Cary Brown model) with respect to the realization doctrine. In example one, assume T owns land long thought essentially worthless with a negligible basis. A valuable mineral deposit is discovered nearby immediately causing the value of T's land to rise to 10,000*u*. The land's value continues to rise at 10 percent annually for three years. At the end of three years, T sells the land (still undeveloped) for 13,310*u*, resulting in 13,310*u* of gain. At a 40 percent tax rate, the tax owed is 5324*u*, leaving T with 7986*u*.

Contrasting the above example with a slightly different variation can best show the tax deferral benefit of the realization doctrine. In example two, assume that T's neighbor, R owns land which is essentially worthless with a negligible basis. After discovery of a similar mineral deposit, R's land immediately increases in value to 10,000*u*. In this second example, however, assume that the 10,000*u* in appreciation is subject to immediate taxation. Therefore, R immediately owes 4000*u* in taxes to the government.

Assume that R disposes of the land for 10,000*u* to satisfy the 4000*u* tax liability so that his after-tax proceeds are 6000*u*. R invests the 6000*u* in a tax-exempt investment yielding 10 percent interest annually, maturing in three years. At the end of year one, the investment will be worth 6600*u*. At the end of year two, the investment will be worth 7260*u*. At the end of year three, the investment will be worth 7986*u* maturing at that time. R will receive 7986*u*, which will not be subject to tax because the investment is tax-exempt. In other words, 6000*u* will grow to 7986*u* in three years at a *pre-tax* rate of return of 10 percent. This example, when contrasted with the first example illustrates, in accordance with the Super Cary Brown model, that by delaying the taxation of gains until realization, the income tax system effectively exempts the future annual return on the appreciation from tax.

The following table summarizes the two examples with the assumption that the 10,000*u* appreciation occurs on 31 December 1995.

The above two examples, (1) T owning originally worthless land suddenly increasing in value and continuing to increase in value and (2) R owing similar land in which appreciation is immediately taxed but investing the after-tax proceeds in a tax-exempt investment, demonstrate an important tax deferral principle. By delaying the taxation of gains until realization, the income tax system effectively exempts the future annual return on the appreciation from tax. As a result, the realization doctrine

---

noting in the case of a short sale of securities, recognition occurs at the closing of the short sale, citing CTL Basic Circular 2-1-23).

[65] See generally Darcy, *supra* note 43, at ¶ 900.10 (citing to Civil Code Art. 555 and CTL Basic Circular 2-1-14); Gomi, *supra* note 6, at ¶ 6-190 (citing to CTL Basic Circular 2-1-14); Kitagawa, *supra* note 59, at § 2.05 (citing to CTL Basic Circular 2-1-14).

	Realization doctrine	Taxation of unrealized appreciation
Fair market value	10,000*u*	10,000*u*
Basis	0*u*	0*u*
Gain on 31 December 1995	0*u*	10,000*u*
Taxes (40%)	0*u*	4000*u*
Investment on 31 December 1995	10,000*u*	6000*u*
Return on investment (10%) for 1996	1000*u*	600*u*
Taxes (40%)	0*u* (no taxes owed because of the application of the realization doctrine)	0*u* (no taxes owed because of the assumption that the return is exempt from taxation)
After-taxes on 31 December 1996	11,000*u*	6600*u*
Return on investment (10%) for 1997	1100*u*	660*u*
Taxes (40%)	0*u* (no taxes owed because of the application of the realization doctrine)	0*u* (no taxes owed because of the assumption that the return is exempt from taxation)
After-taxes on 31 December 1997	12,100*u*	7260*u*
Return on investment (10%) for 1998	1210*u*	726*u*
Taxes (40%)	0*u* (no taxes owed because of the application of the realization doctrine)	0*u* (no taxes owed because of the assumption that the return is exempt from taxation)
Sales proceeds on 31 December 1998	13,310*u*	Not applicable
Taxes on sale (40%)	5324*u*	Not applicable
After-taxes on 31 December 1998	7986*u*	7986*u*

is an example of the Super Cary Brown model. In the first example, T is effectively shielded from taxation (until he sells the land) by the realization doctrine. As shown by the two examples, this is equivalent to R being immediately taxed on the appreciation but investing the after-tax proceeds on a tax-exempt basis.

4. United States' Solution to Preventing Tax Deferral

The United States has attacked the tax deferral that occurs with respect to unrealized appreciation in very few instances, thereby allowing tax deferral opportunities to continue. In the very few situations in which the United States has prevented tax deferral, the United States has used the *Immediate Inclusion in Income Method* to prevent tax deferral with respect to unrealized appreciation. For example, the United States requires dealers in securities mark to market all of their non-inventory securities on the last day of the year. The *Immediate Inclusion in Income Method* is discussed in detail in the following chapter.

D. Installment Sales

1. United States

As stated earlier, the United States income tax system generally does not tax gain until a realization event, such as a sale, has taken place. If a payment on the sale of property is to be received after the end of the seller's taxable year, this is referred to as an installment sale and the gain can generally be reported over time. More specifically, under I.R.C. Section 453, income from an installment sale can generally be reported under the installment method.[66] The installment method spreads the income from the installment sale over the period of time when payments are actually received by the seller.[67] The United States Supreme Court has stated that purpose of the installment sales provision is to:

> [R]elieve taxpayers who adopted it from having to pay an income tax in the year of sale based on the full amount of anticipated profits when in fact they had received in cash only a small portion of the sales price. Another reason was the difficult and time-consuming effort of appraising the uncertain market value of installment obligations.[68]

What makes an installment sale interesting with respect to the Cary Brown model is that a realization event has taken place (i.e., the sale) between the time of appreciation in the property and the recognition of the appreciation as gain.

A number of terms are used in applying the installment method to an installment sale. First, it is important to define what constitutes an installment sale. An installment sale is defined as a disposition of property where at least one payment is to be received after the end of the taxable year in which the disposition occurs.[69] It is not necessarily a series of payments. For example, assume X Company, a calendar-year taxpayer, sells a parcel of land for $100,000 on 3 December 1996, in which one lump-sum payment will be made by the buyer on 3 June 1997. X Company's basis in the land is $40,000 and it is not a dealer in real estate. The buyer, on 3 June 1997,

---

[66] I.R.C. § 453(a). Generally, an installment sale is a disposition of property where at least one payment is to be received after the end of the taxable year in which the disposition occurs. I.R.C. § 453(b)(1).

[67] I.R.C. § 453(c). The installment method is a method under which the income recognized for any taxable year from a disposition is that proportion of the payments received in that year which the gross profit bears to the total contract price. *Id.*

[68] *Commissioner v. So. Tex. Lumber Co.*, 333 U.S. 496, 503 (1948).

[69] I.R.C. § 453(b)(1).

will pay $100,000 plus a market rate of interest for the six month delay in making payment. This is an installment sale because at least one (in this case, only one) payment is to be received after the end of the taxable year in which the sale occurs. If, however, the buyer agreed to pay $50,000 plus a market rate of interest on 3 June 1997 and an additional $50,000 plus a market rate of interest on 3 June 1998, this would also constitute an installment sale. This is because at least one payment (in this case, two payments) was received after the end of 1996. Once it is determined that an installment sale has taken place, the installment method can be used to recognize the gain, subject to a number of exceptions.[70]

The installment method is a method under which the income recognized for any taxable year from an installment sale is that proportion of the payments received in that year that the gross profit bears to the total contract price.[71] An example will demonstrate the mechanics and terminology of installment sales. Assume in 1996, X Company sold property for $5 million, of which $2 million was paid in cash and the remaining $3 million was evidenced by a seven-year interest-only installment obligation (due in the year 2003).[72] X Company's basis in the property at the time of the sale was $1 million. The $3 million note is X Company's only obligation arising during 1996. This is an installment sale because at least one payment is to be received after the end of 1996. The selling price[73] and the total contract price[74] are $5 million. The gross profit[75] is $4 million ($5 million minus $1 million) and the gross profit ratio[76] is 80 percent ($4 million/$5 million).

As a result, X Company will recognize as gain each year, 80 percent of each payment it receives during the year. In 1996, X Company received $2 million cash at the time of the sale. X Company will recognize $1.6 million as gain in 1996 (80 percent times $2 million). The characterization of the gain will depend on the asset that was sold. In 1997 through 2002, X Company will not recognize any gain from the sale of the property because it received no payments during these years. In 2003, X Company receives a $3 million payment and therefore must recognize $2.4 million of gain in that year (80 percent times $3 million). As a result, X Company will recognize total gain of $4 million, $1.6 million in 1996 and $2.4 million in 2003.

---

70 I.R.C. § 453(a). 71 I.R.C. § 453(c).

72 Assume that Sections 483 and 1274 do not apply.

73 Treas. Reg. § 1.453-1(b)(2)(ii). "Selling price" means the gross selling price without reduction to reflect any existing mortgage or other encumbrance on the property and without reduction to reflect any selling expenses. *Id.* In addition, interest, whether stated or unstated, and original issue discount, are not part of the selling price. *Id.*

74 Treas. Reg. § 1.453-1(b)(2)(iii). "Contract price" means the total contract price which is equal to the selling price reduced by the portion of qualifying indebtedness, assumed or taken subject to by the buyer, which does not exceed the seller's adjusted basis in the property. *Id.* Generally, "qualifying indebtedness" means a mortgage or other indebtedness encumbering the property and other types of indebtedness not encumbering the property. Treas. Reg. § 1.453-1(b)(2)(iv).

75 Treas. Reg. § 1.453-1(b)(2)(v). "Gross profit" means the selling price less the adjusted basis. *Id.* Generally, commissions and other selling expenses are added to the basis in determining the gross profit. *Id.*

76 I.R.C. § 453(c); Treas. Reg. § 1.453-1(b)(2)(i). "Gross profit ratio" means the gross profit divided by the total contract price. *Id.*

2. Japan

Japan allows for reporting the sales of property on an installment method, similar in some respects to the United States. These types of sales are generally referred to as "deferred payment sales."[77] Unlike the United States, the Japanese provision can apply to the sale of inventory and the providing of services, in which case it is generally referred to as installment sale.[78]

The special timing treatment for deferred payment sales (and installment sale transactions) dates back to a September 1945 government circular titled "The Treatment of Corporate Taxes."[79] The circular allowed real estate companies that made installment sales of real estate to recognize the profit over time.[80] The provision changed gradually over time, and in 1965, the government passed the Corporation Tax Act of 1965, enacting provisions for deferred payment sales and installment basis treatment, which are similar to the provision in existence today.[81] The Ministry of Finance, through enactment of a cabinet order, has stated that the deferred payment sales provision is a "method to recognize those amounts of consideration of sales and of cost of goods sold and the like and selling commission and the like which correspond to the amount of the profit on the deferred payment sales to be stated in the current term computed in accordance with the following formula[s] as the amount of revenue and the amount of expenses for the said business year."[82] It then gives the following two formulas:

$$\text{Profit} = \text{Consideration} - [\text{Cost of goods sold} + \text{Selling commission}]$$
(A)

$$\text{Current profit} = (A) \times \frac{\text{Consideration due during the current term}}{\text{Total consideration}}$$

Under the deferred payment sales provision, generally three requirements must be met to utilize the provision. First, the sales price must be paid in three or more installments, either monthly, annually, or in some periodic fashion.[83] Second, the period beginning with the day after the due date of delivery of the property subject to the contract and the due date of the last payment under the contract must be at least two years.[84] In other words, at least two years must pass between the day after the due date of delivery of the property and the due date of the last payment. Third, the amount payable by the due date of the delivery of the property cannot exceed two-thirds of the total sales price.[85]

---

[77] CTL Art. 62 (1998). See, e.g., Gomi, *supra* note 5, at ¶ 6-180; Darcy, *supra* note 43, at ¶ 900.10.

[78] Prior to the changes made in 1998, Japan had two provisions that were basically installment sale types of provisions. As part of the tax changes made in 1998, Japan collapsed the two provisions into one, making a few revisions to the unified provision. Old CTL Arts. 62 and 63 (1997) collapsed into CTL Art. 62 (1998).

[79] Kitagawa, *supra* note 59, at § 5.02[14][c][ii][B]. [80] See *id.* [81] *Id.*

[82] CTL Enf. Order Art. 124 (translated in Gomi, *Corporate Tax 1996*, *supra* note 61, at 159–60).

[83] CTL Art. 62(2)(i) (1998). [84] CTL Art. 62(2)(ii) (1998).

[85] CTL Art. 62(2) (iii) (1998) (imposing additional requirements pursuant to Cabinet Order). See Darcy, *supra* note 43, at ¶ 900.10 (citing to CTL Enf. Order Art. 126); Gomi, *supra* note 5, at ¶ 6-180.

An example will demonstrate the deferred payment sales provision. Assume on 1 July 1996, Tanaka Corporation sold property for ¥400 million, of which ¥100 million was paid immediately and the remaining ¥300 million was paid in three equal installments: ¥100 million due on 1 July 1997, ¥100 million due on 1 July 1998, and ¥100 million due on 1 July 1999. The date the contract was entered into is also the due date of the delivery of the property. The buyer will also pay a market rate of interest with each of the installments to compensate Tanaka Corporation for the delay in payment. Tanaka Corporation's basis in the property at the time of the sale was ¥100 million. This is a deferred payment sale because (1) the sales price is paid in three or more installments, in this case, annually, (2) more than two years will pass from the day after the due date of delivery of the property (2 July 1996) and the due date of the last payment under the contract (1 July 1999), and (3) no more than two-thirds of the sales price will be due by 1 July 1996.

The two formulas in the cabinet order yield the following:

$$\text{¥300 million profit} = \text{¥400 million} - [\text{¥100 million} + 0]$$
$$= \text{consideration} - [\text{cost of goods sold} + \text{commission}]$$

$$\text{¥75 million profit each year} = \text{¥300 million} \times \frac{\text{¥100 million}}{\text{¥400 million}}$$

As a result, Tanaka Corporation will recognize as profit (or gain) each year, 75 percent of each payment due during the year. In 1996, Tanaka Corporation received ¥100 million at the time of the sale. Tanaka Corporation will recognize ¥75 million as profit in 1996. In 1997–1999, Tanaka Corporation will recognize as profit ¥75 million each year. As a result, Tanaka Corporation will recognize total profit of ¥300 million – ¥75 million each year for four consecutive years beginning in 1996.

It should be noted that there appears to be an interesting difference between the United States' installment sales provision and the comparable Japanese provision in that the United States focuses on the actual payment while Japan focuses on the due date of the payment. In the United States, gain is recognized as an actual (or constructive) payment is received. In Japan, profit is recognized when the due date of the payment arrives, even if the payment is not made at that time. The Japanese Tax System Council of the National Government wrote in December 1963: "[The reason why the due date basis has been allowed] is the result of consideration that installment sales are unique and are sales over an extended period of time… . It may be admitted that there are no reasons why we should introduce the cash method so we will continue to support the existing treatment."[86] This seems a bit peculiar. If the purpose of deferring profit over time on an installment sale is to consider the seller's ability to pay taxes on the profit, then the focus should be on actual payment and not on the due date of payment.[87] If the purpose of allowing deferral is because collectibility

---

[86] Kitagawa, *supra* note 59, at § 5.02[14].

[87] See *id.* (citing Choku-ho 1-244 (26 December 1959)).

is uncertain, then it is probably still sensible to focus on actual payment rather than the due date of payment.[88]

3. Tax Deferral Principle

It appears that analyzing installment sales by applying the Cary Brown model eluded American tax authorities for a number of years. When the U.S. Treasury released Treasury I in November 1984, it discussed the tax deferral advantage of installment sales but concluded that the seller should not be charged interest by the government on the amount of deferred taxes.[89] Treasury reasoned that many taxpayers would feel that no interest should be owed to the government if a seller did not have the use of the sales proceeds.[90] In other words, sellers would not understand why they were paying interest to the government on money that they had not yet received.[91]

Shortly after the release of Treasury I, Georgetown Professor Martin Ginsburg stated that Treasury's reasoning for not eliminating the tax deferral benefit of installment sales "makes no sense."[92] He also stated that in terms of lost government revenue, the failure to charge interest on the deferral of tax through the use of the installment method is "the biggest trout in the stream" of time value of money problems.[93]

The following two examples will demonstrate the application of the Cary Brown model with respect to installment sales. In example one, assume T owns land long thought essentially worthless with a negligible basis. A valuable mineral deposit is discovered nearby immediately causing the value of T's land to rise to 10,000*u*. At this point, T sells the land to buyer. Buyer will pay 10,000*u* cash at the time of sale. Assume the sale takes place on 31 December 1995, and the tax is due that same day. At a 40 percent tax rate, T will pay 4000*u* in taxes to the government, leaving T with 6000*u* to invest. T invests the 6000*u* at a 10 percent pre-tax rate of return, however, with taxes, the investment return is reduced to a six percent after-tax rate of return. At the end of three years T will have 7146.10*u*, after-taxes ($6000u \times (1.06)^3$).

---

[88] *Id.* (citing to *Koei Kigyokumiai v. The Head of the Okayama Tax Office*, Okayama District Court, 1 March 1973, 69 Zeimu-sosyo-shiryo 607, affirmed, Hiroshima High Court Okayama Division, 11 March 1974, 74 Zeimu-sosyo-shiryo 479. The Okayama District Court stated: the reason why such special treatment is allowed is that collection of receivables over time [from installment sales] are made over an extended period of time, their collectability is highly uncertain, and the requirements for transfer or resumption of ownership of the goods are complex, thus it is necessary to be cautious in confirming such revenue. Installments which become due for the taxable year and their corresponding expenses have, up to now, been treated as includible in gross income and deductible expenses respectively for the year in which they are received. This treatment is sound when the actual circumstances surrounding installment sales are considered.)

[89] United States Department of the Treasury, *Tax Reform for Fairness, Simplicity and Economic Growth* (November 1984) at 129–30. This report has been generally referred to as Treasury I to distinguish it from a second Treasury report released in May 1985 titled, *The President's Proposals to the Congress for Fairness, Growth, and Simplicity* (May 1985).

[90] See *id.* at 129–30. [91] *Id.*

[92] Lee A. Sheppard, "Ginsburg Discusses Taxing the Privilege of Tax Deferral in Installment Sales," 27 *Tax Notes* 457 (29 April 1985).

[93] See *id.*

Contrasting the above example with a slightly different variation can now show the tax deferral benefit of installment sales. In example two, assume that T owns the same land that is essentially worthless with a negligible basis. After discovery of the mineral deposit, T's land increases in value to 10,000*u*. In this second example, however, assume T sells the land to buyer for 10,000*u*, but instead of an all-cash sale, the buyer will pay T 10,000*u* in three years (payment occurring on 31 December 1998). To compensate T for the delay in paying the sales price, buyer will pay T 10 percent each year for the next three years on the outstanding sales price (1000*u* each year for three years with payment occurring on 31 December of each year).

If T is entitled to use the installment method to report the gain on the sale of the land, T will not report any gain on 31 December 1995, and as a result, will owe no taxes to the government. In 1996, T will receive 1000*u* of interest from buyer and pay taxes of 400*u* leaving T with 600*u* at the end of 1996. The 600*u* that T has earned *after-taxes* is the same amount that T earned *before-taxes* in the previous example of the all-cash sale. In 1997, T will receive another 1000*u* of interest from the buyer and pay taxes of 400*u*, leaving T with 600*u* (plus the 600*u* that was earned from 1996, which was also invested in 1997).

In 1998, T will receive another 1000*u* of interest from the buyer and pay taxes of 400*u*, leaving T with 600*u* (plus the amounts that were earned from 1996 and 1997 which were also invested in 1998). In 1998, T will also receive the sales price of 10,000*u* and will then owe 4000*u* in taxes to the government. At the end of 1998, T will have 7910.16*u*.

The following table summarizes the two examples:

	Cash sale	Installment sale
Sales price	10,000*u*	Deferred (10,000*u*)
Basis	0	0
Gain on 31 December 1995	10,000*u*	Deferred (10,000*u*)
Taxes (40 percent)	4000*u*	Deferred
Investment on 31 December 1995	6000*u*	10,000*u*
Return on investment (10 percent) for 1996	600*u*	1000*u*
Taxes (40 percent)	240*u*	400*u*
After-taxes on 31 December 1996	6360*u*	600*u*
Return on investment (10 percent) for 1997	636*u*	1060*u* (60*u* earned on investment plus 1000*u* received from buyer)
Taxes (40 percent)	254.40*u*	424*u*
After-taxes on 31 December 1997	6741.60*u*	1236*u*

Table continued

	Cash sale	Installment sale
Return on investment (10 percent) for 1998	674.16*u*	1123.60*u* (123.60*u* earned on investment plus 1000*u* received from buyer)
Taxes (40 percent)	269.66*u*	449.44*u*
Sales proceeds on installment sale	0*u*	10,000*u*
Taxes on installment sale (40 percent)	0*u*	4000*u*
After-taxes on 31 December 1998	7146.10*u*	7910.16*u*

The two examples can be generalized algebraically. In the case of a cash sale in which tax is immediately imposed (the first example), an amount A of gain is reduced by tax t such that $A(1-t)$ may be invested. At an annual rate of return r, $A(1-t)$ invested will earn $rA(1-t)$ per year, which will be subject to tax at rate t equaling tax each year of $trA(1-t)$. The seller's net annual after-tax position each year will be:

$$rA(1-t) - trA(1-t) \text{ which equals } rA(1-t)(1-t).$$

In the case of an installment sale (the second example), the amount A of gain is not reduced by tax. At an annual rate of return r, A invested will earn rA per year, which will be subject to tax at rate t equaling tax each year of trA. The seller's net annual after-tax position will be:

$$rA - trA \text{ which equals } rA(1-t).$$

This is better than the seller's net annual after-tax position when a cash sale is made and tax is immediately imposed.

The installment sale example is simply an application of the Cary Brown model. By making an installment sale, the seller T is in effect earning interest at a pre-tax rate of return of 10 percent. The installment method allows for deferral of gain thereby deferring the tax on the gain. Cary Brown would describe the government as being a partner with the seller until the tax on the gain is paid to the government.[94]

4. *United States' Solution to Preventing Tax Deferral*

The United States has attacked the tax deferral that occurs in certain installment sales through the *Interest Charge Method*. Generally, the government charges the

[94] See E. Cary Brown, "Business Income Taxation and Investment Incentives" in *Income, Employment and Public Policy: Essays in Honor of Alvin H. Hansen* 300, 309–310 (1948).

seller interest each year on the income tax that is deferred through use of the installment method. This is discussed in detail in the following chapter.

E. Discounted or Zero Coupon Bonds

1. United States

A zero coupon bond is a bond that pays no interest during the life of the bond. At maturity, the corporation makes a single lump-sum payment to the holder of the bond. A corporation may issue a zero coupon bond when it anticipates being strapped for cash during the years that the bond is outstanding. As a result, the corporation will not have to utilize its cash to make interest payments until the bond matures.

For example, assume a corporation issues a bond in the face amount of $1000, maturing in 10 years. The corporation pays no interest on the bond during the 10-year period. An investor purchases the bond at original issue for $385. At maturity, the investor receives $1000, which can be broken down into $385 return of principal and $615 of interest. The interest is referred to as original issue discount or simply OID.

Prior to 1969, an investor would include OID in income based on the investor's method of accounting. If the investor were on the cash method of accounting, the investor would include $615 in income upon receipt at the end of ten years when the bond matures. The corporation issuing the bond would deduct the interest based on its method of accounting, which in many cases would be the accrual method of accounting. As a result, a mismatch was created for timing purposes because almost all individual holders of zero coupon bonds were on the cash method of accounting. As a result, prior to 1969, the individual holder would not include OID in income until maturity (or sale of the bond).[95] From a tax deferral standpoint, this gave individual investors of zero coupon bonds an advantage over holders of bonds paying interest annually.

In 1969, Congress required that an investor include a ratable share of OID in income each year without regard to the investor's method of accounting.[96] In the above example, the investor would include $61.50 in income each year for 10 years even if the investor were on the cash method of accounting. The issuer would receive a deduction in the same amount. In 1982, Congress changed the rules for OID inclusion once again by requiring the investor to include OID in income through use of a constant yield to maturity method rather than a ratable inclusion method.[97] In addition, the issuer of the bond would receive an interest deduction based on a constant yield to maturity method. In the above example, $385 will grow to $1000 in 10 years, using an interest rate of 10 percent compounded annually.

---

[95] See *United States v. Midland Ross*, 381 U.S. 54 (1965) (dealing with pre-1954 tax years in which the Court stated that OID is the functional equivalent of interest). In 1954, the U.S. Congress provided this same result with the enactment of section 1232(a)(2).

[96] Pub. L. No. 91-172, Section 413(a) (1969).

[97] Pub. L. No. 97-248, Section 231(a) (1982).

The following chart demonstrates the income inclusion for the investor each year (and the deduction to the issuer):

Year	Principal plus accrued OID ($)	Yield to maturity (%)	OID inclusion ($)
1	385	10	38.50
2	423.50	10	42.35
3	465.85	10	46.59
4	512.44	10	51.24
5	563.68	10	56.37
6	620.05	10	62.01
7	682.06	10	68.21
8	750.27	10	75.03
9	825.30	10	82.53
10	907.83	10	92.17 (rounded off)

The above chart demonstrates that the income inclusion to the holder of the zero coupon bond increases each year. This is the proper result. If $385 were deposited in a bank at a 10 percent rate of return compounded annually and left in the bank for 10 years, it will grow to about $1000 at the end of 10 years. But it does not grow in equal increments each year. It will grow by compound interest. In other words, interest will be earned on the previous year(s) interest. The $385 deposited in a bank account will grow to $1000 as demonstrated in the above chart. This same methodology should be used for zero coupon bonds, which is the case in the United States since 1982.

2. Japan

The Japanese government, Japanese corporations, and Japanese banks issue discounted bonds with OID. These bonds are generally taxed in one of two ways. The first method is a withholding tax of 18 percent (in several cases, 16 percent) applying to the excess of the redemption price over the purchase price of the bond (this is the OID).[98] This withholding tax applies to certain types of zero coupon bonds, called *waribiki-sai*, which are issued by for example, the Industrial Bank of Japan and the Long-Term Credit Bank of Japan.[99] In the case of an individual resident holder, this excess is not later subject to assessment income tax upon redemption and as a result does not show up on the individual investor's income tax return.[100] In other words, the withholding tax of 18 percent is the final tax liability on the OID.

[98] See, e.g., Darcy, *supra* note 43, at ¶ 430; MOF 1997, *supra* note 6, at 65; Otsuka and Watanabe, *supra* note 64, 3.5A.

[99] See Darcy, *supra* note 43, at ¶ 430.20.

[100] See Otsuka and Watanabe, *supra* note 64, at 3.12.2.2.

The second method of taxing OID bonds, those that are not *waribiki-sai*, is a net basis taxation in which the holder of the bond includes the OID in income at maturity.[101] An individual resident holder does not include the OID in income over the life of the bond even though the issuer of the bond will deduct the OID on a ratable basis over the life of the bond.

For example, assume a Japanese bank issues a discounted bond in the face amount of ¥1 million that is subject to the 18 percent withholding tax rule. An investor purchases the bond for ¥900,000. There is ¥100,000 of OID that is subject to an 18 percent withholding tax. This withholding tax is collected by the issuer upon issuance of the bond and is remitted to the government in the same manner as income tax withheld.[102] As a result, the investor must pay ¥918,000 to the issuer for the bond. The issuer will keep ¥900,000 and remit ¥18,000 to the government. When the investor receives ¥1 million upon maturity of the bond, the investor does not include the ¥100,000 of OID in income as income taxes have already been paid on the OID income.

If the OID bond is not subject to the withholding tax rule, then the investor will include the OID in income upon maturity of the bond. As a result, in the above example, the investor will include ¥100,000 in income upon maturity of the bond. Apparently, the income is treated as miscellaneous income and not as interest income under domestic Japanese tax law.[103]

3. Tax Deferral Principle

In theory, the value of a zero coupon bond increases as the maturity date becomes closer. This is simply based upon the concept of present value and also ignoring market conditions as well as the creditworthiness of the issuer. Ideal income taxation, pursuant to the Haig–Simons definition of income, would require that the holder of the bond include the increase in value in income at least annually. If the holder of a zero coupon bond defers inclusion of OID until maturity of the bond, then the holder would be in a more favorable tax position as compared to the holder of a bond paying interest annually. For example, a zero coupon bond in the face amount of 1000*u*, maturing in 10 years, which is issued for 385*u* yields a rate of return of approximately 10 percent, compounded annually. This is in many ways equivalent to a bond in the face amount of 385*u*, maturing in 10 years, which is issued for 385*u* and paying 10 percent interest annually. The holder of the zero coupon bond and the holder of the bond paying interest annually should be taxed in a similar manner so as not to give one a tax advantage over the other.

4. United States' Solution to Preventing Tax Deferral

The United States has attacked the tax deferral that occurs in zero coupon bonds through the *Immediate Inclusion in Income Method*. This is discussed in detail in the

101 See Darcy, *supra* note 43, at ¶ 430.20; Otsuka and Watanabe, *supra* note 64, at 3.12.2.2 (permanent resident individuals) and 3.15.2.2 (resident corporations).

102 See Otsuka and Watanabe, *supra* note 64, at 3.12.2.2 (permanent resident individuals).

103 See Darcy, *supra* note 43, at ¶ 430.20.

following chapter. Generally, the United States devised a constant yield to maturity method in determining the annual income inclusion rather than appraise the value of the bond at least annually, which can be an administrative burden. The constant yield to maturity method is an approximation of the Haig–Simons definition of income, or more simply a surrogate. The constant yield to maturity method that the United States has adopted for OID is very similar to the theory behind Samuelson depreciation in which an internal rate of return must be calculated from the cash flows.

Under a constant yield to maturity method, the amount of income inclusion annually may deviate slightly from the actual annual increase in value of the bond. But if the investor retains the bond until maturity, then the *total* amount of income inclusion will be equal under the Haig–Simons definition of income or under a constant yield to maturity method. If the investor sells the bond prior to maturity, then the investor will recognize gain or loss on sale of the bond which will equalize the *total* amount of income inclusion under the Haig–Simons definition of income or the constant yield to maturity method although there may be characterization differences.

F. Offshore Investment Funds

1. United States

As a general rule, the United States income tax will not apply to tax a U.S. shareholder on the earnings of a foreign corporation until the earnings are repatriated to the United States by way of dividend, liquidation proceeds, or from the sale of shares of stock of the foreign corporation. The United States has enacted a host of rules designed to prevent United States corporations from shifting earnings offshore to a foreign subsidiary. These rules include the foreign personal holding company (FPHC) rules, which were enacted in 1937, and designed to attack transactions in which a relatively small number of U.S. investors set up a foreign corporation which would generate investment or passive-type of income;[104] the controlled foreign corporation (CFC) rules and subpart F income;[105] the foreign investment company (FIC) rules;[106] the personal holding company (PHC) rules;[107] the accumulated earnings tax;[108] and the passive foreign investment companies (PFIC) rules, which became effective in 1987.[109]

Prior to the Tax Reform Act of 1986, which included the enactment of the PFIC rules, these anti-deferral rules did not apply to a U.S. corporation investing in an offshore investment (or mutual) fund, which had hundreds or maybe even thousands of investors. The offshore investment fund would be located in a no tax or low tax jurisdiction. As a result, the U.S. corporation would avoid paying U.S. income taxes on the earnings of its investment in the offshore investment fund until the earnings were repatriated to the United States. In addition, the earnings would grow in a tax-free environment during the interim period. It was the enactment of the PFIC rules in

[104] I.R.C. §§ 551–557 (1998).
[105] I.R.C. §§ 951–958 (1998).
[106] I.R.C. §§ 1246–1247 (1998).
[107] I.R.C. §§ 541–547 (1998).
[108] I.R.C. §§ 531–537 (1998).
[109] I.R.C. §§ 1291–1297 (1998).

1986, that the United States eliminated the tax deferral benefits of investing in an offshore investment fund.

Generally, the investment in an offshore investment fund would be structured through a two-tier structure.[110] The two-tier structure consisted of a foreign parent corporation and its foreign subsidiary. The foreign corporations were incorporated in a no tax or low tax jurisdiction, such as the British Virgin Islands.[111] The foreign parent issued its stock to investors, the majority of which were foreign investors and a minority of which were U.S. investors.[112] The foreign subsidiary did the actual investing in stocks and securities.[113]

The offshore investment fund (consisting of the two foreign corporations) had a number of additional hurdles to clear to give its U.S. investors tax deferral on their investment. First, it was important that the foreign subsidiary was not engaged in a U.S. trade or business, which would subject it to U.S. corporate income taxation.[114] This was not difficult to accomplish even if the foreign subsidiary was investing in U.S. stocks and securities.[115] It was important that the foreign subsidiary not be treated as a dealer in stocks and securities. This was easily met as U.S. Treasury regulations excluded the typical offshore investment fund as a dealer in stocks and securities.[116] It was also important that the foreign subsidiary not have its principal office in the U.S.[117] This was also easily accomplished by having the foreign investment fund "make an arrangement with a service company in the country of its incorporation [maybe the British Virgin Islands] to provide it with a general business office where its management would be permanently located and from where it would carry on all or a substantial portion" of its functions.[118]

Second, the offshore investment fund had to avoid the accumulated earnings tax, which penalized corporations (including some foreign corporations) that had permitted earnings to accumulate beyond the reasonable needs of the business. The accumulated earnings tax could apply to a foreign corporation's U.S. source income. The offshore investment fund could avoid the accumulated earnings tax by having the foreign subsidiary declare an annual dividend of its U.S. source income to its foreign parent to which it could utilize the dividends paid deduction.[119] The foreign parent's only income was its dividend from its foreign subsidiary.[120] The foreign parent would not be treated as having U.S. source income because the dividend received by the foreign parent from its foreign subsidiary was paid by a corporation not engaged in a U.S. trade or business and also U.S. investors owned less than 50 percent of foreign parent.[121]

---

[110] See Stanley I. Rubenfeld and Jesse R. Rubin, "Passive Foreign Investment Companies: The Pentapus Becomes the Sextapus, Or Does It?," 36 *Tax Notes* 199 (1987) for a detailed description of how U.S. investors structured a pre-1986 offshore investment fund.

[111] Rubenfeld and Rubin, *supra* note 110, at 200. It was also suggested that the foreign parent corporation be incorporated in a different no tax or low tax jurisdiction than its foreign subsidiary to give the structure more credibility and not have it be treated as a sham by the IRS. *Id.* at 202.

[112] See *id.* at 200. [113] *Id.* at 200. [114] *Id.* at 200. [115] *Id.* [116] *Id.* at 200–01.

[117] *Id.* at 201. [118] *Id.* [119] *Id.* [120] *Id.* [121] *Id.*

In addition, the offshore investment fund had to be structured so that the IRS would not treat the two-tier structure as a sham and collapse the structure into one corporation.[122] To avoid sham classification, many two-tier structures contained the following safeguards: (1) the placement of one or more minority foreign shareholders at the foreign subsidiary level to give the dividend from foreign subsidiary to foreign parent more economic significance, (2) the incorporation of foreign parent and foreign subsidiary in two different jurisdictions, (3) having the foreign parent pay a dividend to its investors (shareholders) to the extent the foreign subsidiary's U.S. source income exceeded its U.S. expenses, and (4) having the foreign parent limit its U.S. ownership to substantially less than 50 percent.[123]

Finally, it was important that the offshore investment fund avoid classification as a personal holding company, foreign personal holding company, foreign investment company, or controlled foreign corporation. It could avoid the last three classifications, by restricting the U.S. ownership of the foreign parent to less than 50 percent.[124] In other words, foreign investors owned a majority of the foreign parent. This was generally accomplished by having the foreign parent issue two classes of stock, one for foreign investors and one for U.S. investors. The foreign parent would monitor, control, and restrict ownership of the two classes of stock, particularly the class designed for foreign investors.[125] The offshore investment fund could avoid classification as a personal holding company several different ways, including monitoring the ownership of the foreign parent so that five or fewer U.S. or foreign individuals did not own more than 50 percent of its stock during the last half of the year.[126]

The U.S. investors in the pre-1986 offshore investment fund achieved significant tax savings through deferring U.S. income taxes on the earnings of the fund. For example, assume a U.S. investor invested $1 million in an offshore investment fund. The fund earns a 10 percent rate of return each year and pays no income taxes on its earnings. If the U.S. investor stays in the fund for 10 years, then the value of the U.S. investor's interest in the fund should increase to $2,593,742 ($1 million times $(1.10)^{10}$). If the U.S. investor sells its interest or is redeemed out, then it will have gain of $1,593,742. At a 40 percent tax rate, it will pay taxes of $637,497 (40 percent times $1,593,742) leaving it with $1,956,245 after-taxes ($2,593,742 less $637,497). The U.S. investor has nearly doubled its money after 10 years.

If the U.S. investor's share of the earnings of the fund were subject to U.S. taxation each year, then the U.S. investor's interest in the fund should increase in value to $1,790,848 at the end of 10 years (assuming the fund distributes an amount each year to the U.S. investor equal to the taxes owed on the earnings). If the U.S. investor sells its interest or is redeemed out, it will have no gain leaving it with $1,790,848 after-taxes at the end of 10 years. In other words, $1 million will grow to $1,790,848 in 10 years at an *after-tax* rate of return of 6 percent.

---

[122] *Id.* This was a concern because the foreign parent would generally reinvest the dividend it received from the foreign subsidiary back into the foreign subsidiary. *Id.*

[123] *Id.* at 202. [124] *Id.* at 202–04. [125] *Id.* at 202–03. [126] *Id.* at 203.

In comparing the returns of the two investors, the U.S. investor who was able to defer taxes on the earnings of the fund ended up with $165,397 more cash at the end of 10 years ($1,956,245 less $1,790,848) than the U.S. investor whose investment earnings were taxed annually by the United States.

2. *Japan*

As a general rule, the Japanese income tax, like the U.S. income tax, will not apply to the earnings of a foreign subsidiary until the earnings are repatriated to Japan by way of dividend, liquidation proceeds, or from the sale of shares of stock of the foreign subsidiary.[127] In 1978, Japan enacted its first and only anti-tax haven measure. This provision is based in part on the controlled foreign corporation rules of the United States. It is designed to prevent tax avoidance by Japanese corporations who attempt to divert income to a foreign subsidiary in a no tax or low tax jurisdiction. The anti-tax haven measure prevents tax avoidance by Japanese corporations by immediately taxing the earnings of a foreign subsidiary that has been set up in a no tax or low tax jurisdiction if a number of requirements are met.

The anti-tax haven measure applies to a domestic corporation[128] (or resident individual[129]) that owns five percent or more of a designated tax haven subsidiary. A designated tax haven subsidiary is a foreign related company in which the country where its principal office is located has no income tax or the income tax burden is 25 percent or less of the income. A foreign related company is (1) a company whose principal office is located outside of Japan, in other words, a foreign corporation or a foreign unincorporated association, and (2) more than 50 percent of the stock or voting power is held by domestic corporations (or resident individuals).

There are numerous methods of avoiding the anti-tax haven measure. These include: (1) failing the more than 50 percent requirement of Japanese ownership by having nonresidents or foreign corporations own at least 50 percent of the foreign subsidiary; (2) establishing the foreign subsidiary in a jurisdiction where the income tax burden is above 25 percent but below the Japanese income tax rates; (3) meeting the local country active business exception;[130] and (4) keeping a particular domestic corporation's ownership at less than five percent so that the provision will not apply to that particular domestic corporation.

The Japanese anti-tax haven measure clearly does not apply to a Japanese domestic corporation investing in an offshore investment fund if the Japanese corporation's ownership interest in the fund is kept at less than five percent. Assume Inaba Corporation has generated an excess amount of cash that it wishes to invest. It

---

[127] See Otsuka and Watanabe, *supra* note 64, at 1.7.

[128] Special Taxation Measures Law Arts. 66-6 to 66-9 (1998) (resident corporate shareholders).

[129] See Otsuka and Watanabe, *supra* note 64, at 1.7 (citing to Special Taxation Measures Law Arts. 40-4 to 40-6 (1998) for resident individual shareholders).

[130] Special Taxation Measures Law Art. 66-6(3) (1998). See Darcy, *supra* note 43, at ¶ 745 (citing to Special Taxation Measures Law Arts. 40-4(3) (resident individual shareholders) and 66-6(3) (resident corporate shareholders)).

invests the money in an offshore investment fund in the Cayman Islands. The investment fund is a Cayman Islands corporation that pays no income tax to the Cayman Islands. Inaba Corporation invests ¥100 million in the offshore fund that gives it less than a five percent interest. The Cayman Islands corporation invests the money earning a 10 percent rate of return each year. Assume these earnings are free of Cayman Islands income tax, Japanese income tax, and other income tax, which should be the case. At the end of the first year, Inaba Corporation's investment will have grown from ¥100 million to ¥110 million. At the end of two years, it will grow to ¥121 million. At the end of 10 years, it will grow to ¥259.37 million. If Inaba Corporation were to close out its investment at this time, it will have gain of ¥159.37. Assuming a 34.5 percent tax rate, the tax owed to Japan will be ¥54.98 million, leaving Inaba Corporation with ¥204.39 million. Inaba Corporation has doubled its money in 10 years.

If Japan were to tax the earnings annually at a 34.5 percent tax rate, the investment would grow at an after-tax rate of return of 6.55 percent. At the end of one year, Inaba Corporation's investment will have grown from ¥100 million to ¥106.55 million (assuming the fund distributes an amount each year to Inaba Corporation equal to the taxes owed on the earnings). At the end of two years, it will grow to ¥113.53 million. At the end of 10 years, it will grow to ¥188.60 million. If Inaba Corporation were to close out its investment at this time, it will owe no taxes to Japan (because taxes have already been paid on the earnings), leaving Inaba Corporation with ¥188.60 million.

In comparing the returns of the two investments, Inaba Corporation, when it was able to defer taxes on the earnings of the fund, ended up with ¥15.79 million more at the end of 10 years (¥204.39 less ¥188.60) than when it invested in a fund whose investment earnings were taxed annually by Japan. If the rate of return that the offshore investment fund can earn is increased from 10 percent to 15 percent, the results are even more dramatic. Inaba Corporation, at the end of 10 years, will have ¥299.49 (¥404.56 less ¥105.07 taxes on closing out the investment) if Japan does not tax the earnings annually and will have ¥255.28 million if Japan taxes the earnings annually, a difference of ¥44.21 million.

3. Tax Deferral Principle

a. Super Cary Brown Model

The application of the Super Cary Brown model to an investment in an offshore investment fund should be apparent. The original investment in the fund with after-tax dollars or yen does not result in tax deferral at the time of the investment. However, if the subsequent earnings on that investment are not taxed at least annually, then tax deferral is taking place. This may be a result that a country's taxing authority has no objection to although the United States has exerted its taxing power with respect to investments in offshore investment funds. Japan must decide whether it approves of allowing tax deferral to take place on these types of investments or whether it will follow the path of denying tax deferral similar to the United States' lead. The Organisation for Economic Co-operation and Development ("OECD") has, for example, recommended that countries adopt a foreign investment fund ("FIF") or equivalent rule, such as the United States' PFIC rules.[131] As of 1996, only five OECD countries had adopted a FIF rule.[132]

One factor that may prevent Japan from adopting a FIF rule is that it will actually make the playing field less level in terms of Japanese investors investing in a domestic or offshore investment fund. Japan has two types of trust funds that are similar to U.S. mutual funds.[133] These two funds, which are collectively referred to as securities investment trusts ("*shoken toshi shintaku*"), are: (1) stock investment trusts ("*kabushiki toshi shintaku*"), which may invest in stocks or bonds; and (2) bond investment trusts ("*koshasai toshi shintaku*"), which may invest only in bonds. Japanese investors in these trust funds are taxed at a flat 20 percent withholding tax when receiving distributions from the trust funds. If no distribution is made, then no income tax applies. As a result, income can accumulate in these trust funds for several years with no tax being paid during the interim time.[134] Only at the time of distribution is the withholding tax applicable.[135] In addition, the trust fund itself is not subject to tax.[136] As a result, Japanese investors can invest in domestic funds and achieve tax deferral without the need to go offshore. As a result, enacting a FIF rule will give domestic investment funds a tax deferral advantage over offshore investment funds when the playing field is actually level at the current time without a FIF rule.

In the example of Inaba Corporation, during its first year in the fund, its investment increased in value from ¥100 million to ¥110 million. The increase in value of ¥10 million was due to the investments of the offshore investment fund of which Inaba Corporation was a minority shareholder. During the second year, Inaba Corporation's investment increased in value to ¥121 million. If Japan does not tax the increase in value on say an annual basis, this is identical to not taxing unrealized appreciation. In accordance with the Super Cary Brown model, by delaying the taxation of gains until realization, the income tax system effectively exempts the future annual return on the appreciation from tax.

b. Variation on the Cary Brown Model

It is important at this time to demonstrate another very important principle with respect to tax deferral, which was introduced in the previous chapter. Assume that

---

131 See Organisation for Economic Co-operation and Development, *Harmful Tax Competition: An Emerging Global Issue* at 42–43 (April 1998). See also Brian J. Arnold, "The Taxation of Investments in Passive Foreign Investment Funds in Australia, Canada, New Zealand and the United States," in *Essays on International Taxation* 5 (Herbert H. Albert and Kees van Raad eds., 1993).

132 See Organisation for Economic Co-operation and Development, *Controlled Foreign Company Legislation: Studies in Taxation of Foreign Source Income* at 153–55 (1996).

133 See Darcy, *supra* note 43, at ¶ 385.

134 See Eiki Kawakami, "The Taxation of Investment Funds: Japan," reprinted in 82b *Cahiers de Droit Fiscal International* [*International Fiscal Association*] 561, 565–66 (International Fiscal Association ed., 1997).

135 See *id.*

136 *Id.*

T invested a negligible amount a number of years ago in an offshore investment fund located in a tax haven jurisdiction. Through luck and good investments, T's stock in the fund is now worth 10,000*u*. The offshore investment fund will earn a 10 percent pre-tax rate of return each year for the next three years. Instead of closing out his investment by either selling his stock or having it redeemed, T decides to remain a stockholder for three more years. The realization doctrine prevents T from paying tax on mere appreciation. As a result, T has deferred paying 4000*u* in taxes (40 percent multiplied by 10,000*u* gain). If the deferred income amount of 10,000*u* increases by the after-tax rate of return, however, then there is no tax advantage to deferral.

Assume that the offshore investment fund is now subject to tax on its earnings by the foreign government at a 40 percent tax rate (and T is also in the 40 percent tax bracket). In other words, the foreign country where the foreign investment fund is located is now no longer a tax haven jurisdiction, maybe due to the pressure of the OECD.[137] As a result, T's stock will increase in value by a six percent rate of return each year, which is an after-tax rate of return. Should T immediately close out its investment in the fund or should it wait to do so at the end of three years? If T waits, then at the end of three years, T's stock is worth 11,910.16*u* (10,000*u* multiplied by $(1.06)^3$). If T sold the stock at the end of three years, T's gain would be 11,910.16*u*, and T would owe taxes of 4764.06*u*, leaving T with 7146.10*u*.

If T immediately sold his stock when it was worth 10,000*u* (and not held on to it for three more years), T would have 6000*u* after-taxes (10,000*u* sales proceeds less 4000*u* taxes paid). T could then invest the money and earn an after-tax rate of return of six percent annually. At the end of three years, T will have 7146.10*u* (6000*u* times $(1.06)^3$). T has achieved no tax deferral benefit by deferring taxes on the original appreciation of 10,000*u*. As a result, the example demonstrates that "deferral of income (or deductions) is not advantageous (or disadvantageous) to taxpayers if the deferred amount is increased by the after-income-tax rate of return" during the deferral period.[138]

In terms of expressing deferral of income in formulas, an amount A of income would produce $(1-t)A(1+r(1-t))^y$ after y years where r is the pre-tax rate of return whether (1) the income is included immediately or (2) deferred until a later year. In the case of immediate inclusion in income, the taxpayer would have $(1-t)A$ after taxes, which would compound over the years to $(1-t)A(1+r(1-t))^y$. In the case of deferral of income, the taxpayer would have A which would compound to $A(1+r(1-t))^y$ over the years. At the end of the deferral period, the taxpayer would owe taxes of $A(1+r(1-t))^y$ times t, leaving the taxpayer with $(1-t)A(1+r(1-t))^y$ after payment of the taxes. As a result, the taxpayer ends up in the same position whether the income is included immediately or deferred for a number of years.

If the deferred amount of income increases at a pre-tax rate of return, then in the case of deferral, the taxpayer would have A which would compound to $A(1+r)^y$

[137] See Organization for Economic Cooperation and Development, *Harmful Tax Competition: An Emerging Global Issue* (April 1998).

[138] Alvin C. Warren, "The Timing of Taxes," 39 *Nat'l Tax J.* 499, 501 (1987). See also Daniel I. Halperin, "Interest in Disguise: Taxing the 'Time Value of Money,'" 95 *Yale L. J.* 506, 523–34 (1986).

over the years. At the end of the deferral period, the taxpayer would owe taxes of $A(1+r)^y$ times t, leaving the taxpayer with $(1-t)A(1+r)^y$ after payment of the taxes. As a result, the taxpayer is better off when compared to the immediate inclusion in income.

4. United States' Solution to Preventing Tax Deferral

The United States has attacked the tax deferral that occurs in an offshore investment fund through one of three mutually exclusive methods: the *Interest Charge Method* and the Pass-Through and Mark to Market methods (both categorized as sub-methods under the *Immediate Inclusion in Income Method*). Each of these methods is discussed in detail in the following chapter.

G. Fiscal Year Partnerships and Limited Liability Companies

1. United States

Prior to the Internal Revenue Code of 1954 ("1954 Code"),[139] a partnership could select any taxable year it desired.[140] There were no taxable year conformity rules, and no establishment of a business purpose was required to select a taxable year. Thus, a partnership with calendar year partners could select a taxable year ending 31 January and provide its partners with an eleven month deferral of income. Apparently, a number of partnerships did just that.[141]

In the 1954 Code, the U.S. Congress enacted Section 706(b)(1), which for the first time placed statutory limits on a partnership's taxable year. As enacted, it read:

> The taxable year of a partnership shall be determined as though the partnership were a taxpayer. A partnership may not change to, or adopt, a taxable year other than that of all its principal partners unless it establishes, to the satisfaction of the Secretary or his delegate, a business purpose therefor.[142]

This provision required a new partnership to use the taxable year of all its principal partners. An existing partnership could not change to a taxable year other than that of all its principal partners. Both a new and an existing partnership, however, could use a taxable year other than that of all its principal partners if it could show a business purpose for such a taxable year.

As part of the 1986 Act, Congress again greatly limited the taxable year that a partnership can select. After the 1986 Act, a partnership is subject to a three step analysis, commonly referred to as the taxable year conformity rules.[143] First, a partnership must use a majority interest taxable year if one exists.[144] The term "majority interest taxable year" means the taxable year which, on each testing day, constituted the taxable

---

139 Pub. L. No. 83-591 (1954).

140 See generally Christopher H. Hanna, "A Partnership's Business Purpose Taxable Year: A Deferral Provision Whose Time Has Passed," 45 *Tax Law.* 685, 688 (1992).

141 See Hanna, *supra* note 140, at 688.

142 I.R.C. § 706(b)(1) (1954).

143 I.R.C. § 706(b)(1)(B).

144 I.R.C. § 706(b)(1)(B)(i).

year of one or more partners having on such day an aggregate interest in partnership profits and capital of more than 50 percent.[145] Second, if the partnership does not have a majority interest taxable year, then it must use the taxable year of all the principal partners of the partnership.[146] A principal partner is defined to mean a partner having an interest of five percent or more in partnership profits or capital.[147] Third, if the partnership does not have a majority interest taxable year and does not have a taxable year based on all the principal partners of the partnership, then it must use the calendar year or any other taxable year prescribed by regulations.[148] A partnership can use another taxable year if it can establish a business purpose to the satisfaction of the Secretary.[149]

As a result of the tightening of the rules in 1986, most new and many existing partnerships were forced to use a calendar year.[150] This created considerable controversy with accountants who felt that the taxable year conformity rules would create a large burden on them. Since most partnerships would be required to use a calendar year, much of the accountants' workload would fall during the first three and a half months following the end of the calendar year.[151] In the 1987 Act, Congress responded to this concern by enacting Code Sections 444 and 7519. Code Section 444 provides partnerships with options to elect a taxable year other than the required taxable year.[152] If a partnership makes an election under Code Section 444, however, it must also make a required payment with the Treasury under Code Section 7519.

Under Code Section 444, a new partnership can only elect a taxable year that does not have a deferral period exceeding three months.[153] Assuming the new partnership is required to use a calendar year under Code Section 706(b)(1)(B), which most partnerships are, it can elect a taxable year ending 30 September, 31 October, or 30 November under Code Section 444. As a result, partnerships are faced with extremely limited choices as to what taxable year they may select.

If a partnership has been using a taxable year based on a business purpose, it can continue to use that year without having to make the election under Code Section 444.[154] The obvious advantage is that it is not required to make the required payment

---

[145] I.R.C. § 706(b)(4)(A)(i). The testing day is the first day of the partnership taxable year or the day during such representative period that is prescribed by the Secretary. I.R.C. § 706(b)(4)(A)(ii).

If a partnership changes to a majority interest taxable year, it is not required to change to another taxable year for the two years following the year of change. I.R.C. § 706(b)(4)(B).

[146] I.R.C. § 706(b)(1)(B)(ii). [147] I.R.C. § 706(b)(3). [148] I.R.C. § 706(b)(1)(B)(iii).

[149] I.R.C. §§ 706(b)(1)(C). See generally Hanna, *supra* note 140.

[150] See Hanna, *supra* note 140, at 709–10. [151] See *id.*

[152] "Required taxable year" is defined to mean the taxable year determined under Section 706(b) or 1378 without taking into account any taxable year which is allowable by reason of a business purpose. I.R.C. § 444(e).

[153] No mention is made in the legislative history as to why a deferral period of up to three months was allowed. See Hanna, *supra* note 140, at 711.

[154] Temp. Treas. Reg. § 1.444-1T(a)(3). The business purpose must have been established under Rev. Proc. 87-32 or any successor revenue ruling or revenue procedure, e.g., Rev. Rul. 87-57. Temp. Treas. Reg. § 1.444-1T(a)(3)(i). However, a taxable year that is a grandfathered fiscal year under Rev. Proc. 87-32 or any successor revenue ruling or revenue procedure will also suffice. Temp. Treas. Reg. § 1.444-1T(a)(3)(ii).

under Code Section 7519. In addition, a new partnership that can establish a taxable year based on a business purpose does not have to make the Code Section 444 election and, therefore, is not required to make the required payment under Code Section 7519.

2. Japan

Japan has four major business entities: *kabushiki kaisha*, *yūgen kaisha*, *gōmei kaisha*, and *gōshi kaisha*, all of which are categorized as ordinary corporations under the Japanese corporate income tax system.[155] Japan also has several additional categories of corporations (public interest corporations, cooperatives, public corporations, and nonjuridical organizations). But there are two additional business entities which are somewhat unique in that they are treated as flow-through or conduits for Japanese income tax purposes (or generally the equivalent of flow-through entities) similar in some respects to United States partnerships. These two entities are the *nin-i kumiai* and the *tokumei kumiai*. It should be noted that these two entities are not in widespread use in Japan, and, as a result, there are many unresolved issues with respect to the use of these entities, particularly tax issues.[156] It will be interesting to see whether these two entities, particularly the *tokumei kumiai*, will become more popular during the next 10 or 20 years in a manner similar to the rise in popularity of the limited partnership in the United States in the 1970s and continuing with the limited liability company in the 1990s.[157]

The first flow-through entity is the *nin-i kumiai*, which is a Civil Code association.[158] It is a contract of partnership that becomes effective when each of the parties ("*kumiai in*") has agreed to carry on a joint undertaking by making a contribution to the partnership.[159] The contribution may be in the form of cash, property, or services.[160] The contribution made by each partner and the other property of the partnership belongs to all the partners jointly.[161] Corporations may be partners in the *nin-i kumiai*, which is not recognized as a corporation (company) under the Commercial Code.[162] It is treated as an aggregate of the partners and not as a separate legal entity.[163]

The conduct of the affairs of the partnership is decided by a majority of the partners.[164] However, one or more persons may be appointed to conduct the affairs of the

---

155 CTL Art. 2(1)(ix) (1996).

156 See generally Ichiro Otsuka, "International Income Tax Problems of Partnerships: Japan," reprinted in 80a *Cahiers De Droit Fiscal International* [*Studies of International Fiscal Law*] 317 (International Fiscal Association ed., 1995).

157 The *tokumei kumiai* has been used quite extensively with respect to the Japanese leveraged lease transaction. See, e.g., Darcy, *supra* note 43, at ¶ 630.20; Richard S. Koffey and Richard L. Umbrecht, "Japanese Cross-Border Leasing into the United States," 43 *Tax Law.* 149 (1989); Todd M. Landau, "Japan's New Wave of Advantages," 7 *Int'l Tax Review* 40–43 (March 1996).

158 Civil Code Section 12 (Articles 667–688).

159 Civil Code Art. 667.

160 Civil Code Art. 667(2).

161 Civil Code Art. 668.

162 See Takashi Kuboi and Yoichi Asakawa, "Partnering in Japan: Form of Entry and Recent Tax Issues," 13 *Tax Notes Int'l* 446, 447 (1996); Griffith Way et al., *Business Operations in Japan*, in Tax Management (BNA Portfolio 51-7th 1990) at A-22.

163 See Kuboi and Asakawa, *supra* note 162, at 318; Otsuka, *supra* note 156, at 317–18.

164 Civil Code Art. 670(1).

partnership.[165] As a result, the *nin-i kumiai* is "essentially a contractual relationship among the members with respect to a common undertaking, and thus bears some resemblance to an American partnership."[166] One commentator has pointed out that the *nin-i kumiai* has four common basic features of a partnership: "(1) a contractual arrangement, (2) between two or more persons (individuals or legal entities), (3) with a view to sharing profits (or losses as the case may be), and (4) in cooperation with and on a proportionate basis for each of them resulting in a personal relationship in a commercial or professional activity."[167]

The *nin-i kumiai* is not a separate taxable entity and is not subject to the Japanese corporate income tax.[168] In addition, it does not file a tax return.[169] In the absence of an agreement, the allocation of profits and losses is made in proportion to the value of the contribution of each partner.[170] As a result, it appears that an agreement can be entered into among the partners to allocate profits and losses in a manner different than their relative contributions to the partnerships. If an allocation has been entered into for only the sharing of profits (or losses), then that allocation ratio is presumed to apply both to profits and losses.[171] It appears that the partners can specify an allocation ratio for profits and a different allocation ratio for losses. It also appears that the partnership can amend the association contract to change the allocation ratios from time to time.[172]

Each partner must include in its taxable income its ratable share of the *nin-i kumiai's* profit (or loss) during the partner's year that includes the last day of the *nin-i kumiai's* accounting period.[173] In other words, the *nin-i kumiai's* profit (or loss)

---

[165] Civil Code Art. 670(2). [166] See Way, *supra* note 162, at A-22.

[167] See Otsuka, *supra* note 156, at 318.

[168] See, e.g., Darcy, *supra* note 43, at ¶ 105.10 (citing to CTL Basic Circular 1-1-1); Gomi, supra note 5, at ¶ 3-120; Otsuka, *supra* note 156, at 317–19; Morio Uematsu, "Computation of Income in Japanese Income Taxation: A Study in the Adjustment of Theory to Reality in Law," in *Japan: The Legal Order in a Changing Society* 566, 583 (Arthur Taylor von Mehren ed., 1963). The income of the *nin-i kumiai* is taxed to the partners, whether or not the income is actually distributed to them.

[169] See Kuboi and Asakawa, *supra* note 162, at 447; Otsuka, *supra* note 156, at 320; Way, *supra* note 162, at A-22.

[170] Civil Code Art. 674(1). [171] Civil Code Art. 674(2).

[172] The Japanese income tax system, like the United States, has adopted the principle of substance over form. Care must be taken in structuring a transaction that will not be successfully challenged by the Japanese National Tax Agency. See Income Tax Law Art. 12; Corporation Tax Law Art. 11; MOF 1997, *supra* note 6, at 27; Dean A. Yoost and Richard R. McGinnis, "Using Japan's Tokumei Kumiai," 7 *Int'l Tax Review* 15, 16 (November 1996).

[173] See Darcy, *supra* note 43, at ¶ 630.10 (citing CTL Basic Circular 14-1-1); Kuboi and Asakawa, *supra* note 162, at 447 (citing ITL Basic Circular 36.37-19 and CTL Basic Circular 14-1-1); Otsuka and Watanabe, *supra* note 64, at 2.17 (citing ITL Basic Circular 36.37 and CTL Basic Circular 14-1-1); Way et al., *supra* note 162, at A-53 (citing CTL Basic Circulars 14-1-1 and 14-1-2).

Japan provides for three methods in which the partner of the *nin-i kumiai* accounts for its ratable share of the income or loss. The first method is referred to as the net income method, net result method, or simply the net method. As its name implies, the partner reports its share of the net income or net loss of the *nin-i kumiai*. The second method is referred to as the partial flow-through method or hybrid method. Under this method, the partner reports its share of revenues and expenses. The third method is the pass-through method or flow-through method. Under this method, the partner reports its share of each

flows through to the partners on the last day of the *nin-i kumiai's* accounting period.[174] The partner must include its ratable share of the profit even if no distribution of the profit has been made by the *nin-i kumiai*.[175] This must be done annually.[176] The timing of the flow-through of profits and losses appears to be identical or almost identical to the rule in the United States for partnerships.[177]

The partners are liable for the obligations of the *nin-i kumiai* in proportion to how they share losses, which is generally based on their contributions to the *nin-i kumiai* unless the association contract otherwise provides.[178] A creditor who was unaware of the loss sharing agreement among the partners at the time his claim came into existence may exercise his right against each partner in equal shares.[179]

The second type of flow-through entity is the *tokumei kumiai* (secret or anonymous association), which is formed under the Commercial Code.[180] It is not really a flow-through entity but is generally equivalent to a flow-through entity. It is similar in some respects to the United States limited partnership, however, for Japanese legal purposes, it is not exactly a partnership or a corporation.[181] It has been compared to the German "*stille gesellschaft*" and the French "*association commerciale en participation*" or "*societe en participation*."[182]

In the *tokumei kumiai*, the entrepreneur ("*eigyosha*") enters into contracts with investors ("*tokumei kumiai in*") who contribute cash or property in exchange for a share of profits.[183] Each investor enters into a separate contract with the entrepreneur.[184] There is no contractual relationship among all the investors.[185] The cash or property contributed by the investors becomes the property of the entrepreneur.[186]

The entrepreneur conducts the business entirely on its own behalf. The investors do not participate in the administrative affairs of the business or represent the business.[187] The entrepreneur owns all the assets (including those contributed by the

---

item of the *nin-i kumiai's* revenues, expenses, assets, and liabilities. See, e.g., Darcy, *supra* note 43, at ¶ 630.10; Kuboi and Asakawa, *supra* note 162, at 446–47; Otsuka and Watanabe, *supra* note 64, at 2.17; Way et al., *supra* note 162, at A-52 to A-53.

174 See, e.g., Darcy, *supra* note 43, at ¶ 630.10; Kuboi and Asakawa, *supra* note 162, at 447; Otsuka, supra note 156, at 320–21; Way et al., *supra* note 162, at A-53.

175 See Darcy, *supra* note 43, at ¶ 630.10: Otsuka, *supra* note 156, at 320–21.

176 See Otsuka and Watanabe, *supra* note 64, at 2.17.

177 See Internal Revenue Code § 706(a).

178 Civil Code Art. 674–75. See Way et al., *supra* note 162, at A-22.

179 Civil Code Art. 675.

180 Commercial Code Chapter IV (Articles 535–42).

181 See Yoost and McGinnis, *supra* note 172, at 15.

182 See, e.g., Otsuka and Watanabe, *supra* note 64, at 1.2.1.4; Uematsu, *supra* note 168, at 583 n. 94.

183 Commercial Code Arts. 150, 535 and 542. Many times the investors also agree to share in the losses, if any, of the *tokumei kumiai*. See generally Hugh J. Ault, *Comparative Income Taxation* 292 (1997); Kuboi and Asakawa, *supra* note 162, at 448; Otsuka and Watanabe, *supra* note 64, at 1.2.1.4; Gary M. Thomas, "Structure of Japanese Operations and Other Selected Japanese Tax Issues," *Intertax* 33, 36–37 (January 1992); Yoost and McGinnis, *supra* note 172, at 15.

184 See Otsuka and Watanabe, *supra* note 64, at 1.2.1.4; Yoost and McGinnis, *supra* note 172, at 15.

185 See Way et al., *supra* note 162, at A-23; Yoost and McGinnis, *supra* note 172, at 15.

186 Commercial Code Art. 536.

187 Commercial Code Arts. 156 and 542.

investors) and is liable for all the debts of the business.[188] The investors have limited liability to the extent of their contributions unless the *tokumei kumiai* contract provides for an investor to bear responsibility for a portion of the liabilities.[189] An investor may transfer its interest in the *tokumei kumiai* with the consent of the entrepreneur, or without consent if the *tokumei kumiai* contract so provides.[190]

For Japanese income tax purposes, the entrepreneur reports all of the profits (or losses) of the *tokumei kumiai* and then deducts the portion of the profits allocated to the investors.[191] The investor is treated as receiving its share of the profits on the last day of the *tokumei kumiai's* year. As a result, an investor must report its share of the *tokumei kumiai's* profit in its taxable year which includes the last day of the *tokumei kumiai's* year even if no actual distribution of profits takes place.

When the *tokumei kumiai* distributes the profits to the investors, the distribution is subject to withholding under the Japanese income tax laws unless the number of investors is less than ten.[192] As a result, most *tokumei kumiai* are formed with nine or less investors.[193]

The *nin-i kumiai* and the *tokumei kumiai* are not in widespread use in Japan at the present time.[194] Many of the reasons for the lack of interest in these two entities are the same reasons given for the lack of interest in the *yugen kaisha*, such as the lack of prestige and the lack of familiarity. Other reasons given for the lack of interest in the *nin-i kumiai* and the *tokumei kumiai* include the difference in tax culture, differences between book and tax accounting, and the reporting of financial performance on a single company basis as opposed to a consolidated basis.[195] In addition, the *nin-i kumiai* has several serious disadvantages that the *tokumei kumiai* does not. For

---

[188] Commercial Code Arts. 536(2) and 537. See, e.g., Kuboi and Asakawa, *supra* note 162, at 448; Otsuka, *supra* note 156, at 318; Otsuka and Watanabe, *supra* note 64, at 1.2.1.4; Way et al., *supra* note 162, at A-23.

[189] Commercial Code Arts. 153, 156, 536, 537 and 542. See, e.g., Kuboi and Asakawa, *supra* note 162, at 448; Otsuka, *supra* note 156, at 318; Way et al., *supra* note 162, at A-23; Yoost and McGinnis, *supra* note 172, at 15.

[190] See Yoost and McGinnis, *supra* note 172, at 16.

[191] See, e.g., Otsuka, *supra* note 156, at 318 (citing ITL Basic Circular 36.37-21 and CTL Basic Circular 14-1-3); Yoost and McGinnis, *supra* note 172, at 16 ("The allocation of profits or losses to the investor under a TK agreement is considered a deductible expense or taxable income for the proprietor.")

[192] See Darcy, *supra* note 43, at 630.20 (citing ITL Art. 210 and ITL Enf. Order Arts. 288(1)(i), 327); Otsuka, *supra* note 156, at 321 (citing ITL Art. 161(12) and ITL Enf. Order Art. 288); Yoost and McGinnis, *supra* note 172, at 16.

[193] See, e.g., Darcy, *supra* note 43, 630.20; Robert Tomkin, Lease-Backs on Offer in Finance Boutiques, Japan Economic Journal, 13 April. 1991, at 10. Apparently, there is support for the position that if a *tokumei kumiai* is conducting business in Japan and the 20 percent withholding tax applies (because there are 10 or more investors), it will be the only tax that applies to an American investor if the American investor does not have a permanent establishment in Japan. If so, this may be more advantageous than having an American investor subject to the progressive Japanese income tax rates. As a result, a *tokumei kumiai* may be intentionally structured to have 10 or more investors. See Otsuka and Watanabe, *supra* note 64, at 2.18.

[194] See, e.g., Kuboi and Asakawa, *supra* note 162, at 448; Otsuka, *supra* note 156, at 332. But see *supra* note 157.

[195] See Kuboi and Asakawa, *supra* note 162, at 448.

example, all of the members of the *nin-i kumiai* have unlimited liability. In addition, foreign members of the *nin-i kumiai* may be treated as having a permanent establishment in Japan if the *nin-i kumiai* itself is treated as having a permanent establishment in Japan while foreign investors in the *tokumei kumiai* apparently will not be treated as having a permanent establishment in Japan.[196]

It appears that the *nin-i kumiai* is free to select any taxable year its members' desire. There are no taxable year conformity rules like in the United States. As a result, a *nin-i kumiai* could select a taxable year ending on 31 January giving its calendar year members 11 months of deferral.

Like the *nin-i kumiai*, there are no taxable year conformity rules for the *tokumei kumiai*. As a result, it appears that the *tokumei kumiai* can select any taxable year its members' desire. The *tokumei kumiai*, however, may be treated differently than the *nin-i kumiai* for purposes of determining its taxable year. In some sense, the *tokumei kumiai* and the entrepreneur are one and the same. For example, all of the property of the *tokumei kumiai* is owned by the entrepreneur. This applies even to the property contributed by the investors. The entrepreneur is liable for all of the debts of the *tokumei kumiai*. In addition, the income of the *tokumei kumiai* does not flow through to the investors. Rather, the income is treated as entirely that of the entrepreneur. The entrepreneur deducts the portion of the income allocated to investors. As a result, the taxable year of the *tokumei kumiai* may be required to be the same as that of the entrepreneur. So, for example, if the entrepreneur is a Japanese corporation using a 31 March year end, the *tokumei kumiai* may also be treated as having a 31 March year end. The calendar year investors in the *tokumei kumiai* would receive nine months of deferral. As a result, it is not entirely clear whether the *tokumei kumiai* can select any taxable year or whether its taxable year must be the same as that of the entrepreneur.

3. Tax Deferral Principle

By selecting a taxable year different than the owners of the pass through entity, the entity is providing deferral of income. For example, assume a pass through entity is

---

[196] See Otsuka, *supra* note 156, at 328–29; Otsuka and Watanabe, *supra* note 64, at 2.18. The Japanese National Tax Administration appears to take the position that the income from a *tokumei kumiai* conducting business in Japan will be taxed to an American investor even if the American investor does not have a permanent establishment in Japan because the term "Industrial or Commercial Profits" in article 8 of the U.S.–Japan Income Tax Treaty does not include income from a *tokumei kumiai* conducting business in Japan. The income of the *tokumei kumiai* conducting business in Japan is taxed to an American investor as income from the utilization or holding of assets in Japan. See CTL Art. 138(11); CTL Enf. Order 177(1)(iv); Art. 6(9) of the U.S.–Japan Income Tax Treaty; Darcy, *supra* note 43, 405.20 (citing CTL Enf. Order Art. 177(1)(iv) and ITL Enf. Order Art. 280(1)(iv)); Otsuka, *supra* note 156, at 3.4; Otsuka and Watanabe, *supra* note 64, at 2.18. The taxation of an American investor is in sharp contrast to the taxation of a United Kingdom investor or Swiss investor. Apparently the income from a *tokumei kumiai* conducting business in Japan is completely exempt from Japanese income taxation under the Japan–United Kingdom Income Tax Treaty for U.K. investors and the Japan–Switzerland Income Tax Treaty for Swiss investors if the U.K. or Swiss investors do not have a permanent establishment in Japan. See Darcy, *supra* note 43, at 1270; Otsuka and Watanabe, *supra* note 64, at 2.18 n. 342.

formed on 1 January 1997. All of its owners are calendar year individuals. The entity selects a taxable year ending on 31 August. During the year 1997, eight months of income (1 January through 31 August) will flow through the entity on 31 August 1997. The remaining four months of income will be deferred until the next year. However, the next taxable year will end on 31 August 1998, at which time 12 months (and not 16 months) of income will flow through to the partners. As a result, four months of income is still being deferred.

When a pass through entity uses a taxable year different than its owners, it presents its owner with *indefinite* tax deferral. The deferral period continues for an owner of the entity until the owner departs the entity or the entity is terminated. In the above example, when the partnership terminates at some point in the future, the owners will take the four months of deferred income into income and pay taxes on it. At that point in time, the deferral will end. But this may be many years in the future.

4. United States' Solution to Preventing Tax Deferral

The United States has attacked the tax deferral that occurs with a pass through entity using a taxable year different than its owners through use of the *Deposit Method.* This method is discussed in detail in the following chapter.

H. Advance Receipt for Services

1. United States

In the United States, generally an accrual method taxpayer must include in income amounts currently received for services to be performed in the future.[197] This has become a well-accepted principle of tax law, commonly referred to as the *Schlude* doctrine, with very few exceptions.[198] The *Schlude* doctrine is based on the case of *Schlude v. Commissioner*, decided by the U.S. Supreme Court in 1963. The U.S. Supreme Court had previously decided two earlier cases involving prepaid service income, *Automobile Club of Michigan v. Commissioner* in 1957 and *American Automobile Association v. Commissioner* in 1961, and ruled in each case that the prepayment constituted income at the time of receipt, not when the services would

[197] See, e.g., *Automobile Club of Michigan v. United States*, 353 U.S. 180 (1957); *American Automobile Association v. United States*, 367 U.S. 687 (1961); *Commissioner v. Schlude*, 372 U.S. 128 (1963). The Supreme Court's holding in these three cases is sometimes referred to as the *Schlude* doctrine. This doctrine basically states that an accrual method taxpayer that receives an advance payment for services must include the advance payment in gross income at the time of receipt. This doctrine has also been applied to advance payment for goods. See, e.g., *Hagen Advertising Displays, Inc. v. Commissioner*, 407 F.2d 1105 (6th Cir. 1969); Treas. Reg. § 1.451-5 (1971).

[198] But see, e.g., I.R.C. § 455 (prepaid subscription income); I.R.C. § 456 (prepaid dues income of certain membership organizations); Rev. Proc. 71-21, 1971-2 C.B. 549; Treas. Reg. § 1.446-3; Treas. Reg. § 1.451-5; Notice 89-21, 1989-1 C.B. 651; *Artnell Co. v. Commissioner*, 400 F.2d 981 (7th Cir. 1968); *Collegiate Cap & Gown Co. v. Commissioner*, 37 T.C.M. (CCH) 960 (1978); *Boise Cascade Corp. v. United States*, 530 F.2d 1367, *cert. denied*, 429 U.S. 867 (1976).

later be performed by the recipient accrual method corporation. These three cases are collectively referred to as The Trilogy.

In *Schlude v. Commissioner*, the U.S. Supreme Court once again held that a prepayment for services is income at the time of receipt to an accrual method taxpayer. In *Schlude*, a dance studio on the accrual method of accounting received advance payments from customers for dance lessons to be given in the future. The advance payments related to a specific period of time when the lessons had to be taken, but there was no schedule of specific dates. The dance studio included the advance payments in income when the dance lessons were actually given to the customers. The U.S. Supreme Court held that the dance studio had to include the advance payments in income at the time of receipt to clearly reflect income. The Court reasoned that some or all of the customers might allow some of the lessons to lapse and as a result, "At the end of each period, while the number of lessons taught had been meticulously reflected, the [dance] studio was uncertain whether none, some or all of the remaining lessons would be rendered."[199]

In 1970, the Internal Revenue Service allowed partial relief from the *Schlude* doctrine. In Revenue Procedure 71-21,[200] the Service provided that an accrual method taxpayer may defer an advance payment received for services to be rendered in the future if the services are required to be performed by the end of the year following the year of receipt. If this requirement is met, the accrual method taxpayer will include the advance payment in income as services are rendered with the entire amount being included by the end of the year following the year of receipt. As a result, Revenue Procedure 71-21 provides at most a one year deferral of income.

2. *Japan*

Japan does not appear to have a clear cut rule for prepaid service income for accrual method taxpayers, in the way that the United States has with its *Schlude* doctrine. There seems to be very little authority in the area of prepaid service income. As a result, there is a lot of tension between the National Tax Administration and taxpayers as to when prepaid service income must be included in gross income by an accrual method taxpayer. The NTA has released several circulars describing the timing of the realization event with respect to the performance of personal services by an accrual method taxpayer.

The Income Tax law provides that the amount of income included in the current taxable year, except as otherwise provided, is the income that belongs to the current year (if the income is non-cash, rights, or economic benefits, then value should be used).[201] A circular, which is issued under the Income Tax laws, provides that the time of realization in the case of personal services is when the services are completed.[202] If a contract or usual business custom shows the relationship between the compensation

[199] 372 U.S. 128, 136 (1963).

[200] 1971-2 C.B. 549 (superseding Revenue Procedure 70-21, 1970-2 C.B. 501).

[201] ITL Art. 36-1 (1998).

[202] ITL Basic Circular 36-8, para. 5.

and periods of performance or extent of performance, then the timing of income recognition should be the date when the performance occurs.[203]

The Corporate Tax law provides that income should generally be calculated in accordance with Generally Accepted Accounting Principles (GAAP).[204] A circular, issued under the Corporate Tax laws, provides that "revenue from work undertaken is included in gross income in the business year of the date of completion and delivery of the subject property if the work includes delivery of the property, or the date of completion of all services promised if the work does not include delivery of the property."[205]

Several leading commentators, most notably University of Tokyo Professor Emeritus Hiroshi Kaneko, have written that the recipient of an advance payment for services can defer the income over the period of time to which the services relate.[206] This seems to be based on the principle in Japan that Generally Accepted Accounting Principles (GAAP) are used in determining the timing of income unless the income tax law specifically provides otherwise, as for example, installment sales and deferred payment sales.[207]

As a result, it appears that there is some authority to allow deferral of prepaid income. It also appears that the deferred income will be recognized either as the services are performed or when the services are completed.

3. Tax Deferral Principle

Deferral is only taking place with respect to an advance payment for services if one concludes that the proper result is to include the advance payment in income at the time of receipt. As a result, the United States would view Japan as allowing tax deferral for advance payments for services while Japan would argue that no deferral is taking place in its income tax system. The issue appears to be whether the accrual method recipient has an undeniable accession to wealth upon receiving the advance payment or whether the advance payment is more in the nature of a loan that is being repaid in the form of services.[208]

But, even under the Japanese point of view, there is a time value of money component to the advance payment for services, which needs to be considered. In other words, it is not appropriate to treat the advance payment as a *non-interest* bearing loan. Professor Halperin has suggested the following method that takes into account the time value of money. Professor Halperin argues that the customer should be treated as earning interest on the prepayment before the prepayment is earned. As a result, he would impute an interest payment from the business to the customer thereby forcing the customer to pay taxes on the deemed interest income payment.

An example will best illustrate Professor Halperin's method. Assume a business on the accrual method of accounting receives an advance payment for services

[203] ITL Basic Circular 36-8, para. 5. [204] CTL Art. 22-4 (1998).

[205] See Kitagawa, *supra* note 59, at ¶ 2.05 (citing to CTL Basic Circulars 2-1-5 and 2-1-6).

[206] See Hiroshi Kaneko, *Sozeiho* (in Japanese) at 216–17, 240–41, 244–47 (6th ed., 1997); Hugh J. Ault, *Comparative Income Taxation* 258 (1997).

[207] See Kitagawa, *supra* note 59, at ¶ 2.05.

[208] See Calvin H. Johnson, "The Illegitimate Earned Requirement in Tax and Nontax Accounting," 50 *Tax L. Rev.* (1995); Halperin, *supra* note 138.

on 31 December of year zero. The payment is 1000*u* and is for five years' worth of services. The services will be performed in equal amounts each year for five years. The following table shows the results for the 1000*u* advance payment if it is treated, in essence, as a loan:

Year	Imputed loan balance	Imputed interest expense	Service income	Service income net of interest expense
1	1000*u*	100*u*	263.80*u*	163.80*u*
2	836.20*u*	83.62*u*	263.80*u*	180.18*u*
3	656.26*u*	65.60*u*	263.80*u*	198.19*u*
4	457.83*u*	45.78*u*	263.80*u*	218.01*u*
5	239.82*u*	23.98*u*	263.80*u*	239.82*u*
Total		318.99*u*	1318.99*u*	1000.00*u*

Assuming that the business performs an equal amount of services each year with respect to the advance payment, the business would have compensation of 263.80*u* each year, not 200*u* each year. The reason is that 263.80*u* is the annuity needed to give the customer who made the advance payment 10 percent interest on a 1000*u* loan in which payments (covering principal and interest) are constant over five years.[209] Professor Halperin maintains that the business should include in year one 263.80*u* of service income. It should also be allowed a deemed interest deduction of 100*u* (the customer will have 100*u* of deemed interest income). The business will also include 100*u* of interest income by investing the 1000*u* advance payment at a 10 percent rate of return. As a result, the business' net income inclusion for year one is 263.80*u*. In year two, the business should include 263.80*u* of service income and be allowed a deemed interest deduction of 83.62*u* (the customer will have 83.62*u* of deemed interest income). The business will also include 99.45*u* of interest income by investing 994.49*u* (1000*u* advance payment plus 100*u* return on the advance payment minus 105.51*u* taxes paid (263.80*u* multiplied by 40 percent tax rate)) at a 10 percent rate of return. Providing for interest each year shifts the tax burden on the interest income from the business to the customer.

The following table demonstrates the results to the business each year by, in essence, treating the advance payment as a loan and also focusing on the investment earnings of the advance payment.[210]

At the end of five years, the business will have 892.23*u*. This amount represents a growth of 8.26 percent compounded annually if the advance payment were included in income upon receipt (600*u* multiplied by $(1+0.0826)^5$). If it were required to include the advance payment in income upon receipt, the business will have 802.94*u* at the end of five years (600*u* multiplied by $(1+0.06)^5$). Professor Halperin's

209 See Johnson, *supra* note 208, at 406 n. 108.

210 See *id.* at 407 n. 114.

Year	1	2	3	4	5	6
A. Investment amount	1000*u*	994.48*u*	982.08*u*	961.73*u*	932.22*u*	892.23*u*
B. Interest (10%)	100*u*	99.45*u*	98.21*u*	96.17*u*	93.22*u*	
C. Outstanding deemed debt	1000*u*	836.20*u*	656.03*u*	457.83*u*	239.82*u*	
D. Deemed compensation	263.80*u*	263.80*u*	263.80*u*	263.80*u*	263.80*u*	
E. Deemed interest (C × 10%)	100*u*	83.62*u*	65.60*u*	45.78*u*	23.98*u*	
F. Reduction of outstanding deemed debt (D – E)	163.80*u*	180.18*u*	198.20*u*	218.01*u*	239.82*u*	
G. Taxable income	263.80*u*	279.63*u*	296.40*u*	314.19*u*	333.04*u*	
H. Tax (40%)	105.52*u*	111.85*u*	118.56*u*	125.68*u*	133.22*u*	
I. After-tax growth of investment amount	(5.52*u*)	(12.40*u*)	(20.35*u*)	(29.50*u*)	(39.99*u*)	

methodology shifts the tax burden on the interest during the five-year period from the business to the customer.

4. United States' Solution to Preventing Tax Deferral

As previously stated, the United States requires that the recipient of an advance payment for services include the payment in income at the time of receipt, even though the recipient is on the accrual method. There are several exceptions to this rule with Revenue Procedure 71-21 being among the most notable. In 1992, the United States developed another exception to the *Schlude* doctrine by allowing deferral but preventing the taxpayer from receiving a time value of money advantage to the deferral. This is referred to as the *Deferral of Income with Imputed Interest Method* and will be discussed in the next chapter.

I. Reserves

1. United States

As a general rule, the United States does not permit taxpayers to establish reserves for estimated expenses.[211] Historically, many accrual method taxpayers attempted to

[211] I.R.C. § 461(h)(5) (generally no reserves are permitted unless specifically provided for in the tax laws).

establish reserves for estimated expenses because the United States required prepaid income of accrual method taxpayers to be immediately included in income pursuant to the *Schlude* doctrine. In other words, accrual method taxpayers were in a sense being whipsawed: immediate inclusion of prepaid income and deferral of deductions relating to estimated expenses. A few courts, however, permitted accrual method taxpayers to deduct amounts for estimated expenses, such as the estimated costs of workers' compensation claims and the estimated costs of surface mining reclamation.[212]

In 1984, the United States Congress enacted Section 461(h) that reinforced the general rule of no reserves for estimated expenses.[213] This provision requires that economic performance take place before a deduction is permitted to an accrual method taxpayer. For example, if the accrual method taxpayer is required to perform a service in the future, economic performance occurs as the services are performed. As a result, the taxpayer is not permitted a deduction until the year when the services are performed. The example given by the Joint Committee on Taxation is that of a contractor who is engaged by a highway construction company to repair damaged properties.[214] Economic performance occurs as the contractor performs the repair work. If the highway construction company itself performs the work, then economic performance occurs as it makes the repairs.

There are some exceptions to the general rule of no reserves for estimated expenses. For example, special rules apply to banking institutions and life insurance companies permitting them to establish reserves in certain cases. But there are also several other provisions that are essentially reserve types of provisions. What is interesting is that each provision has a different manner of eliminating the time value of money benefit of tax deferral.

The first provision, enacted in 1984, relates to mining reclamation expenses.[215] Mining reclamation expenses are costs that a taxpayer must incur in the future to restore areas that the taxpayer has been mining. Generally, a taxpayer can elect to deduct mining reclamation expenses currently. The currently deducted amount is treated as being deposited in a fund that earns interest at an apparently, pre-tax rate of return.[216] The balance of the fund is then calculated at the end of each year. If the balance exceeds the estimated mining reclamation expenses, then the excess is included in income. As Professor Halperin has noted, it appears that the U.S. Congress should treat the fund as earning interest at an after-tax rate of return instead

---

212 See, e.g., *Crescent Wharf & Warehouse Co. v. Commissioner*, 518 F.2d 772 (9th Cir. 1075); *Harrold v. Commissioner*, 192 F.2d 1002 (4th Cir. 1951).

213 P.L. No. 98-369, Section 91(a) (1984).

214 Staff of the Joint Committee on Taxation, *General Explanation of the Tax Reform Act of 1984* (1984) at 258–67.

215 I.R.C. § 468.

216 I.R.C. § 468(a)(2)(B) (the reserve is increased each taxable year by the amount of interest which would have been earned on the opening balance of the reserve if the interest were computed at the applicable federal short-term rate, compounded semi-annually).

of a pre-tax rate of return.[217] As a result, this special reserve provision actually treats a taxpayer worse than the general rule for accruing deductions (unless the after-tax rate of return is greater than the pre-tax rate of return).

An example will best illustrate this special provision. Assume in 1994, the taxpayer deducts $1000 as a mining reclamation expense. The taxpayer will actually pay $1000 in 1997 to restore the land where the mining has taken place and the restoration will take place that same year. The currently deducted amount of $1000 is treated as being deposited in a fund earning interest at a pre-tax rate of return. Assuming a 10 percent pre-tax rate of return, the fund is treated as earning $100 in 1995. Therefore, the balance of the fund is $1100, which is $100 greater than the estimated mining reclamation expense of $1000. The taxpayer must include $100 in income in 1995. In 1996, the taxpayer will include another $100 in income. In 1997, the reserve is terminated. The taxpayer will pay $1000 for mining reclamation expenses but will not be allowed a deduction because the taxpayer already deducted it in 1994.

A second special reserve provision, also enacted in 1984, relates to nuclear power plant decommissioning costs.[218] Generally, a taxpayer can deduct amounts set aside for nuclear power plant decommissioning costs, which are costs that will be incurred in the future to dismantle a nuclear power plant. The deduction reflects amounts actually contributed into a fund. The fund is treated as a separate taxpayer and is therefore taxed on the earnings of the fund at a flat 20 percent rate. As a result, the fund grows at an after-tax rate of return although the after-tax rate of return may differ from the taxpayer's after-tax rate of return. Any amounts withdrawn from the fund, except for the payment of taxes and management costs, are includible in the taxpayer's income. But the withdrawal may then be deducted if paid for nuclear decommissioning costs, which should be the case.

An example will illustrate the reserve for nuclear decommissioning costs. Assume in 1994, the taxpayer deducts $1000 actually set aside in a reserve for nuclear decommissioning costs. The taxpayer will pay $1000 in 1997 to decommission the nuclear plant and the decommissioning will take place that same year. Assuming a 10 percent pre-tax rate of return, the fund will grow at an eight percent after-tax rate of return. In 1995, the fund will increase to $1080 and in 1996, to $1166.40. In 1997, the fund is terminated. The taxpayer will include $1166.40 in income but will also deduct $1000 paid and incurred for nuclear decommissioning. The net result is that the taxpayer will include $166.40 in income.

The third type of reserve provision was proposed by the Treasury Department in 1990 but was subsequently withdrawn in 1992. It is included here because it is very similar to the two previously described reserve provisions but interestingly Treasury utilized a different method to eliminate tax deferral. Some background information is necessary to understand this provision. Generally, an accrual method taxpayer may deduct an item only when the all events test is met, i.e., when all events have

[217] See Halperin, *supra* note 138, at 530–31.
[218] I.R.C. § 468A.

occurred which establish the fact of the deduction and it can be determined with reasonable accuracy.[219] In addition, this test is not met until economic performance also has taken place.[220] Generally, a cash method taxpayer may deduct an item when payment is made.[221] Section 461(f) provides rules with respect to contested liabilities. It reads:

> If (1) the taxpayer contests an asserted liability, (2) the taxpayer transfers money or other property to provide for satisfaction of the asserted liability, (3) the contest with respect to the asserted liability exists after the time of the transfer, and (4) but for the fact that the asserted liability is contested, a deduction would be allowed for the taxable year of the transfer (or for an earlier taxable year) determined after application of subsection (h) [section 461(h)], then the deduction shall be allowed for the taxable year of the transfer. This subsection shall not apply in respect of the deduction for income, war profits, and excess profits taxes imposed by the authority of any foreign country or possession of the United States.[222]

To qualify under Section 461(f), the taxpayer must transfer the money or other property beyond his control by relinquishing all authority over such money or other property.[223] Examples include transferring the money or other property (i) to the person who is asserting the liability, (ii) to an escrowee or trustee pursuant to a written agreement that the money or other property be delivered in accordance with the settlement of the contest, or (iii) to a court or public agency that the money or other property be delivered in accordance with the settlement of the contest.[224]

Treasury issued proposed regulations on the taxation of 461(f) settlement funds on 6 June 1990.[225] The proposed regulations were subsequently withdrawn pending the issuance of final regulations under Section 468B (dealing with designated settlement funds).[226] The proposed regulations, however, contained an interesting and apparently controversial example involving the taxation of 461(f) settlement funds. Many commentators wrote to Treasury and the Service complaining that the example was simply wrong.[227]

In a simplified version of the example, the taxpayer X transferred in January 1991, $9000 of cash into a fund in a transaction treated as a contested liability.

---

219 I.R.C. §§ 461(h)(1) and 461(h)(4).
220 I.R.C. § 461(h)(1).
221 Treas. Regs. §§ 1.446-1(c)(1)(i) and 1.461-1(a)(1).
222 I.R.C. § 461(f).
223 Treas. Reg. § 1.461-2(c)(1).
224 *Id.*
225 IA-258-84, 1990-2 C.B. 805; 55 Fed. Reg. 23235 (7 June 1990).
226 T.D. 8408, 1992-1 C.B. 155, 162; 57 Fed. Reg. 12411 (10 April 1992). The final Section 468B regulations were filed by the Office of Federal Register on 18 December 1992 and published in the Federal Register on 23 December 1992. T.D. 8459, 1993-8 I.R.B. 6; 57 Fed. Reg. 60983 as corrected by 58 Fed. Reg. 7865.
227 Marianne Evans, "IRS' Kempson Explains Contested Liabilities Under Economic Performance Test," 48 *Tax Notes* 1463 (1990). The example in its entirety is as follows:

> X, an accrual basis, calendar year taxpayer, contests a $9000 liability asserted against X by Y for hazardous waste disposal services rendered by Y during 1990. In January 1991, X transfers assets having a

X deducted the entire $9000 in 1991. During 1991, the fund earned $600, for which X paid taxes on and deducted the taxes. During 1992, X settled the contested liability for $8000. As a result, $8000 was transferred from the fund to settle the liability and the remaining $1600 in the fund was returned to X. X included the entire $1600 in income in 1992.

Many commentators argued that X was being double-taxed on $600 of the fund's earnings.[228] In other words, X was taxed on $600 of the fund's income in 1991. Then X is taxed on $1600 of the fund's assets in 1992. This latter amount appears to include the $600 of income that X was previously taxed on in 1991. Several commentators argued that X should only be taxed on $1000 of income in 1992. The reason for this apparent double taxation is to compensate for the fact that X took too large a deduction in 1991 at too early in time. In other words, X should have taken an $8000 deduction in 1992 or the present value of $8000 discounted by one year to 1991. Because the $9000 deduction for 1991 essentially includes an expensing of an amount returned to X in 1992, an inclusion of this returned amount and income thereon in 1992 brings X to a zero tax situation and a greater inclusion is necessary to provide the government with a tax on X's pretax income on the amount. As a result, the example is really nothing new. Rather it is a somewhat complex variation of the Cary Brown model.

What makes this third type of reserve provision interesting is that it is really a combination of the provisions for mining reclamation expenses and nuclear decommissioning costs. Under the rules for mining reclamation expenses, the deemed fund was treated as growing at a pretax rate of return, which appears to be inaccurate. Under the rules for nuclear decommissioning costs, the fund actually grows at an after-tax rate of return, which is correct. This third reserve provision, involving contested liabilities, actually grows at a pretax rate of return. So, in terms of growth rate, it is similar to mining reclamation expenses but it is also similar to nuclear decommissioning costs in that it is an actual fund (not a hypothetical or deemed fund). This third reserve provision accurately eliminates tax deferral even though it grows at a

---

fair market value of $9000 and an adjusted basis of $7000 to a trust in a transaction that satisfies the requirements of § 1.461-2(c). Under section 461(f), X is allowed a $9000 deduction for 1991. In addition, the asset transfer is considered a disposition of the assets for fair market value for purposes of Section 1001. Thus, for 1991, X recognizes a $2000 gain from the transfer and has a new basis of $9000 in the assets.

During 1991, the fund assets earn $600, which is included in X's gross income for 1991. X pays, and takes a deduction for, taxes attributable to this amount. The only other deduction X is allowed with respect to the fund is a deduction for administrative expenses.

The fair market value of the transferred assets remain the same. In 1992, the contest is settled and assets having a fair market value of $8000 are transferred from the fund to Y. X must include in gross income for the 1992 taxable year the $1600 remaining in the fund. Any amounts earned by the fund in 1992 must also be included in X's gross income for 1992. The transfer to Y of assets having a fair market value of $8000 is considered a disposition of the assets for purposes of Section 1001. Because the fair market value of the assets has not changed, the disposition does not require X to recognize additional gain or loss for 1992.

[228] See *supra* note 227.

pretax rate of return because the taxpayer who establishes the fund pays taxes on the pretax earnings of the fund *and is permitted to deduct the taxes*. In addition, this third reserve provision is similar to the nuclear decommissioning reserve in that the income inclusion to offset the benefits of deferral occurs at the termination of the reserve, not annually like the mining reclamation reserve.

2. *Japan*

In Japan, the tax base of a corporation in each accounting period is the amount of income in that accounting period.[229] The amount of income of a domestic corporation in each accounting period is obtained by deducting the amount of expense in the accounting period from the amount of gross revenue in the accounting period.[230]

Expenses are generally deductible under one of three categories: (1) cost of sales, cost of completed construction work, cost of services provided, cost of transfer, and other similar costs with regard to revenue in the accounting period;[231] (2) selling expenses, general administrative expenses, and other expenses but not including expenses (other than depreciation) for which the liability is not definite by the last day of the accounting period;[232] and (3) losses in the accounting period other than transactions relating to the corporation's capital.[233]

A liability is definite by the last day of the accounting period if it satisfies the following three conditions: (1) the liability pertaining to the expense is realized by the end of the term; (2) the fact which causes a definite payment based on the expense shall occur by the end of the term; and (3) the amount of the expense shall be able to be computed reasonably by the end of the term.[234]

Japan has two broad categories of reserve provisions. The first type is contained in the Corporate Tax Law and is based on generally accepted accounting principles.[235] The Ministry of Finance has noted that "among the reserves justified by the generally accepted accounting principles, only those enlisted under the law are eligible reserves for tax purposes."[236] These reserves are called *hikiatekin*. The second type of reserve provision is contained in the Special Taxation Measures Law.[237] The

---

[229] CTL Art. 21 (1998). [230] CTL Art. 22(1) (1998). [231] CTL Art. 22(3)(i) (1998).

[232] CTL Art. 22(3)(ii) (1998). [233] CTL Arts. 22(3)(iii) and 22(5) (1998).

[234] See Gomi, Corporate Tax 1996, *supra* note 61, at 41.

[235] See, e.g., CTL Arts. 52 (1998) (reserve for bad debts); 53 (1998) (reserve for loss on returned goods); and 54 (1998) (reserve for retirement allowances).

[236] MOF 1997, supra note 6, at 95.

[237] See, e.g., STML Arts. 55 (1998) (reserve for overseas investment loss); 55-3 (1998) (reserve for investment loss in the Okinawa Free Trade Zone); 55-4 (1998) (reserve for investment loss in newly-formed small and medium-sized enterprises); 55-5 (1998) (reserve for metal mining pollution control); 55-6 (1998) (reserve for shutdown of offshore oil or gas fields); 55-7 (1998) (reserve for prevention of specified disasters); 56 (1998) (reserve for improvement of railroad systems in specified urban areas); 56-2 (1998) (reserve for calorie change of gas); 56-3 (1998) (reserve for programmed forestation reserve); 56-4 (1998) (reserve for losses from the repurchase of electronic computers); 57 (1998) (reserve for electronic computer programs); 57-2 (1998) (reserve for droughts); 57-3 (1998) (reserve for spent nuclear fuel reprocessing); 57-4 (1998) (reserve for nuclear power plan dismantling); 57-5 (1998)

Ministry of Finance has noted that these reserves are not justified by generally accepted accounting principles but rather are designed to attain specific policy goals.[238] These reserves are called *junbikin*. The Ministry of Finance has noted that "these reserves [*hikiatekin* and *junbikin*] provide tax deferral but not tax exemption."[239]

The tax mechanics of the reserves are generally handled in one of two ways. The first method, which commentators refer to as the wash and exchange method or the wash down method,[240] involves a current deduction in establishing the reserve at the end of the year followed by reversing it at the beginning of the following year by including the amount of the reserve in income. An example of this method is the reserve for bad debts.[241] Corporations may deduct an amount as a reserve for bad debts based upon actual experience or based on a fixed percentage.[242] For example, manufacturing businesses may deduct 0.8 percent of the accounts receivable outstanding at the end of the accounting period.[243] This amount, however, must then be included in income the following accounting period.[244] Assume a manufacturing business has ¥1000 of outstanding accounts receivables at the end of the year. It may deduct eight yen in setting up a reserve for bad debts. At the beginning of the next year (year two), the manufacturing business must include eight yen in income. But assume that outstanding accounts receivables remain at ¥1000. The business will deduct eight yen in the second year in again setting up the reserve for bad debts. In essence, this eight yen deduction will offset the eight yen included in income so that there is no net effect on income in year two. As a result, a corporation gets an indefinite deferral assuming the amount of outstanding accounts receivables does not change. Any actual bad debt losses may be deducted when the receivables become uncollectible.

Japan, like the United States, also allows a reserve for nuclear power plant decommissioning/dismantling.[245] This reserve is an example of the accumulation method of reserves. An electric company is permitted to deduct, within limits, amounts relating to future expenditures for dismantling specified nuclear power plants. These deductible amounts are credited to a reserve account and are allowed to accumulate. This reserve is not deemed to grow at either a pretax or after-tax rate of return. When amounts are actually paid out at some point in the future for dismantling of nuclear power plants, the reserve amount is decreased with a corresponding increase to income.[246] If dismantling of the nuclear power plant has been

(extraordinary risk reserve of insurance companies); 57-6 (1998) (extraordinary risk reserve for nuclear insurance or earthquake insurance); 57-7 (1998) (reserve for construction of Kansai International Airport); 57-8 (reserve for special repairs); and 57-9 (1998) (reserve for bad debts of small and medium-sized enterprises).

238 MOF 1997, *supra* note 6, at 95.

239 MOF 1997, *supra* note 6, at 95.

240 Gomi, Corporate Tax 1996, *supra* note 61, at 511; Way, *supra* note 162, at A-37.

241 CTL Art. 52 (1998).

242 CTL Art. 52 (1998).

243 This percentage is being phased out over a five-year period as a result of changes made in 1998. The percentages are as follows: 1998 (0.65 percent), 1999 (0.5 percent), 2000 (0.4 percent), 2001 (0.25 percent), and 2002 (0.1 percent). See Gomi, *supra* note 5, at ¶ 6-360.

244 CTL Art. 52(2) (1998).

245 STML Art. 57-4 (1998).

246 STML Art. 57-4(3) (1998).

completed and there is still an amount in the reserve, then the amount of the reserve must be taken into income.[247] As a result, a corporation may receive deferral for a number of years under this provision.

3. Tax Deferral Principle

Generally, reserves involve claiming a current deduction for the full amount of a future liability when payment may not be made for many years. There is no time value of money benefit to accelerating a deduction if the deduction is discounted to present value. But currently allowing the full amount of a future liability as a deduction overstates the deduction. As a result, the full amount of the liability can be bifurcated into two components: (1) the present value component, which can be currently allowed as a deduction, and (2) the excess of the full amount of the liability over its present value. If this excess is allowed as a current deduction, it is equivalent to expensing. Expensing is of course the classic example of the Cary Brown model.

An example will best illustrate the tax deferral involved with a reserve provision. Assume a taxpayer pays 8000*u* in year two and receives a deduction for this amount. An equivalent result can be achieved by permitting the taxpayer a deduction in year one for the present value of 8000*u*. Using a six percent after-tax rate of return, the present value is 7547.17*u*. As a result, if a deduction is permitted in year one, the amount of the deduction should be 7547.17*u*, not 8000*u*. If an 8000*u* deduction is permitted in year one (for an 8000*u* liability to be paid in year two), then the taxpayer has, in essence, expensed an asset of 452.83*u* (8000*u* less 7547.17*u*).

Assume, however, the taxpayer does deduct 8000*u* in year one by establishing a reserve. As demonstrated, this will result in an expensing of 452.83*u*. In year two, the taxpayer pays 8000*u* in satisfaction of the liability and the reserve is terminated. The taxpayer will receive a time value of money benefit if the taxpayer is permitted to charge the 8000*u* payment in year two to the reserve account thereby giving the reserve a zero ending balance at the end of year two. The taxpayer should include 480*u* in income in year two, not simply 452.83*u*, which is the expensed amount from year one. The 480*u* reflects the growth of 452.83*u* at a six percent after-tax rate of return for one year. By requiring the taxpayer to include 480*u* in income in year two, the time value of money benefit of tax deferral of the reserve has been eliminated.

4. United States' Solution to Preventing Tax Deferral

The United States has attacked the tax deferral benefit provided by reserves in several different ways. First, the U.S. has eliminated a number of reserve provisions. For example, the reserve for bad debts was repealed in 1986. Second, the U.S. utilizes a method allowing deferral but preventing the taxpayer from receiving a time value of money advantage to the deferral. The U.S. accomplishes this by imputing income to the taxpayer but the U.S. has stumbled on the issue of whether to impute income at a pretax or after-tax rate of return. This method of imputing income is referred to as

---

[247] STML Art. 57-4(5)(i) (1998).

the *Deferral of Income with Imputed Interest Method* and will be discussed in the next chapter demonstrating whether pretax or after-tax is the proper rate of return. Finally, the U.S. utilizes a method that will be referred to as the *Double Inclusion in Income Method* to prevent the benefit of tax deferral. Under this method, the investment income appears to be double-taxed to prevent the time value of money benefit of tax deferral. This method is also discussed in detail in the next chapter.

J. 401(k) plans

1. United States

In 1978, the United States Congress provided for 401(k) plans, sometimes referred to as cash or deferred arrangements (CODAs).[248] A 401(k) plan is part of a qualified retirement plan, which generally means that a number of requirements must be met for an employer to establish such a plan and also that a number of very favorable tax consequences will result. For example, there are participation rules so as not to discriminate against certain classes of employees.[249] Also, generally distributions from a 401(k) plan cannot be made until the employee reaches age 59 1/2, dies, becomes disabled, or leaves the employer's service.[250] The primary tax advantages are that the employee is not taxed on compensation that is contributed to the 401(k) plan until the amount is distributed at some time in the future, and the earnings of the plan are not taxed until distributed.

If the requirements of a 401(k) plan are met, then an employee is given a choice between accepting current compensation or electing to defer the compensation. If the employee elects to receive current compensation, then the employee is taxed upon receiving the compensation. If, however, the employee elects to defer part of the compensation, then the employee will not be taxed on the deferred compensation until the employee receives it as a distribution at a later point in time. In other words, the employee chooses whether to receive currently taxable compensation or defer compensation until a later time.

An example will best demonstrate the deferral that occurs in a 401(k) plan. Assume an employee elects to participate in her employer's 401(k) plan. The employee's salary for the year 1997 is $70,000. The employee elects to receive $68,000 of salary and contribute $2000 to the plan. The $2000 contribution is called an elective deferral. The employee will only be taxed on $68,000 of income for 1997. The $2000 of elective deferral is held in a tax-exempt trust fund. When the employee receives the $2000 contributed to the plan, for example, in the year 2030, *at that time* the employee will be taxed on the $2000 (plus any earnings on the $2000 that are distributed to the employee).

There is a limitation on the amount of elective deferrals each year. Generally, the maximum annual amount of elective deferrals by an employee is $7000.[251] This

---

[248] The U.S. Congress' enactment of section 401(k) was actually a codification of earlier IRS rulings permitting CODAs. See Bittker and Lokken, *supra* note 53, at ¶ 61.8.1.

[249] I.R.C. § 401(k)(3). [250] I.R.C. § 401(k)(2). [251] I.R.C. § 402(g)(1).

amount, however, is indexed for inflation for years after 1987.[252] In 1997, the amount is $9,500;[253] in 1998 it is $10,000;[254] and in 1999 it is $10,000.[255]

In many 401(k) plans, the employer will match part or all of the employee's contribution. In other words, if an employee contributes $2000 to a 401(k) plan in the way of an elective deferral, the employer may match 25 percent or $500 by also contributing it into the plan for the benefit of the employee. It is estimated that approximately 25 million Americans participate in a 401(k) plan. Total assets held in 401(k) plans are probably in excess of $1 trillion.

2. *Japan*

Japan does not have 401(k) plans. However, there has been a lot of discussion among Japanese politicians and bureaucrats about the possibility of the Japanese government allowing the use of qualified retirement plans similar to 401(k) plans. The Japanese government has been studying 401(k) plans and refers to them as "*yon-maru-ichi-k*" plans.[256] It is likely that Japan will adopt some sort of CODA, although it will in all likelihood differ in some respects from 401(k) plans.

It should be noted that Japan has qualified retirement pension plans. Prior to 1962, the employer received a deduction upon transferring the money into the plan and the employee was immediately taxed. In 1962, the government changed the tax treatment so employees would not be taxed until receipt of the money. But to offset the tax deferral benefit, a one percent annual tax of the pension plan funds was adopted. The MOF has written that "[t]his tax is considered as interest on income tax during the period of tax deferral."[257] If Japan were to introduce 401(k) plans, then it may need to reconsider the issue of imposing a tax to prevent the time value of money benefits of tax deferral. It appears that Japan should be consistent in its view towards tax deferral with respect to qualified plans. Japan should either permit tax deferral and therefore eliminate the one percent annual tax on qualified retirement pension plans or eliminate some or all of the benefits of tax deferral by also adopting the tax for 401(k) plans.

3. *Tax Deferral Principle*

An elective deferral pursuant to a 401(k) plan is an example of the Super Cary Brown Model. An example will demonstrate the application of the Super Cary Brown Model to funds set aside in a qualified plan. Assume individual T receives 30,000*u* salary from her employer. T will contribute 1000*u* to a qualified 401(k) plan. The end result is that T will only have 29,000*u* of taxable income for the year. The 1000*u* contributed to the 401(k) plan is excluded from gross income. In other words, the money in the 401(k) plan is comprised of pre-tax dollars. At a 10 percent pre-tax rate of return, the 1000*u* in the qualified plan will grow to 1100*u* at the end of one year; 1210*u* at the end of two years; 1331*u* at the end of three years; and so on. It will continue to grow at a 10 pre-tax rate of return each year. At the end of x years, the fund will have $1000u(1+r)^x$. When the money is distributed to T from the qualified plan, T will

[252] I.R.C. § 402(g)(5). [253] Notice 96-55, 1996-2 C.B. 222.
[254] Notice 97-58, 1997-45 I.R.B. 7. [255] Notice 98-53, 1998-46 I.R.B. 23.
[256] These plans are also referred to as "*kakutei kyoshutsugata nenkin*" defined contribution plans.
[257] MOF 1997, *supra* note 6, at 118.

receive 60 percent of the total funds and the government will receive 40 percent based on the application of the partnership analogy to the Super Cary Brown model.

4. United States' Solution to Preventing Tax Deferral

The permissibility of a 401(k) plan is an affirmative action by the U.S. government to allow employees to defer compensation without being currently taxed on the deferred amount. The obvious solution to eliminating the tax deferral benefits of 401(k) plans is to simply reduce the amount that an employee can defer or eliminate 401(k) plans. The United States limits the tax deferral benefit by limiting the amount of elective deferral per year. As stated earlier, for 1999, the maximum amount of elective deferral is $10,000.

K. Premiums Received for Options

1. United States

The premium received by the writer of an option (generally referred to as the "optionor") is not taxed until the option is either exercised or allowed to lapse.[258] If the option is exercised, then the premium is added to the optionor's amount realized thereby increasing the gain or decreasing the loss on the sale of the underlying property.[259] If the option lapses unexercised, then the optionor includes the premium in income at the time the option lapses unexercised, not at the time of the receipt. The rationale appears to be that only at the time of exercise or lapse is it possible to determine whether the premium should be included as part of the amount realized on sale of the underlying property or simply income upon lapse of an option.[260]

For example, assume X issues an option for 1000*u* to Y. Y, the holder of the option, is allowed to buy property held by X for 100,000*u*. The option must be exercised within the next 90 days or it will lapse unexercised. The premium of 1000*u* received by X will not be included in X's income at the issuance of the option. Rather, X will wait until the option is exercised or lapses unexercised. Assume, at the end of 90 days, Y exercises the option and purchases X's property for 100,000*u*. X's amount realized on the sale will be 101,000*u* (100,000*u* plus 1000*u*), and this amount will be used to calculate X's gain or loss on sale of the underlying property. Y's basis in the property will be 101,000*u* (100,000*u* plus 1000*u*). If the option expires at the end of 90 days, then X will include 1000*u* in income at the end of the 90-day period. Y will have a deduction of 1000*u* at the time the option expires.

2. Japan

Japan has recently amended its rules for option premiums so that they are generally identical to the United States' rules. This is a complete reversal of the NTA's position with respect to option premiums. Prior to 1993, the NTA required that option

---

[258] See generally Bittker and Lokken, *supra* note 53, at ¶51.8.

[259] In the case of an option to sell property, the premium is added to the optionor's cost basis in the property.

[260] See generally Boris I. Bittker and Martin J. McMahon, Jr., *Federal Income Taxation of Individuals* ¶28.7[1] (2d. ed. 1995).

premiums be included in income *at the time of receipt* by the optionor.[261] The purchaser of the option was entitled to an immediate deduction. In 1993, this treatment of immediate recognition was altered by a decision of the National Tax Tribunal.

On 30 October 1998, the NTA issued a corporate tax law circular addressing a number of financial transactions, including the tax treatment of option premiums.[262] Under the circular, the optionor includes the premium as part of the amount realized from the sale of the underlying property if the option is exercised. If the option lapses without exercise, then the optionor includes the premium in income at the time the option lapses without exercise.

3. Tax Deferral Principle

When the optionor receives the option premium, the optionor is under no obligation to return it to the holder. As a result, the optionor can immediately invest the premium and earn a return on it. As a general rule in the United States, prepaid income is taxed upon receipt. If this rule applied to the optionor, then the optionor would include the premium in income upon receipt.[263] This immediate inclusion would eliminate the time value of money benefit of tax deferral in an option. The holder of the option should not be permitted a deduction even if the optionor included the premium in income upon receipt. The holder of the option has made a capital expenditure when it pays the premium to the optionor. The tax consequences to the holder with respect to the premium should be taken into account at the time the option is exercised (add it to the basis of the property) or lapses unexercised (a deduction at that time).

An alternative way of viewing the time value of an option is to recognize that as a general rule, the value of an option is expected to increase over time.[264] The premium paid by the holder to the optionor is equal to the present value of the expected return from the option. Under this view, the holder of an option would be taxed on imputed income that is taken into account over the life of the option. The optionor would accrue a deduction over the same period. For example, assume X issues an option for 1000*u* to Y. The option must be exercised within the next two years or it will lapse unexercised. Assume a discount rate of 10 percent so that the expected value of the option is 1210*u*. The premium of 1000*u* received by X will not be included in X's income at the issuance of the option. Rather, X will wait until the option is exercised or lapses unexercised. During the two-year option period, Y, the holder, should include 100*u* in income for the first year (1000*u* times 10 percent) and 110*u* in income for the second year (1100*u* times 10 percent). X, the optionor, would accrue a 100*u* deduction for the first year and a 110*u* deduction for the second year.

4. United States' Solution to Preventing Tax Deferral

The United States has taken no action to eliminate the tax deferral with respect to option premiums. It is, however, an issue that has been recognized in the tax literature during the past 10 years. The United States will probably address the issue in the not too distant future.

---

261 See Fujitani, *supra* note 58, at 335.

262 CTL Basic Circular 2-11.

263 See Calvin H. Johnson, Taxing the Income from Writing Options, 73 *Tax Notes* 203 (1996).

264 See Reed Shuldiner, A General Approach to the Taxation of Financial Instruments, 71 *Tex. L. Rev.* 243, 337s (1992).

Chapter 6

Various Methods in Preventing Tax Deferral

I. Introduction

In the last 10–15 years, the United States has devoted a lot of attention to issues of tax deferral and time value of money. As a number of academics and practitioners have recognized, tax deferral is the next best thing to tax exemption.[1] As a result of this awareness, the U.S. has developed and implemented a number of methods for preventing tax deferral. Each method has its advantages and disadvantages. In addition and more importantly, each method is not on an even plane with the other methods therefore leading to inequity in the tax system. In other words, one method may be quite favorable to the taxpayer while another method may be quite draconian. It appears that ideally each method of preventing the time value of money of tax deferral should do just that and no more.

In this chapter, five different methods of preventing tax deferral will be discussed. Some of these five methods will be broken down into various sub-methods. Each method and sub-method will be discussed in the context of the U.S. income tax system. An historical overview will be given of each method along with an example and comments. In addition, thoughts for Japan if it decides to adopt a particular method will be given. It should be noted that the thoughts for the Japanese government are simply that and are designed to point out to Japan some of the problems that the United States has encountered with respect to the various methods of preventing tax deferral.

II. Interest Charge Method

A. *Introduction*

In the previous chapter, the Interest Charge Method of preventing tax deferral was briefly mentioned with respect to installment sales and offshore investment

[1] William D. Andrews, "The Achilles Heel of the Comprehensive Income Tax" in *New Directions in Federal Tax Policy for the 1980s* 278, 280 (Charls E. Walker and Mark A. Bloomfield, eds. 1983).

funds. Generally, the idea behind the Interest Charge Method is to compensate the government for the tax deferral that is taking place with respect to a particular transaction. Under the Interest Charge Method, the government requires the taxpayer to determine the taxes that are being deferred, multiply this amount by an interest rate, and remit this amount to the government. The taxpayer does not get this amount back. This continues for each year that taxes are deferred. The actual mechanics of the Interest Charge Method can vary with each type of transaction, which is one criticism of the U.S. government's implementation of the Interest Charge Method. It would be much easier if the U.S. government could apply the Interest Charge Method in a mechanically identical manner to each transaction resulting in tax deferral. In any event, however, the substance of the Interest Charge Method remains the same: tax deferral is viewed as a loan from the government to the taxpayer and the taxpayer must pay interest on the deemed loan.

B. *Installment Sales – Interest Charge Method I ("Annual Method")*

Apparently, the idea of requiring sellers to pay interest to the government on the tax deferral arising from an installment sale was developed a number of years before the U.S. Congress finally acted on it in 1987.[2] One of the reasons that the U.S. Congress was reluctant to impose an Interest Charge Method on installment sales was its concern that many taxpayers would feel that no interest should be owed to the government if a seller did not have the use of the sales proceeds.[3] In other words, sellers would not understand why they were paying interest to the government on money that they had not yet received.[4]

The idea of requiring sellers to pay interest to the government on installment sales is simply a solution to the tax deferral benefit identified by the Cary Brown model, which has been in existence since 1948. In other words, *the Interest Charge Method represents a congressional judgment that the taxpayer can reasonably be thought of as owing the tax on the gain from the time of the installment sale and that the deferral of recognition is only a matter of legislative grace.*

An example will best illustrate the Interest Charge Method for installment sales. Assume, in 1997, X Corporation sold investment property worth $1000 for cash. X Corporation's basis in the property is assumed to be zero and therefore has gain

---

[2] See Christopher H. Hanna and Samuel Olchyk, "Interest Under Section 453A(c): Is It or Isn't It?," 56 *Tax Notes* 1345 (1992); Interview with Martin D. Ginsburg, Professor of Law, Georgetown University Law Center, 12 *ABA Section of Taxation Newsletter* 6, 10 (Fall 1992) ("The 1985 date [Professor Ginsburg discussed the Interest Charge Method in *Tax Notes*], I guess, comes from something that was in *Tax Notes*. Actually, I think the proposal, to the extent I was involved in it, goes back some time, and appeared first – Lord help us – in an Eagle Lodge paper [invitation only tax conference hosted by NYU Law School during the 1970s and 1980s].").

[3] See United States Department of the Treasury, *Tax Reform for Fairness, Simplicity, and Economic Growth* (November 1984) ("Treasury I") at 129–130; Lee A. Sheppard, "Ginsburg Discusses Taxing the Privilege of Tax Deferral in Installment Sales," 27 *Tax Notes* 457 (29 April 1985).

[4] See Treasury I, *supra* note 3, at 129–30.

of $1000. Assuming a 40 percent tax rate, X Corporation will pay tax of $400 (40 percent multiplied by $1000 gain).[5] If X Corporation invests the remaining $600 at an interest rate of 10 percent annually, X Corporation will earn $60 the following year. After X Corporation pays tax of $24 (40 percent tax rate multiplied by $60) on the interest, X Corporation will be left with $36 ($60 minus $24).

If instead of receiving $1000 cash, X Corporation received a $1000 installment obligation due in several years paying 10 percent interest annually, X Corporation would not report any gain in the year of sale under the installment sale rules. X Corporation will earn, however, $100 in interest the following year on the installment obligation. X Corporation will pay tax of $40, thereby leaving X Corporation with $60 ($100 minus $40). This is exactly the same position that X Corporation would be in if it made a cash sale and was not taxed on the earnings of the after-tax proceeds of the sale. In other words, by making an installment sale, X Corporation is in effect earning interest at a pre-tax rate of return of 10 percent. This example is simply an application of the Cary Brown model. The installment method allows for deferral of gain thereby deferring the tax on the gain. In essence, under the Interest Charge Method, the government is making a loan to the seller equal to the amount of tax on the deferred gain of $1000, which in this example is $400. The loan is outstanding until the seller pays the $400 tax to the government. Or, in the alternative, Cary Brown would describe the government as being a partner with the seller.[6]

The following table summarizes the two options:

	Cash sale ($)	Installment sale
Sales price	1000	Deferred ($1000)
Basis	0	0
Gain	1000	Deferred ($1000)
Taxes (40%)	400	Deferred
Investment	600	$1000
Return on investment (10%)	60	$100
Taxes (40%)	24	$40
After-taxes	36	$60

In 1987, the U.S. government apparently decided that it did not want sellers using the installment method for large sales of property to reap the benefits of the Cary Brown model, i.e., excluding from income the future annual return on the asset. It apparently was faced with at least two choices: (1) eliminate use of the installment method for large installment sales or (2) charge the seller interest on the tax that is being deferred through use of the installment method. The U.S. Congress had

[5] Assume the sale takes place on 31 December and the tax is due the same day.

[6] See E. Cary Brown, "Business Income Taxation and Investment Incentives" in *Income, Employment and Public Policy: Essays in Honor of Alvin H. Hansen*, 300, 309–310 (1948).

eliminated the use of the installment method in a number of situations, including the sale of inventory,[7] the sale of marketable securities,[8] and the sale of depreciable property between related entities.[9] The U.S. Congress opted for the second alternative with respect to large installment sales (those over $5 million) by enacting a provision requiring sellers to pay interest to the U.S. government on large installment sales.[10] According to the U.S. Treasury Department, "[c]harging interest on the amount of the deferred tax liability for taxpayers electing the installment method would make the tax law neutral as to the financing of property sales and would end use of installment sales as a vehicle for tax deferral."[11]

Returning to the above example, the seller should pay interest to the government on the deferred taxes. Using an interest rate of 10 percent (and ignoring the $5 million threshold), X Corporation will pay $40 as interest on deferred taxes ($400 taxes deferred multiplied by 10 percent interest rate). This will be paid every year until taxes are no longer deferred. If this amount is not deductible, X Corporation will be left with $20 ($60 less $40) each year with respect to the installment obligation. If the interest on deferred taxes is deductible, however, then X Corporation will be left with $36 ($60 less $40 plus ($40 multiplied by 40 percent)) each year with respect to the installment obligation. *By deducting the interest on deferred taxes, X Corporation will be in the same economic position as if it had received cash in the year of sale.* Consequently, in an ideal income tax system, deductibility of the interest on deferred tax liability should be the proper result.[12]

The following table summarizes the three options:

	Cash sale ($)	Installment sale	Installment sale with deductible interest charge
Sales price	1000	Deferred	Deferred
Basis	0	0	0
Gain	1000	Deferred	Deferred
Taxes (40%)	400	Deferred	Deferred

[7] I.R.C. §§453(b)(2) and (l)(1). The term "installment sale" does not include a dealer disposition or a disposition of personal property of a kind which is required to be included in the inventory of the taxpayer if on hand at the close of the taxable year. *Id.*

[8] I.R.C. §453(k)(2). If stock or securities are traded on an established securities market, then all payments to be received on the sale of the stock or securities are treated as received in the year of disposition. *Id.*

[9] I.R.C. §453(g). In the case of an installment sale of depreciable property between related persons, all payments to be received are treated as received in the year of disposition. I.R.C. §453(g)(1). An exception is provided where tax avoidance is not one of the principal purposes. I.R.C. §453(g)(2). "Related persons" is defined in section 1239(b). I.R.C. §453(g)(3).

[10] I.R.C. §453A(c).

[11] Treasury I, *supra* note 3, at 129.

[12] See, e.g., Martin D. Ginsburg, "Teaching Tax Law After Tax Reform," 65 *Wash. L. Rev.* 595, 617 (1990); Hanna and Olchyk, *supra* note 2, at 1348.

Table *Continued*

	Cash sale ($)	Installment sale ($)	Installment sale with deductible interest charge ($)
Investment	600	1000	1000
Return on investment (10%)	60	100	100
Taxes (40%)	24	40	40
Deductible interest on deferred tax liability	0	0	40 (tax savings of $16)
After-taxes	36	60	36

This example can be generalized algebraically. In the case of a cash sale in which tax is immediately imposed, an amount A of gain is reduced by tax t such that $A(1-t)$ may be invested. At an annual rate of return r, $A(1-t)$ invested will earn $rA(1-t)$ per year, which will be subject to tax at rate t equaling tax each year of $trA(1-t)$. The seller's net annual after-tax position each year will be:

$$rA(1-t) - trA(1-t) \text{ which equals } rA(1-t)(1-t).$$

In the case of an installment sale to which the Interest Charge Method applies, the amount A of gain is not reduced by tax. At an annual rate of return r, A invested will earn rA per year, which will be subject to tax at rate t equaling tax each year of trA. If interest r is charged on the tax of tA, then the interest on deferred tax liability is rtA.[13] The deduction of the interest on deferred tax liability will be $trAt$, leaving the seller with an interest burden of $rAt - trAt$ which equals $rAt(1-t)$. The seller's net annual after-tax position will be:

$$rA(1-t) - rAt(1-t) \text{ which equals } rA(1-t)(1-t).$$

This is equal to the seller's net annual after-tax position when a cash sale is made and tax is immediately imposed.

If the seller cannot deduct the interest on deferred tax liability, then the seller's net annual after-tax position is $rA(1-t) - rAt$. The seller is worse off by the amount of tax that would be saved by the deduction of the interest on deferred tax liability.

C. *Installment Sales – Interest Charge Method II ("Daily Method")*

It is interesting to note that the U.S. Congress has utilized an interest charge rule in a number of different areas of the Internal Revenue Code. For example, the U.S. Congress has also enacted an interest charge on installment sales of certain time-shares and residential lots as part of the ordinary course of the taxpayer's trade or business.[14] Somewhat strangely, the computation of the interest under this provision

[13] For purposes of the formulas, the rate of return r is assumed to equal the rate of interest imposed by the government on the deferred tax liability.

[14] I.R.C. § 453(l)(3).

is completely different than the computation of interest for installment sales over $5 million.[15] Yet, they are both installment sale provisions, both interest charge methods, and are both intended to reach the same result, i.e., to deny the seller the time value of money benefit of tax deferral. Under this second method, which will be referred to as the Daily Method, the interest is computed from the date of sale to the date the payments on the obligation are received.[16]

An example will best illustrate the Daily Method.[17] Taxpayer A, an accrual method corporation, is a calendar year dealer in undeveloped residential lots. In 1997, A receives an installment obligation to which the Daily Method applies. More specifically, A sells an undeveloped residential lot with a basis of $100 and a sales price of $1000. Therefore, the face amount of the installment obligation is $1000. The obligation provides for adequate interest and monthly principal payments of $100 for a period of 10 months. The date of the sale is 1 June 1997. The first monthly payment is due on 1 July 1997 and on the first day of every month thereafter until satisfied.

Under this Daily Method, no interest is imposed on payments received in the year of sale, i.e., 1997.[18] The first payments on which interest is imposed occur on 1 January 1998. The first payment for which interest is due is received seven whole monthly compounding periods from the date of the sale (1 June 1997 until 1 January 1998). The gross profit ratio for the sale is 90 percent ($900 gross profit divided by $1000 sales price). Assume in 1998 that A has taxable income unrelated to the installment sale of $21,000.

With respect to the 1 June 1997 installment sale, A receives a $100 payment on 1 January 1998, of which $90 is gain and $10 is recovery of basis. A's total gain on the other three payments received in 1998 (1 February 1998, 1 March 1998, and 1 April 1998) is $270 ($90 multiplied by three months). Therefore, A recognizes total gain of $360 in 1998 from the installment sale ($90 multiplied by four months).

A's tax liability for 1998 is $3204 (using the 15 percent actual tax rate multiplied by $21,360 (total income of $21,000 plus $360)).[19] A's tax liability determined without regard to the gain on the installment obligation is $3150 (15 percent multiplied by $21,000). The excess of A's tax liability with regard to the installment payments over its tax liability without regard to such payments is $54 ($3204 minus $3150). Of this excess, $13.50 ($54 multiplied by $90/$360) is allocated to and treated as the tax liability attributable to the 1 January 1998 payment on the 1 June 1997 obligation.

Assume the applicable Federal rate in effect on the date of the 1 June 1997 sale is 10 percent, compounded monthly. The amount of interest due with respect to the

---

[15] It should not be possible for both the Annual Method and the Daily Method to apply to a particular installment sale. The Annual Method is applicable to non-dealers in property while the Daily Method is applicable to dealers in timeshares and residential lots.

[16] I.R.C. § 453(l)(3)(B)(i).

[17] This example is adopted from Temp. Treas. Reg. § 1.453C-8T(c). See T.D. 8224, 1988–2 C.B. 103, 53 Fed. Reg. 34716 (September 8, 1988). Temp. Treas. Reg. § 1.453C-8T has been removed but see *infra* note 21.

[18] See also Temp. Treas. Reg. § 1.453C-8T(b)(1) (removed).

[19] Assume A has no alternative minimum tax liability for the year.

1 January 1998 payment on the 1 June 1997 obligation is $0.81. This computation must also be done with respect to the 1 February 1998 payment on the 1 June 1997 obligation ($0.93), 1 March 1998 payment on the 1 June 1997 obligation ($1.05), and the 1 April 1998 payment on the 1 June 1997 obligation ($1.17). These payments are treated as interest on an underpayment of tax for purposes of deductibility and are treated as additions to tax due on the due date of A's 1998 tax return.[20]

As this example demonstrates, the computation of interest under the Daily Method is much more complex than the interest computation under the Annual Method. Under the Daily Method, the seller must count the number of days from the sale until each payment in a subsequent year is made and also must determine the tax liability with and without the gain recognized on the installment sale. There is also no threshold rule under the Daily Method comparable to the $5 million threshold of the Annual Method, but of course this could easily be corrected. Under both methods, however, the interest is treated as interest on an underpayment of tax and therefore apparently nondeductible personal interest for an individual.[21] Ideally, it should be treated as deductible interest so as to achieve parity with a cash sale.

D. Passive foreign investment companies – interest charge method III

Some other areas where the U.S. Congress has enacted interest charge rules, include the domestic international sales corporation provisions ("DISC"),[22] accumulation distributions from foreign trusts,[23] long-term contracts,[24] and the income forecast method for depreciation.[25] The U.S. Congress has also provided for an interest charge rule relating to passive foreign investment companies ("PFIC"), sometimes referred to as foreign investment funds ("FIF").[26] Generally, this interest charge can be avoided if the shareholder elects pass-through treatment for the PFIC.[27] The pass-through type of PFIC is referred to as a qualified electing fund or simply a QEF PFIC.[28] If the shareholder does not make the QEF election, then the PFIC is referred to as a non-QEF PFIC.

---

[20] A may, however, adopt the midpoint method and treat all 1998 payments as being received on 1 July 1998. Temp. Treas. Reg. § 1.453C-8T(b)(3(ii) (removed).

[21] See Temp. Treas. Regs. §§ 1.453C-8T(b)(6), 1.453C-8T(c) Example (v), and 1.163-9T(b)(2)(i)(B). The legislative history to section 453(l)(3) states that "[t]he installment method rules applicable to dispositions of residential lots or 'timeshares' with respect to which interest is paid ... are not affected by the [1987] amendment." S. Rep. No. 63, 100th Cong., 1st Sess. 146 (1987). See also H.R. Rep. (Conf. Rep.) No. 495, 100th Cong., 1st Sess. 929 (1987), reprinted in 1987–3 C.B. 209. As a result, Temp. Treas. Reg. § 1.453C-8T should still be effective today. See generally Blake D. Rubin, "Taxable Dispositions of Real Estate: Planning Under the Passive Loss and Installment Sale Rules," 48 *N.Y.U. Inst. on Federal Tax'n* section 30.02[3] (1990).

[22] I.R.C. § 995(f). [23] I.R.C. § 668. [24] I.R.C. § 460. [25] I.R.C. § 167(g).

[26] I.R.C. § 1291. See Organisation for Economic Co-operation and Development, *Controlled Foreign Company Legislation: Studies in Taxation of Foreign Source Income* 153–55 (1996) (discussion of foreign investment funds).

[27] I.R.C. § 1291(d)(1). [28] I.R.C. § 1295.

The U.S. Congress enacted the PFIC rules in 1986.[29] The PFIC rules apply to a shareholder of a foreign corporation if 75 percent or more of the corporation's income is passive income or if 50 percent or more of the corporation's assets produce passive income.[30] The PFIC rules only apply to U.S. persons who are shareholders of the PFIC. In addition, no minimum ownership amount is required for the U.S. person to be subject to the PFIC rules. The U.S. Congress enacted the PFIC regime because it concluded that "eliminating the economic benefit of deferral is necessary to eliminate the tax advantages that U.S. shareholders in foreign investment funds have heretofore had over U.S. persons investing in domestic investment funds."[31]

Under the PFIC regime, the computation of interest is different than the computation under either the Annual Method for large installment sales or the Daily Method for installment sales of certain timeshares and residential lots. Generally, under the PFIC rules, the computation period is based on the *due date of the tax return* for the current and previous years to which the deferred tax is attributable.[32] For example,[33] assume X is a calendar year U.S. corporation. On 31 December 1993, X acquires a share of stock of Foreign Corporation ("FC") for $500. FC has been a Section 1291 fund since FC's taxable year that began on 1 January 1994. Generally, a Section 1291 fund is a PFIC in which the shareholder has not elected pass-through treatment, i.e., it is a non-QEF PFIC.[34] On 31 December 1997, X sold the FC stock for $1000 incurring no foreign tax on the disposition. X's gain on the sale of $500 is taxed as an excess distribution and is allocated pro rata over X's four year holding period. Therefore, $125 is allocated to each year. Generally, an excess distribution is the excess of the amount of the distribution over 125 percent of the average amount received by the shareholder over the previous three years.[35] The $125 allocated to 1997, the current shareholder year, is included in ordinary income for that year with no interest charge. The allocations to 1994, 1995, and 1996, the prior PFIC years, are subject to the deferred tax amount as follows:

Year	Increase in tax($)	Interest period
1994	43.75 (125 × 35%)[36]	3/15/95 to 3/15/98 (three years)
1995	43.75 (125 × 35%)	3/15/96 to 3/15/98 (two years)
1996	43.75 (125 × 35%)	3/15/97 to 3/15/98 (one year)

[29] Pub. L. No. 99-514, Section 1235(a) (1986).

For a comprehensive discussion of the PFIC rules, see, e.g., Joel D. Kuntz and Robert J. Peroni, *U.S. International Taxation* ¶B 2.08 (1992); 3 Boris I. Bittker and Lawrence Lokken, *Federal Taxation of Income, Estates and Gifts* ¶68.5 (1991).

[30] I.R.C. § 1296(a).

[31] H.R. Rep. (Conf. Rep.) No. 841, 99th Cong., 2d Sess. at II-641 (1986).

[32] I.R.C. § 1291(c)(3)(A); Prop. Reg. § 1.1291-4(d)(1).

[33] This example is adopted from Prop. Reg. § 1.1291-4(e) Example 1.

[34] Prop. Reg. § 1.1291-1(b)(2)(v). [35] I.R.C. § 1291(b).

[36] The 35% tax rate represents the highest corporate tax rate. I.R.C. § 11(b).

Under the PFIC regime, an interest charge is computed separately for each net increase in tax (using the rates and methods provided in Section 6621).[37] The increase in tax of $43.75 attributable to 1994 would be subject to three years' interest charge. The increase in tax of $43.75 attributable to 1995 would be subject to two years' interest charge, and the increase in tax of $43.75 attributable to 1996 would be subject to one year's interest charge. The tax plus the interest would be remitted to the U.S. government. The interest is treated as interest on an underpayment of tax[38] and therefore apparently nondeductible personal interest for non-corporate taxpayers.[39]

E. Japanese Version of Interest Charge Method

Prior to 1962, an employer who established a qualified retirement pension plan for its employees would receive a deduction upon contributing the amounts to the plan and the employee would be immediately taxed on the transfer.[40] In 1962, a change was made to permit employees to defer income until receipt. But to eliminate the tax deferral benefit, the Japanese government enacted a new annual tax on pension funds.[41] The tax was equal to one percent of the assets of the pension fund contributed by the employer.[42] The MOF has written that "[t]his tax is considered as interest on income tax during the period of tax deferral."[43] What is interesting is that the United States and Japan have taken completely opposite views on tax deferral with respect to qualified plans. The United States permits the tax deferral benefit while Japan attempts to eliminate it.

It appears that the one percent annual tax on pension funds had its origin from a similar proposal advanced by the Shoup Mission.[44] In 1949, the Shoup Mission proposed a one percent annual tax on retained profits of a corporation. The tax was not meant to discourage profit retention but rather to eliminate some of the tax deferral benefit associated with it. In 1950, Japan adopted the Shoup Mission's recommendation but increased the tax to two percent annually on retained earnings. The tax was repealed just two years later.

The one percent tax on pension funds appears to be a very rough justice method in eliminating the benefits of tax deferral, which is certainly understandable given the year in which it was adopted. In fact, the Japanese were quite innovative to utilize an interest charge method at such an early date. The Japanese interest charge is similar to what Professor Halperin has suggested with respect to *nonqualified* plans.[45] To eliminate the potential tax deferral benefit of *nonqualified* plans, Professor Halperin has suggested a special tax on the investment income generated by a nonqualified

[37] Prop. Reg. § 1.1291-4(d)(1). [38] Prop. Reg. § 1.1291-4(b).

[39] Temp. Reg. § 1.163-9T(b)(2)(i)(B).

[40] Tax Bureau of the Ministry of Finance, *An Outline of Japanese Taxes 1997* (1997) at 118.

[41] CTL Art. 8 (1996) (the tax is imposed on a domestic corporation engaged in retirement pension fund business).

[42] CTL Art. 87 (1996). [43] MOF 1997, *supra* note 40, at 118. [44] See Appendix.

[45] See Daniel I. Halperin, Interest in Disguise: Taxing the 'Time Value of Money,' 95 *Yale L. J.* 506, 539–550 (1986).

plan. Japan has done something similar in eliminating the tax deferral benefit of *qualified* plans by imposing an interest-like tax not on the investment income though but on the assets of the plan that are contributed by the employer.[46] But the amount is extremely low possibly to reflect the fact that it is on the assets of the plan and not just on the investment income currently being generated by the assets of the plan.

If Japan adopts 401(k) types of plans, which is currently being considered by politicians and bureaucrats, it will be interesting to see if the one percent tax will also apply to these new types of plans. It is possible that Japan may simply head in the opposite direction and repeal the one percent interest like tax on qualified retirement pension plans.

F. Comments on the U.S. Interest Charge Methods

It would seem much simpler if the U.S. Congress were to adopt one interest computation scheme where an Interest Charge Method is utilized. This, however, may not be possible. Under the installment sale rules, interest accrues on gain from the date of sale (i.e., realization) until the date of recognition. Under the PFIC rules, gain on the sale is prorated over the period from when the stock was acquired until it is sold. Consequently, gain prorated to each year bears interest from the return due date for that year until the return due date for the year of sale. In other words, the installment sale rules deal with post-realization periods, while the PFIC rules deal with pre-realization periods, and the two do not appear similar enough to allow one set of rules to be used for both purposes. It does, however, seem unnecessary to have different types of interest charge regimes for installment sales (Annual Method and Daily Method) when they are both intended to reach the same result, i.e., eliminate the time value of money benefit of tax deferral.

For installment sales in which an interest charge is imposed, the Annual Method would appear to be the more preferable scheme because of its simplicity. It is a relatively simple calculation done once at the end of each year the installment obligation is outstanding. Despite its simplicity, it also adequately achieves its goal of eliminating the time value of money benefit of tax deferral. U.S. commentators have questioned whether the simplicity of the Annual Method makes it less desirable than the Daily Method, which appears to be extremely precise by charging interest on the number of days from the date of the installment sale until payments are made.[47] The Annual Method, however, is quite precise. The interest on deferred taxes under

---

[46] CTL Arts. 83 and 84 (1996).

[47] See, e.g., *Comments Regarding Selected Provisions of the Omnibus Budget Reconciliation Act*, prepared by the Sales and Financial Transactions Committee, Section of Taxation, American Bar Association (full text available in Tax Analysts Highlights & Documents, 11 July 1988; available electronically 88 TNT 142-14). The authors of the report believe that section 453(l)(3) is simpler and fairer than section 453A(c). As a result, they believe that the interest regime used under section 453(l)(3) should also be used under section 453A(c).

the Annual Method relates to the delay in paying tax on the gain through use of the installment method.[48] If, for example, a sale is made on 1 January and the sales price is collected on 31 December, interest on deferred tax liability is not owed to the government because an installment sale has not taken place. If, however, the sales price is collected on 1 January of year two, one year's interest on deferred tax liability is owed to the government. A one-day difference has resulted in one year's interest. The reason appears to be that the one-day difference has resulted in a delay of exactly one year in paying the tax. The interest on deferred tax liability relates to the delay in paying the tax from 31 December of year one to 31 December of year two. Under the Annual Method, the interest computation scheme would result in one year's interest owed to the government because of the one-year delay in paying the tax. This is why the interest is not prorated in the year of sale and also why no interest is owed in the year when the gain is fully recognized.[49]

It also appears that the interest charge on deferred taxes should be deductible. As the above formulas demonstrate, in the case of an installment sale, the seller's net annual after tax position each year will be: $rA(1-t)-trA(1-t)$ which equals $rA(1-t)(1-t)$. If the seller cannot deduct the interest on deferred tax liability, then the seller's net annual after tax position is $rA(1-t)-rAt$. The seller is worse off by the amount of tax that would be saved by the deduction of the interest on deferred tax liability. Only by allowing deductibility of interest on deferred taxes does the U.S. government achieve parity between a seller who sells property for cash and one who sells using the installment method.[50] In fact, the goal of achieving parity was U.S. Treasury's rationale for the enactment of the Interest Charge Method in 1987. In addition, under the PFIC regime, the interest charge should be deductible. If the interest is not deductible, then looking solely at the deductibility of interest under the PFIC regime versus immediate income under QEF PFIC, it would appear to be more advantageous to elect QEF PFIC status.[51]

The U.S. government has taken the position that the interest paid by an individual under the Interest Charge Method is personal interest and therefore not deductible.[52] Apparently, to compensate for the non-deductibility of interest on deferred taxes for individuals, the first $5 million of installment sales each year are excluded from the interest charge method. If so, this appears to be one bad rule trying to compensate for another bad rule. As one leading commentator describes it, "Essentially what we

---

[48] See Hanna and Olchyk, *supra* note 2, at 1349. [49] See *id.*

[50] See *infra* text at notes 12–13.

[51] See, e.g., Joseph Isenbergh, *International Taxation*, ¶ 31.9.3 (1990) ("The QEF regime is likely, on balance, to be the more benign [in comparison to PFIC taxation], especially if the interest on deferred taxes paid to the Treasury is itself not deductible in full.").

[52] See I.R.C. § 163(h)(1) (personal interest is not deductible); Temp. Reg. § 1.163-9T(b)(2)(i) (interest on deferred tax liability is treated as interest on a tax deficiency, which is treated as personal interest).

See, e.g., *Miller v. United States*, 65 F.3d 687, 691 (8th Cir. 1995) (regulation § 1.163-9T is valid); *Redlark v. Commissioner*, 141 F.3d 936, 942 (9th Cir. 1997), *rev'g* 106 T.C. 31 (1996); *Stecher v. United States*, 1998 U.S. Dist. LEXIS 10173 (D. Colo. 1998). But see, e.g., *Allen v. United States*, 987 F. Supp. 460, 468 (E.D.N.C. 1997) (regulation § 1.163-9T is invalid); *Kikalos v. Commissioner*, T.C. Memo. 1998–92 (1998).

have is called chaos."[53] Alternatively, perhaps the $5 million threshold is to simply confine the rules to sellers with large amounts of installment sales.

The issue of deductibility of interest on installment sales and under the PFIC regime in a sense leads to the broader issue as to whether interest on tax deficiencies in general should be deductible.[54] For non-corporate taxpayers, the non-deductibility of interest on tax deficiencies generally operates as a penalty to the taxpayer. Perhaps, however, a distinction can be drawn between interest on installment sales and interest on tax deficiencies. Taxpayers generally have the ability to pay their taxes on time and avoid all interest. A penalty on tax deficiencies may therefore be appropriate. As to the interest on installment sales, there is no U.S. Congressional policy to discourage use of the installment method. In fact, it is mandatory in the absence of a timely election not to use it.[55] Arguably, the installment method interest charge should be deductible, even if interest on tax deficiencies is not, so that use of the installment method is not penalized. The same argument can be made for the non-QEF PFIC regime. This regime is also mandatory in the absence of a timely election not to use it.[56] As a result, arguably the interest charge on non-QEF PFICs should also be deductible so that their use is not penalized. Although the government should limit the use of targeted legislation, i.e., "fixing" what it perceives to be problems without thoroughly thinking through all the ramifications, it appears to be appropriate with respect to deductibility of interest on installment sales and PFICs while retaining general non-deductibility of interest on tax deficiencies.[57]

In addition, the Interest Charge Method under the installment method only achieves parity to an all-cash sale if interest is imposed by the government at the same rate as the seller's rate of return on investments (or possibly the seller's borrowing rate if the assumption is that the seller can avoid borrowing).[58] The rationale is that the benefit of the deferral is equal to the taxpayer's rate of return on investment by being allowed to invest the deferred taxes. For example, if the government charges interest at a 10 percent rate and the seller's rate of return is only 8 percent, the seller is better off by making an all cash sale and avoiding the interest charge to the government. The seller will earn a rate of return of eight percent and avoid paying interest of 10 percent. If the government's interest rate is less than the seller's rate of return, however, then the seller is better off making an installment sale earning the higher rate of return on the sale and paying the government at a lower rate of return as opposed to an all cash sale.

It is possible that the government could look to the seller's rate of return on the particular installment obligation and use that figure as the seller's rate of return.

[53] See Ginsburg Interview, *supra* note 2, at 10.

[54] See Bittker and Lokken, *supra* note 29, at ¶ 31.2.

[55] I.R.C. § 453(d). [56] I.R.C. § 1295(b).

[57] See generally Christopher H. Hanna, "Partnership Distributions: Whatever Happened to Nonrecognition?" 82 *Kent L. J.* 465 (1993) (arguing that the U.S. Congress in recent years has adopted targeted legislation in partnership taxation that corrects one problem but raises a host of additional issues thereby adding complexity to an already difficult area).

[58] See, e.g., David F. Bradford and the U.S. Treasury Tax Policy Staff, *Blueprints for Basic Tax Reform* 73–74 (2d ed., 1984); Bittker and Lokken, *supra* note 29, at ¶ 3.5.2.

Focusing in on each installment seller's rate of return, however, would lead to tremendous administrative difficulties for the government. It appears that the only practical solution is the one currently in use, which is a uniform rate for all sellers.[59]

In fact, the comparison of the interest rates is not an entirely accurate picture. If the government is charging interest at 10 percent with no deductibility for the interest, then the 10 percent figure should remain at that amount. If the seller is earning a rate of return of also 10 percent, this figure must be reduced by the seller's tax rate because the interest earned is subject to tax. If, for example, the seller is in a 40 percent tax bracket, the seller's rate of return is more accurately the after-tax rate of return of six percent. Therefore, the comparison is between a 10 percent interest charge by the government and a six percent rate of return earned by the seller. Clearly, the seller is better off making a cash sale and avoid paying 10 percent to the government in after-tax dollars.

To achieve parity in a world where the interest charge is not deductible, the comparison is between the government's rate of interest charge, which is based on a pre-tax rate of return, and the seller's after-tax rate of return. For example, assume a seller makes an installment sale subject to an interest charge rule. Assume the interest rate on the installment obligation is 10 percent, resulting in interest for the year of $100,000, and the seller is in the 40 percent tax bracket. If the government also charges 10 percent interest resulting in $100,000 of interest and the interest is deductible, then the interest income and deduction wash against each other. If the interest is not deductible, then the seller will end up in a negative cash flow of $40,000 equal to the amount of taxes that would be saved by deducting the interest paid to the government.

G. Thoughts for Japan

The Interest Charge Method appears to be the U.S. government's preferred method for eliminating tax deferral. It is generally a quite simple and straightforward calculation. The Annual Method adopted for large installment sales seems to be the easiest. The amount of taxes deferred at the end of each year is multiplied by the applicable interest rate and remitted to the government. This is done each year until the taxes are paid off. Japan would need to determine what tax rate to use in computing the amount of deferred taxes and also what interest rate is applicable. The possibilities for the tax rate appear to be: (1) a fixed rate for all sellers, such as the highest capital gains tax rate, or (2) the seller's marginal tax rate. The possibilities for the interest rate are along the same lines: (1) a fixed rate based upon the length of the deferral period[60] or (2) the seller's rate of return on investments or the seller's borrowing rate. Obviously, fixed rates for the tax rate and for the interest rate (based upon the length of the deferral period) would

---

[59] I.R.C. §§453A(c)(2)(B) and 6621(a)(2).

[60] A fixed rate may not be entirely accurate because of the term structure of debt. In other words, the interest rate should change as the deferral period becomes shorter. See, e.g., Joseph Bankman and William A. Klein, "Accurate Taxation of Long-Term Debt: Taking Into Account the Term Structure of Interest," 44 *Tax L. Rev.* 335 (1989); Bruce Kayle, "Where Has All the Income Gone? The Mysterious Relocation of Interest and Principal in Coupon Stripping and Related Transactions," 7 *Va. Tax Rev.* 303 (1987); Theodore S. Sims, "Long-Term Debt, the Term Structure of Interest and the Case for Accrual Taxation," 47 *Tax L. Rev.* 313 (1992).

be extremely simple to administer while using the seller's marginal tax rate and rate of return (or borrowing rate) could be an administrative nightmare.

If Japan were to adopt a PFIC-type regime, which has been recommended by the OECD,[61] then it would encounter the same problems that the U.S. has in terms of adopting an Interest Charge Method. The Annual Method used for large installment sales does not appear to be applicable to a PFIC-type regime. If Japan were to adopt a PFIC-type regime, it may want to avoid the Interest Charge Method altogether and use an Immediate Inclusion in Income Method (pass-through, mark-to-market, or deemed return), which the United States allows (pass-through or mark-to-market) as an alternative to the Interest Charge Method. The stated advantage of the Interest Charge Method for PFICs, however, is that shareholders of a PFIC may be unable to obtain the information necessary to comply with treating the PFIC as a pass-through (transparent) entity or marking to market the stock of the PFIC if it is not publicly traded.[62]

It would also make sense for Japan to allow deductibility of the interest. As stated earlier, the United States is wrong to deny an individual taxpayer an interest deduction on deferred taxes. One solution to this problem would be to charge interest at an after-tax rate of return as opposed to a pre-tax rate of return. If the government were to do this, then there would be no need to allow deductibility of the interest as it has already in essence been deducted when using an after-tax rate of return.

Finally, from a theoretical standpoint, it appears that interest should be charged on deferred taxes beginning with the first dollar of deferred taxes. In other words, the United States government does not charge interest on installment sales until the amount of the sales exceed $5 million in a given year. This seems way too high and appears to benefit solely wealthy taxpayers. It may make sense to have some sort of threshold rule but the U.S. threshold is excessively high. Japan may want to consider a more reasonable amount.

III. Immediate Inclusion of Income Method

A. *Introduction*

Rather than impose an interest charge, the government could repeal each provision in the tax law allowing deferral and consequently require immediate inclusion in income. This is a sledgehammer approach to eliminating tax deferral. This will obviously eliminate the time value of money benefit that accompanies tax deferral because no tax deferral is taking place. For example, the U.S. Congress and the

---

[61] Organisation for Economic Co-operation and Development, *Harmful Tax Competition: An Emerging Global Issue* 42–43 (1998).

[62] Australia, Canada, and New Zealand utilize a deemed return method (in additional to other methods) with respect to PFICs. See Brian J. Arnold, "The Taxation of Investments in Passive Foreign Investment Funds in Australia, Canada, New Zealand and the United States" in *Essays on International Taxation* (Herbert H. Alpert and Kees van Raad, eds. 1993) at 5, 58.

Japanese government could simply repeal the installment method rules and require immediate recognition of gain on an installment sale of property. If this were done, sellers would not be allowed to defer gain on an installment sale. In fact, in recent years, the U.S. Congress has repealed the use of the installment method for dealers in personal property as well as dealers in real property (with the limited exception for dealers in timeshares and residential lots who pay the interest charge).[63] As a result, the installment method can no longer be used for sales of inventory.[64] A seller of inventory must use the accrual method of accounting with respect to the inventory.[65] This means that the income on each sale is included at the time of the sale. In 1998, Japan repealed its installment basis provision, which permitted deferral of income on an installment sale of inventory or services.[66] Japan has retained its deferred payment sales provision permitting deferral of gain on the sale of property.[67]

The U.S. Congress has prevented the use of the installment method in a number of other different situations, including an installment sale of marketable securities[68] and an installment sale of depreciable property between related persons.[69] For example, if a taxpayer sells 100 shares of IBM stock at a $10,000 gain, the entire gain must be included in income at the time of the sale even though payment of the sales price occurs over time.[70] This example can be generalized algebraically. In the case of a cash sale in which tax is immediately imposed, an amount A of gain is reduced by tax t such that $A(1-t)$ may be invested. At an annual rate of return r, $A(1-t)$ invested will earn $rA(1-t)$ per year, which will be subject to tax at rate t equaling tax each year of $trA(1-t)$. The seller's net annual after-tax position each year will be:

$$rA(1-t) - trA(1-t) \text{ which equals } rA(1-t)(1-t).$$

Requiring an immediate inclusion in income by repealing any provision allowing deferral, such as the installment sale rules, is obviously an easy method of preventing tax deferral. Complete elimination of the installment method of accounting, however, could have harsh results by creating severe liquidity problems for taxpayers who would otherwise be eligible to use it. As a result, the U.S. Congress and the Japanese government should retain the installment method but simply eliminate the tax deferral benefits that accompany it. For the most part, this is what the U.S. Congress has done through enactment of the Interest Charge Method. If the seller does not want to pay the interest charge for an installment sale, then the seller can simply elect out of using the installment method.

The U.S. Congress has also eliminated deferral in other areas by simply repealing the applicable provision. For example, it repealed the reserve for bad debts in

---

[63] I.R.C. §§ 453(b)(2) and (l)(1). See also sections 10202(b)(1) and (c) of the Revenue Reconciliation Act of 1987 (Pub. L. No. 100-203, 22 December 1987).

[64] I.R.C. §§ 453(b)(2) and (l)(1).

[65] See Treas. Reg. § 1.446-1(c)(2)(i). But see Treas. Reg. § 1.446-1(c)(2)(ii) for a very limited exception to the use of the accrual method.

[66] CTL Art. 62 (1997) (repealed in 1998).

[67] CTL Art. 63 (1997) has been renumbered as CTL Art. 62 (1998). This provision is generally referred to as the deferred payment sales provision.

[68] I.R.C. § 453(k)(2). [69] I.R.C. § 453(g). [70] I.R.C. § 453(k)(2).

1986.[71] The same year, it eliminated almost all flexibility partnerships had in selecting a taxable year.[72] In 1989, the U.S. Congress completely eliminated the use of the completed contract method with respect to long-term contracts.[73] In the case of a long-term contract, the taxpayer must use the percentage of completion method.[74] So a number of provisions that have allowed deferral have simply been repealed over the years.

B. Flow-through method (transparency)

Rather than repealing every deferral provision, which as stated earlier would be a sledgehammer approach to eliminating tax deferral, a different type of Immediate Inclusion in Income Method is a flow-through method of taxation. This is most commonly illustrated by the partnership taxation rules. The United States and Japan treat partnerships as transparent entities, meaning that the income of the partnership flows through the partnership to each of its partners.[75] The partners must pay taxes on the income of the partnership. By forcing the partners to pay taxes on the income that flows through the partnership, generally no tax deferral is taking place. The United States and Japan both require that the partners of the partnership include their share of partnership income on at least an annual basis.

The qualified election fund provisions under the United States PFIC rules further illustrate the *equivalence* of imposing an interest charge rule or requiring immediate inclusion in income by the flow-through method. Under the PFIC rules, a taxpayer may elect to treat a PFIC as a QEF. If the election is made, the earnings of this QEF PFIC, in essence, flow-through to the electing shareholders of the QEF PFIC. In other words, the entity is treated as transparent like a partnership. The electing shareholders are taxed on the earnings each year and no tax deferral is generally taking place. As a result, no interest needs to be charged by the government. Although electing QEF status (transparent status) with no interest charge versus non-QEF PFIC status (non-transparent status) with the interest charge does not necessarily achieve complete parity to the PFIC shareholders, it is reasonably close.[76]

For example,[77] assume a U.S. shareholder owns one percent of a PFIC, is in the 40 percent tax bracket, and earns a pre-tax rate of return of 10 percent annually on all investments. The PFIC also earns a rate of return of 10 percent and has $100,000

---

[71] Pub. L. No. 99-514, section 805(a) (1986).

[72] Pub. L. No. 99-514, sections 806(a)(1), (2), and (3) (1986).

[73] Pub. L. No. 101-239, section 7621(a) (1986). [74] I.R.C. § 460.

[75] See chapter 5, part g (describing the income tax consequences of Japanese partnerships).

[76] One reason that parity is not accurately achieved is that the interest charge under the PFIC regime is treated as interest on an underpayment of tax and therefore personal interest for individuals. See Temp. Treas. Reg. § 1.163-9T(b)(2)(i)(B). In addition, under the PFIC regime, section 1291(a) requires that the excess distribution be allocated ratably over the applicable period. This may not accurately reflect the timing of the earnings of the PFIC. Finally, under the PFIC regime, gain on the sale of PFIC stock is treated as ordinary income. If the QEF election is made, however, the gain may be taxed as capital gain. See, e.g., Bittker and Lokken, *supra* note 29, at ¶ 68.5.1.

[77] This example is adapted from that given in Isenbergh, *supra* note at 51, ¶ 31.5.3 (1993 Supplement).

in assets. The U.S. shareholder has made the QEF election, meaning that the PFIC is treated as transparent as to the U.S. shareholder. During year one, the PFIC earns $10,000. The U.S. shareholder must include $100 in gross income and pay $40 in taxes. During year two, the U.S. shareholder includes another $100 in gross income and pays another $40 in taxes. At the end of two years, the U.S. shareholder has $123.60 ($60 from year one invested at an after-tax rate of return of six percent equaling $63.60 plus $60 from year two) if cash was distributed each year representing the U.S. shareholder's income.

If the QEF election is not made and an excess distribution of $210 took place at the end of year two, it would be allocated $105 to year one and $105 to year two. At a 40 percent tax rate, $84 in taxes would be owed to the government. However, an interest charge would also be imposed. If the interest rate is 10 percent, the amount of the interest charge is as follows:

Year	Increase in tax	Interest rate	Interest owed
1	$42 ($105 × 40%)	10%	$4.20

At a 10 percent interest rate, $4.20 is owed to the government. If it is not deductible, the PFIC shareholder has $121.80 ($126 minus $4.20). If the interest is deductible, then the PFIC shareholder has $123.48 ($126 minus $4.20 plus $1.68). This latter amount is almost the same amount as current taxation under the QEF regime ($123.48 versus $123.60). The slight difference of $0.12 is attributable to the timing of the earnings under the QEF election ($100 each year) versus the ratable allocation under the PFIC regime ($105 each year instead of $100 in year one and $110 in year two). If, under the PFIC regime, the income was allocated in the actual manner that it was earned (in essence, based on the assumptions, using a constant yield to maturity method), $100 in year one ($1000 assets multiplied by 10 percent rate of return) and $110 in year two ($1100 assets multiplied by 10 percent rate of return), and the interest charge to the government was deductible, then the PFIC shareholder would have $123.60 at the end of the second year. This would be the same amount as if the QEF election was made.

C. Mark-to-market

The idea of requiring immediate inclusion in income can be extended even further by eliminating the realization requirement and utilizing a mark-to-market method of accounting, sometimes referred to as an accretion method of accounting.[78] While the use of such an accounting method would dramatically change the income tax system currently in place, mark-to-market accounting is not unprecedented in the United

[78] Professor Andrews has described the realization doctrine as the "Achilles heel" of the income tax system. See Andrews, *supra* note 1.

States or Japan. The U.S. Congress has eliminated the realization requirement in certain areas beginning with the tax treatment of commodities futures contracts in 1981.[79] In fact, as to dealers in securities, the U.S. Congress eliminated the realization requirement in 1993[80] with the enactment of Section 475. Under Section 475, any dealer in securities must recognize gain or loss on any security which is not inventory in the hands of the dealer and which is held at the close of the taxable year.[81] The recognized gain or loss is determined as if the non-inventory security is sold for its fair market value on the last business day of the taxable year.[82] If the gain or loss is required to be recognized at the end of each year, no tax deferral may take place except within the course of a particular year.

The U.S. Congress has most recently permitted mark-to-market in the case of publicly traded PFIC stock. As a result, there are three possible taxing regimes for a U.S. shareholder owning PFIC stock. The U.S. shareholder could be subject to the Interest Charge Method for owning the PFIC stock. Alternatively, the U.S. shareholder could elect to treat the PFIC as a transparent entity, a QEF PFIC, in which case the earnings of the PFIC flow through to the U.S. shareholder. Finally, if the stock of the PFIC is publicly traded, the U.S. shareholder could elect mark-to-market treatment with respect to ownership of the PFIC stock. All three of these taxing schemes are designed to prevent the time value of money benefit of tax deferral.

In 1990, Japan implemented a mark-to-market accounting method for foreign exchange licensed banks with respect to currency futures and options.[83] This applies to trading activities with respect to the foreign exchange licensed banks as opposed to investment activities of the banks.[84] One commentator has described the 1990 change as "epoch-making in the history of accounting practice in Japan in that it introduced mark-to-market accounting for off-balance transaction and the concept of discounted present value."[85]

A mark-to-market accounting method (and elimination of the realization requirement) is consistent with the Haig–Simons definition of income.[86] Under the Haig–Simons definition of income, "[p]ersonal income may be defined as the algebraic sum of (1) the market value of rights exercised in consumption and

---

[79] See, e.g., Note, "Realizing Appreciation Without Sale: Accrual Taxation of Capital Gains on Marketable Securities," 34 *Stan. L. Rev.* 857 (1982); Karla W. Simon, "Revenue or Religion? Issues and Answers on Tax Deferral," 68 *Taxes* 1015, 1028 (December 1990).

[80] Pub. L. No. 103-66, section 13223(a) (1993).

[81] I.R.C. § 475(a)(2). [82] I.R.C. § 475(a)(2)(A).

[83] See Charles T. Plambeck, H. David Rosenbloom and Diane M. Ring, "General Report, Tax Aspects of Derivative Financial Instruments" reprinted in 80b *Cahiers de Droit Fiscal International [International Fiscal Association]* 653, 682 n. 61 (International Fiscal Association ed., 1995); Shigeki Fujitani, "Tax Aspects of Derivative Financial Instruments: Japan" reprinted in 80b *Cahiers de Droit Fiscal International* [*International Fiscal Association*] 327, 332–33 (International Fiscal Association ed., 1995); Masatami Otsuka and Kenju Watanabe, *Butterworths International Taxation of Financial Instruments and Transactions: Japan* 1.4.4 (2nd ed., 1994).

[84] See Fujitani, *supra* note 83, at 332–33. [85] See *id.* at 333.

[86] See, e.g., Noel B. Cunningham & Deborah H. Schenk, "Taxation Without Realization: A "Revolutionary" Approach to Ownership," 47 *Tax L. Rev.* 725, 733 (1992) ("a pure Haig–Simons system would use a mark-to-market approach").

(2) the change in the value of the store of property rights between the beginning and end of the period in question."[87] This definition of income appears to be the widely accepted definition among tax academics and economists.[88] For example, if a taxpayer bought General Motors stock for $1000 on 1 January 1997, and the U.S. Congress required that the taxpayer utilize a year end mark-to-market method of accounting and the stock was worth $1500 on 31 December 1997, then the taxpayer would include $500 in income for 1997 with respect to the General Motors stock.

The obvious advantage to adopting the Haig–Simons definition of income is that tax deferral is eliminated and no need exists for an Interest Charge Method or any other prophylactic method of eliminating tax deferral.[89] In other words, adoption of the Haig–Simons definition of income would eliminate the benefits of the Cary Brown model. Utilizing an earlier example, assume T owns assets long thought essentially worthless with a negligible basis. The assets immediately rise in value to 10,000*u*. Then the assets' values continue to rise at 10 percent annually for three years. At the end of three years, T sells the assets for 13,310*u* resulting in 13,310*u* of gain. At a 40 percent tax rate, the tax owed is 5324*u* leaving T with cash of 7986*u* (13,310*u* minus 5324*u*). If the realization requirement is eliminated for the original appreciation of 10,000*u* and it is immediately taxed at a 40 percent tax rate, then T owes 4000*u* in taxes to the government. T would have 6000*u* in assets remaining. At a 10 percent *pre-tax* rate of return, T will have 7986*u* at the end of three years, the same amount as when the tax on the gain is delayed until realization. This is consistent with the Super Cary Brown model.

Eliminating the realization requirement, however, and implementing an income tax on changes in the value of a taxpayer's assets could lead to numerous problems, including liquidity in terms of paying the resulting income tax, administrability in determining the changes in fair market value of the taxpayer's assets (particularly those not traded on a publicly traded exchange), and possible constitutional (or

---

[87] Henry C. Simons, *Personal Income Taxation: The Definition of Income as a Problem of Fiscal Policy* 50 (1938). See also Robert M. Haig, "The Concept of Income – Economic and Legal Aspects," in *The Federal Income Tax* 1, 7 (R.M. Haig ed. 1921) reprinted in *Readings in the Economics of Taxation* 54, 55 (Richard A. Musgrave and Carl S. Shoup, eds. 1959) ("Income is the money value of the net accretion to one's economic power between two points of time.").

[88] See, e.g., Bittker and Lokken, *supra* note 29, at ¶ 3.1.1 ("Among contemporary American economists, however, the so-called Haig–Simons definition of income is the most widely accepted."); Cunningham and Schenk, *supra* note 87, at 733 (1992) ("Tax theorists generally have accepted the so-called Haig–Simons definition of income."); Michael J. Graetz and Deborah H. Schenk, *Federal Income Taxation: Principles and Policies* 107 (3rd ed., 1995) ("The Simons definition, which is considered a refinement of the Haig definition, is the most widely accepted."); Alvin C. Warren, Jr., "Financial Contract Innovation and Income Tax Policy," 107 *Harv. L. Rev.* 460, 462 n. 9 (1993) ("The classic exposition of the concept of income is Henry C. Simons, *Personal Income Taxation* 41–58 (1938).").

[89] See, e.g., Stanley S. Surrey, "The Supreme Court and the Federal Income Tax: Some Implications of the Recent Decisions," 35 *Ill. L. Rev.* 779 (1941) (economic gain occurs each year as an asset appreciates and therefore the realization doctrine, which delays taxing the appreciation, is really a matter of timing); Michael J. Graetz, *Federal Income Taxation: Principles and Policies* 206–07 (1988) ("As Surrey indicates, realization is a question of the timing of taxation.").

political) problems.[90] In addition, some period of time, most often assumed to be a year, would have to be adopted in which to make the fair market value determinations.[91] Most commentators have agreed that it is impractical to eliminate the realization requirement and adopt a complete mark-to-market approach.[92] A more realistic approach would be to either adopt mark-to-market on a limited scale or to adopt a substantially different taxing scheme such as a cash flow tax, sometimes referred to as a consumption tax.[93] Professor Halperin has suggested the former approach arguing that mark-to-market needs to be adopted for all instruments whose value is related to traded securities.[94] Professor Andrews, however, believes that it makes sense to adopt a cash flow tax, in large part, because of the tax deferral problems caused by the realization doctrine.[95]

D. Deemed Rate of Return

In 1982, the United States introduced the concept of constant yield to maturity for accruing interest income on debt instruments issued at a discount. The principle behind the constant yield to maturity method is to determine a single interest rate to accrue interest on a discounted debt instrument. By using this single rate, the amount of interest accrual will increase each year in a manner similar to the growth of funds in a bank account. The reason, of course, is the principle of compound interest.

In understanding why the United States adopted the constant yield to maturity method for discounted debt instruments, it is helpful to look at the period prior to 1982. From 1954 to 1969, an investor included accrued interest in income under the

---

[90] See Warren, *supra* note 88, at 462. But see David J. Shakow, "Taxation Without Realization: A Proposal for Accrual Taxation," 134 *U. Pa. L. Rev.* 1111 (1986).

[91] See, e.g., Halperin, *supra* note 45; Shakow, *supra* note 90; David Slawson, "Taxing as Ordinary Income the Appreciation of Publicly Held Stock," 76 *Yale L. J.* 623 (1967); Jeff Strnad, "Tax Timing and the Haig–Simons Ideal: A Rejoinder to Professor Popkin," 62 *Ind. L. J.* 79 (1986); Jeff Strnad, "Periodicity and Accretion Taxation: Norms and Implementation," 99 *Yale L. J.* 1817 (1990).

[92] See, e.g., Haig, *supra* note 87, at 66–69; Simons, *supra* note 87, at 103; Daniel N. Shaviro, "An Efficiency Analysis of Realization and Recognition Rules Under the Federal Income Tax," 47 *Tax L. Rev.* 1, 3 (1992). But see, e.g., Shakow, *supra* note 90 (advocating a partial accrual system); Thomas L. Evans, "The Evolution of Federal Income Tax Accounting – A Growing Trend Towards Mark-to-Market," 67 *Taxes* 824 (1989) (the tax system is moving away from the realization doctrine and going more towards a mark-to-market approach); Thomas L. Evans, "The Realization Doctrine After Cottage Savings," 70 *Taxes* 897, 909–10 (1992) (proposing changes to the income tax laws that would reduce the difficulties created by the realization doctrine).

[93] Under cash flow taxation, an investment is deducted when the cost of the investment is paid and is included in income when cash receipts are received. As to the literature on cash flow taxation, see, e.g., Andrews, *supra* note 1; William D. Andrews, "A Consumption-Type or Cash Flow Personal Income Tax," 87 *Harv. L. Rev.* 1113 (1974); William D. Andrews, "Fairness and the Personal Income Tax: A Reply to Professor Warren," 88 *Harv. L. Rev.* 947 (1975); Michael J. Graetz, "Implementing a Progressive Consumption Tax," 92 *Harv. L. Rev.* 1575 (1979); Alvin C. Warren, "Fairness and a Consumption-Type or Cash Flow Personal Income Tax," 88 *Harv. L. Rev.* 931 (1975); Alvin C. Warren, "Would a Consumption Tax Be Fairer Than an Income Tax?," 89 *Yale L. J.* 1081 (1980).

[94] See Daniel I. Halperin, "Saving the Income Tax: An Agenda for Research," 77 *Tax Notes* 967, 968 (24 November 1997).

[95] See Andrews, *supra* note 93.

investor's method of accounting. Because almost all individual investors were on the cash method of accounting, they would include the accrued interest in income upon receipt, which occurred at maturity (or, if earlier, on sale of the bond).[96] This was, in essence, a realization approach to accrued interest. The issuer would deduct accrue interest under its method of accounting, which in many cases was the accrual method of accounting. This created a timing mismatch as to the investor's income inclusion and the issuer's deduction.

In 1969, the United States implemented a ratable inclusion method of accruing interest, which overstated the interest in the early years and understated it in the later years.[97] Assume for example, that a corporation issued a zero coupon bond maturing in 10 years with a face amount of $1000. An investor pays $385 for the bond at issuance. There is $615 of accrued interest built into the bond, or what the United States refers to as "original issue discount" or simply OID. This OID should be treated as interest because it is compensation for the use of money. Under the realization doctrine (pre-1969 approach), the investor would not include the $615 of accrued interest in income until the bond matured at the end of 10 years (or earlier, if the investor sold the bond). In 1969, the U.S. Congress forced the investor to include the interest in income but under a ratable approach rather than a constant yield to maturity approach. Consequently, the investor would include $61.50 in income each year for 10 years.

In 1982, the U.S. Congress required the investor to use the constant yield to maturity approach.[98] Under this approach, the yield is determined by looking at the cash flows of the debt instrument. In the above example, the yield is approximately 10 percent compounded annually because that is the rate at which $385 will grow to $1000 at the end of 10 years. The following chart demonstrates the income inclusion for the investor each year (and the deduction to the issuer):

Year	Principal plus accrued OID ($)	Yield to maturity (%)	OID inclusion ($)
1	385	10	38.50
2	423.50	10	42.35
3	465.85	10	46.59
4	512.44	10	51.24
5	563.68	10	56.37
6	620.05	10	62.01
7	682.06	10	68.21
8	750.27	10	75.03
9	825.30	10	82.53
10	907.83	10	92.17 (rounded off)

[96] See *United States v. Midland Ross*, 381 U.S. 54 (1965) (in pre-1954 years, the investor could not report gain on selling a discounted bond as capital gain where the gain was attributable to earned discount; this result was codified in 1954).

[97] Pub. L. No. 91-172, section 413(a) (1969).

[98] Pub. L. No. 97-248, section 231(c) (1982).

The above chart demonstrates that the income inclusion to the holder of the zero coupon bond increases each year. This is the proper result. If $385 were deposited in a bank at a 10 percent rate of return and left in the bank for 10 years, it will grow to about $1000 at the end of 10 years. But it does not grow in equal increments each year. It will grow by compound interest. In other words, interest will be earned on the previous year(s) interest. The $385 deposited in a bank account will grow to $1000 as demonstrated in the above chart. This same methodology should be used for zero coupon bonds, which is the case in the United States since 1982 (and 1984 for zero coupon bonds issued for non-publicly traded property).

The constant yield to maturity method is a kind of surrogate for mark-to-market. Mark-to-market has administrative difficulties in that the bond's value needs to be determined at least annually. Under the constant yield to maturity method, the value of the bond is deemed to increase by the yield each year. While this may not be the exact amount that the bond's value increases each year, it should, in most cases, be reasonably close.[98a] In any event, the constant yield to maturity is superior to the realization doctrine in eliminating the time value of money benefit of tax deferral with respect to a discounted bond.

Contingent payment debt instruments pose a special problem under the constant yield to maturity method. It is not possible to determine the exact yield because the payments under the debt instrument are not fixed at the time of issuance. As a result, a couple of approaches are possible. The first is to take a wait-and-see approach.[99] In other words, wait until the payments are fixed and then determine the constant yield to maturity in accruing interest each year. But this approach by its very name leads to deferral of the interest inclusion. In other words, this approach has some of the same problems as the realization doctrine.

The second approach is to determine a comparable yield to maturity and make adjustments as the payments become fixed. This is the approach that the U.S. Treasury has currently taken in regulations.[100] An example will best demonstrate the comparable yield to maturity method.[101] Assume on 31 December 1996, Y Corporation issues to Z for $1 million a debt instrument that matures on 31 December 2000. The debt instrument has a stated principal amount of $1 million, payable at maturity, and provides for payments on 31 December of each year (1997–2000) of $20,000 *plus*

[98a] The two major differences between the constant yield to maturity method and mark-to-market are the "unanticipated changes in the value of the instrument due to changes in interest rates or credit quality" and the term structure of interest rates. See David A. Weisbach, A Partial Mark-to-Market Tax System, 53 Tax L. Rev. 95, 109(1999). Professors Strnad and Gergen have shown that these differences can lead to strategic trading of debt instruments to accelerate losses and defer gains. This can lead to substantial tax savings. See Jeff Strnad, The Taxation of Bonds: The Tax Trading Dimension, 81 Virginia Law Review 47, 53 (1995): Mark P. Gergen, The Effects of Price Volatility and Strategic Trading under Realization, Expected Return, and Retrospective Taxation, 49 Tax L. Rev. 209, 212 (1994).
As to the term structure of interest rates, see supra note 60.

[99] The U.S. Treasury initially adopted this approach for contingent payment debt obligations. See Prop. Reg. § 1.1275-4(c)(3)(i), 51 Fed. Reg. 12022, 12087 (1986) (withdrawn).

[100] Treas. Reg. § 1.1274-4, 61 Fed. Reg. 30133 (1996).

[101] This example is adopted from Treas. Reg. § 1.1274-4(b)(4)(iv) Example 2.

1 percent of Y's gross receipts, if any, for the year. As a result, this is a contingent payment debt instrument.[102]

The key determination that needs to be made is the comparable yield for this debt instrument. Assume Y has outstanding fixed rate debt instruments with maturities from 2 to 10 years that trade at a price that reflects an average of 100 basis points (one percent) over U.S. Treasury bonds. Y's outstanding fixed rate debt instruments have terms and conditions similar to those of the contingent payment debt obligation. Also assume that on 31 December 1996, four-year U.S. Treasury bonds have a yield of 6.5 percent, compounded annually. As a result, the comparable yield for the contingent payment debt obligation is 7.5 percent compounded annually (the yield on four-year U.S. Treasury bonds of 6.5 percent plus the spread on Y's debt instruments of one percent).

Once the comparable yield is determined, a projected payment schedule is set up using that comparable yield. Assume that Y anticipates having no gross receipts in 1997 but will have gross receipts in years following 1997. In addition, the gross receipts will grow each year from 1998 to 2000 and that it is not unreasonable to expect that gross receipts in 1999 and each year thereafter will grow from six percent to 13 percent over the previous year. These expectations must be taken into account in setting up the projected payment schedule so that the debt instrument will have a yield of 7.5 percent compounded annually.

Date	Non-contingent payment ($)	Contingent payment ($)
31 December 1997	20,000	0
31 December 1998	20,000	70,000
31 December 1999	20,000	75,600
31 December 2000	20,000	83,850

If the amount of contingent payment is greater than the projected amount, then the difference is treated as additional interest for the year.[103] If the amount of contingent payment is less than the projected amount, then the difference is used to reduce the interest for the year. For example, assume in 1997, the amount of contingent payment is $10,000, which is $10,000 greater than the projected amount of zero. Therefore, Z's interest inclusion in 1997 will be: $1 million issue price times 7.5 percent yield equaling $75,000 plus $10,000 (additional interest) totaling $85,000.

The comparable yield method for contingent payment debt obligations is, like the constant yield to maturity method, a surrogate for mark-to-market. The constant yield to maturity method allocated a known amount of income (OID) over a period

[102] A variable rate debt instrument is not treated as a contingent payment debt instrument. Treas. Reg. § 1.1274-4(a)(2)(ii).

[103] Treas. Reg. § 1.1274-4(b)(6).

of time. The comparable yield method, however, creates income that may never arise or that may be too little. In the end, the system is self-correcting for the comparable yield method. If the income never arises, then the investor will be allowed an offsetting loss deduction. If the actual income is greater than the projection, then the investor has additional income. In other words, "any deviation between estimates and actual events ultimately is corrected by an appropriate amount of gain or loss that is reported when the contingency is resolved."[104]

It is important to note that the timing of the correction under the comparable yield method occurs at the time the contingency is resolved. As a result, the comparable yield to maturity may deviate wildly from year to year from a mark-to-market approach (the Haig–Simons definition) although in the end the total amount of income included under the comparable yield method will equal the total amount included under a mark-to-market approach.

IV. Deferral of Income with Imputed Interest Method

A. Introduction

Under the Deferral of Income with Imputed Interest Method, the government selects a rate of return and uses that rate to impute or create income to prevent the time value of money benefit of tax deferral. This method is similar to the discussion of debt instruments under the Immediate Inclusion in Income Method because a rate of return is selected to prevent the time value of money benefit of tax deferral. But it differs in one important respect. Under the Immediate Inclusion in Income Method, the various sub-methods either implemented the Haig–Simons definition of income (elimination of a deferral provision, pass-through, or mark-to-market) or attempted to closely follow it when valuation was not reasonably possible (constant yield to maturity or comparable yield to maturity for discounted debt instruments).

Under the Deferral of Income with Imputed Interest Method, the taxpayer has income that is measurable and under the Haig–Simons definition should be immediately included in income. But this method allows deferral of that income so that it will be included at a later point in time. To account for the deferral that is permitted, the later inclusion will be a greater amount than current inclusion because it has been increased by a deemed rate of return.

The Deferral of Income with Imputed Interest Method of preventing tax deferral was mentioned with respect to accrual method taxpayers receiving prepaid income and taxpayers establishing a reserve for mining reclamation expenses. Generally, the theory behind this method is to require the taxpayer to include an interest component in income to compensate the government for deferral of income. The actual mechanics are quite straightforward.

---

[104] Stephen B. Land, "Defeating Deferral: A Proposal for Retrospective Taxation," 52 *Tax L. Rev.* 45, 63 (1996).

B. Income Side – Automobile Dealers

Generally, under U.S. tax law, an accrual method taxpayer must include in income amounts currently received for services to be performed in the future.[105] This has become a well-accepted principle of tax law, commonly referred to as the *Schlude* doctrine, with very few exceptions.[106] In 1992, however, the Internal Revenue Service issued Technical Advice Memorandum 92-18-004 ("TAM"),[107] which created much controversy and uncertainty in the automobile industry. In the T.A.M., an automobile dealer sold extended service warranty contracts along with its automobiles. It received a lump-sum payment from each customer for the extended contract. The dealer would then keep a portion of the payment as a commission and remit the remaining portion to an insurance subsidiary of the automobile manufacturer to cover the warranty obligation to each of the customers. The dealer treated the lump-sum payment from the customer as income and included it upon receipt. But it also immediately deducted the payment that was made to the insurance subsidiary of the manufacturer.

The Service, in the T.A.M., concluded that the automobile dealer must include the lump-sum payment from the customers in income upon receipt. But, the Service also concluded that the dealer must deduct the payment to the manufacturer's insurance subsidiary over the life of the contract rather than immediately deducting it. Automobile dealers argued that this tax treatment created a mismatch of income and deduction and would generate cash flow problems. In other words, the automobile dealer had to pay tax on the entire lump-sum payment received from the customer when in actuality the dealer only kept a relatively small portion of the payment. In addition, the major portion of the payment, which was paid to the manufacturer's insurance subsidiary, could only be deducted over several years. This was the worst of both worlds – full income inclusion with delayed deductions.

The automobile dealers requested relief from the results of the T.A.M. A number of U.S. tax lawyers commented on the T.A.M. with one concluding that it "is so simple [and correct] that a second-year law student could answer it correctly."[108] Another tax lawyer immediately responded that "[i]f that is so, I suggest that it is

---

[105] See, e.g., *Automobile Club of Michigan*, 353 U.S. 180 (1957); *American Automobile Association v. United States*, 367 U.S. 687 (1961); *Commissioner v. Schlude*, 372 U.S. 128 (1963). The U.S. Supreme Court's holding in these three cases is sometimes referred to as the *Schlude* doctrine. This doctrine basically states that an accrual method taxpayer that receives an advance payment for services must include the advance payment in gross income at the time of receipt. This doctrine has also been applied to advance payment for goods. See, e.g., *Hagen Advertising Displays, Inc. v. Commissioner*, 407 F.2d 1105 (6th Cir. 1969); Treas. Reg. § 1.451-5 (1971).

[106] See, e.g., Rev. Proc. 71-21, 1971-2 C.B. 549; Treas. Reg. § 1.446-3; Treas. Reg. § 1.451-5; Notice 89-21, 1989-1 C.B. 651; *Artnell Co. v. Commissioner*, 400 F.2d 981 (7th Cir. 1968); *Collegiate Cap & Gown Co. v. Commissioner*, 37 T.C.M. (CCH) 960 (1978); *Boise Cascade Corp. v. United States*, 530 F.2d 1367, *cert. denied*, 429 U.S. 867 (1976).

[107] Technical Advice Memorandum 92-18-004 (23 January 1992).

[108] See Lee A. Sheppard, "The Goldberg Variation, Or: Giving Away the Store," 58 *Tax Notes* 530 (1 February 1993).

because such a student has had her good sense corrupted by a first year of law school."[109]

In response to the outcry from automobile dealers, the Internal Revenue Service issued Rev. Proc. 92–97[110] and Rev. Proc. 92–98[111] providing relief to the dealers, at least in terms of cash flow. Under the revenue procedures, automobile dealers are permitted to change their accounting method and defer inclusion of the lump-sum payment in income. This is in direct contrast to the *Schlude* doctrine. The cost of the deferral is that the dealers must also include imputed interest income each year along with a portion of the lump-sum payment. The imputed interest income requirement removes the time value of money benefit of tax deferral. Without it, the dealers would, in essence, be receiving the equivalence of exempting from gross income the return on part of the lump-sum payment that was deferred into later years. The Internal Revenue Service clearly did not want to give automobile dealers the benefit of exempting part of the income of the lump-sum payment from tax. More specifically, the Internal Revenue Service did not want to give automobile dealers the benefits of the Cary Brown model. The U.S. government had convinced the U.S. Supreme Court many years earlier that an advance payment for services must be included in income upon receipt.[112] The Internal Revenue Service did not want to alter this rule. At the same time, the Internal Revenue Service wanted to provide some relief to automobile dealers. As a result, the Internal Revenue Service required dealers to include an imputed interest amount in gross income based on the length of deferral and the current interest rate.

The Internal Revenue Service has given an example in Rev. Proc. 92-98 illustrating the mechanics of the deferral of income method with imputed income. The facts of the example, greatly simplified, are as follows:[113]

---

[109] See Letter from James P. Holden, "Lee Sheppard's Grumpy Attack," 58 *Tax Notes* 1130 (22 February 1993). See also Letter from Sheldon S. Cohen, "In Defense of Lee Sheppard," 58 *Tax Notes* 1386 (8 March 1993) (defending Lee Sheppard's analysis of TAM 92-18-004 and Rev. Proc. 92-98); Letter from Milton Cerny, "Sheppard Variations," 58 *Tax Notes* 981 (15 February 1993); Letter from James P. Fuller, "In Defense of Fred Goldberg," 58 *Tax Notes* 1259 (1 March 1993); Letter from George K. Yin, "The Tax Administrator's Duty to Take Pro-Government Positions," 58 *Tax Notes* 1387 (8 March 1993).

[110] 1992-2 C.B. 510. [111] 1992-2 C.B. 512. [112] See *supra* note 105.

[113] 1992-2 C.B. 515. The example reads as follows:

A, a calendar year accrual basis taxpayer, elects... to use the service warranty income method of accounting for its qualified advance payment amounts on service warranty contracts. A sold 5 service warranty contracts on 1 January 1992, for $800 each. A also sold 5 service warranty contracts on 31 December 1992, for $800 each. All the service warranty contracts sold by A in 1992 carry a term of 5 years and run concurrently with the manufacturer's warranties. Further, A pays, within 60 days of the receipt of each advance payment, $600 per contract to an unrelated third party to insure ... its obligations under the service warranty contracts. The applicable interest rate, determined in accordance with section 5.04 of this revenue procedure, is 10 percent.

A aggregates all its qualified advance payment amounts on its 5-year service warranty contracts, thus determining that $6,000 of qualified advance payment amounts were received in 1992 with respect to the class of 5-year service warranty contracts. Applying the "10% and 5-year" table factor of .2398 ..., A

A is an automobile dealer on the accrual method of accounting. In 1992, it receives a total of $8000 from customers for five-year service warranty contracts. A has paid $6000 of that amount to an unrelated third party who will, in essence, take over the service warranty contracts for A. A has retained $2000. Clearly, A must include $2000 in income. But according to the Internal Revenue Service pursuant to the *Schlude* doctrine, A must also include the $6000 immediately in income even though A has paid it to a third party. A can also deduct the $6000 but only over a five-year time period ($1200 per year) because that is the duration of the service warranty contracts which the third party has taken over for A. In other words, the $6000 that A pays to the third party gives A a benefit for five years because that is the length of time that the third party will be responsible for the service warranty contracts, i.e., it is a capital expenditure. Therefore, A's tax results would be as follows:

Item	1992 ($)	1993 ($)	1994 ($)	1995 ($)	1996 ($)
Gross income	8000	0	0	0	0
Deduction	1200	1200	1200	1200	1200
Taxable income	6800	<1200>	<1200>	<1200>	<1200>

As the above chart demonstrates, A has $6800 of taxable income in 1992. If A is subject to a 35 percent tax on this income, the taxes owed would equal $2380 which is more than the $2000 that A retained from selling the service warranty contracts. In other words, A may be forced to borrow money to pay the taxes for the first year. This is part of the cash flow problem over which the automobile dealers expressed outrage.

If A elected to have the Deferral of Income with Imputed Interest Method apply pursuant to the revenue procedure, taxable income is reported by A as follows:

Item	1992 ($)	1993 ($)	1994 ($)	1995 ($)	1996 ($)
Non-deferred income	2000	0	0	0	0
Deferred income	1439	1439	1439	1439	1439
Gross income	3439	1439	1439	1439	1439
Deductions	1200	1200	1200	1200	1200
Taxable income	2239	239	239	239	239

As the above chart demonstrates, under the revenue procedure, A still includes the $2000 it has retained in its gross income in 1992. But the $6000 is not entirely

determines that it must report income of $1,439 in 1992 through 1996 .... In addition, A must include in gross income in 1992 the $2,000 payment received for services that is not deferred ....

Revenue Procedure 97-38, 1997-2 C.B. 479, has superseded Revenue Procedure 92-98. However, no substantive differences exist between the two revenue procedures.

included in gross income in 1992. Rather it is included in gross income over the five-year time frame to which the service warranty contracts relate. But the Internal Revenue Service will not simply allow A to include the $6000 at $1200 per year in gross income. It will be more than that to reflect the imputed interest that the Internal Revenue Service insists upon to eliminate the time value of money benefit of tax deferral. Using an interest rate of 10 percent in computing the imputed interest amounts, A will include $1439 each year for five years, not $1200 each year.

The Internal Revenue Service uses the applicable federal rate ("AFR") in determining the amount of imputed income[114] that must be included each year. The AFR is the rate determined by the U.S. Secretary of the Treasury based on the average market yield on outstanding marketable obligations of the United States.[115] In the above example, it was assumed that the AFR was 10 percent interest annually. The AFR, however, seems to be a pre-tax rate of return. Assuming that it is, this would seem to be too high for use in the Deferral of Income with Imputed Interest Method. The Internal Revenue Service should use an *after-tax* rate of return in computing imputed income. The following table demonstrates the erroneous result reached if a pre-tax rate of return is used.

	Immediate inclusion of prepaid income ($)	Deferral of income with imputed interest method using a pre-tax rate of return ($)
Advance payment	8000	8000
Gross income less deduction of $1200	6800	2238.90
Taxes (40%)	2720	895.56
Investment	<720>	1104.44
After-tax return on investment (6%)	<43.20>	66.27
Investment (year two)	<763.20>	1170.71
Gross income less deduction of $1200	<1200>	238.90
Taxes (40%)	<480>	95.56
After-tax return on investment (6%)	<16.99>	64.51
Investment (year three)	<300.19>	1139.66
Gross income	<1200>	238.90
Taxes (40%)	<480>	95.56
After-tax return on investment (6%)	10.79	62.65
Investment (year four)	190.60	1106.75
Gross income	<1200>	238.90

[114] In the Service's example, the precise amount would be $1438.90.

[115] I.R.C. § 1274(d).

Table *Continued*

	Immediate inclusion of prepaid income ($)	Deferral of income with imputed interest method using a pre-tax rate of return ($)
Taxes (40%)	<480>	95.56
After-tax return on investment (6%)	40.24	60.67
Investment (year five)	710.84	1071.86
Gross income	<1200>	238.90
Taxes (40%)	<480>	95.56
After-Tax Return on investment (6%)	71.45	58.58
Total after-taxes at the end of five years	1262.29	1034.88

In the above example, the automobile dealer was better off from a tax standpoint by immediately including the entire $8000 prepayment in income. Parity has not been achieved between immediate inclusion and the Deferral of Income with Imputed Interest Method because the pre-tax rate of return that was used in imputing interest income was too high. *The automobile dealer ends up being overtaxed.*

Assume that taxpayer A in the example in the revenue procedure is in the 40 percent tax bracket. If the pre-tax rate of return is 10 percent annually, the after-tax rate of return would therefore be six percent annually. Applying the "6 percent and 5-year" table factor of 0.2240 ..., A determines that it must report income of $1344 in 1992 through 1996 ....[116] In addition, A must include in gross income in 1992 the $2000 payment received for services that is not deferred .... Taxable income is reported by A as follows:

Item	1992 ($)	1993 ($)	1994 ($)	1995 ($)	1996 ($)
Non-deferred income	2000	0	0	0	0
Deferred income	1344	1344	1344	1344	1344
Gross income	3344	1344	1344	1344	1344
Deductions	1200	1200	1200	1200	1200
Taxable income	2144	144	144	144	144

If A included the entire $8000 prepayment as gross income in the first year upon receipt with a $1200 deduction in the first year (and each of the next four years), A would pay taxes of $2720 leaving A with a negative investment amount of $720. A would owe interest at an after-tax rate of six percent (assuming the interest was

[116] The precise amount would be $1343.75.

deductible) until the investment amount became positive at which time A could then invest it at an after-tax rate of return of six percent annually. At the end of five years, A would still have $1262.29. Under the Deferral of Income with Imputed Interest Method, using an after-tax rate of return of six percent for five years, A would also have $1262.29 at the end of five years. The following table demonstrates this equivalence if an after-tax rate of return is used.

	Immediate inclusion ($)	Deferral of income with imputed interest method using an after-tax rate of return ($)
Advance payment	8000	8000
Gross income less deduction of 1200	6800	2143.75
Taxes (40%)	2720	857.50
Investment	<720>	1142.50
After-tax return on investment (6%)	<43.20>	68.55
Investment (year two)	<763.20>	1211.05
Gross income	<1200>	143.75
Taxes (40%)	<480>	57.50
After-tax return on investment (6%)	<16.99>	69.21
Investment (year three)	<300.19>	1222.76
Gross income	<1200>	143.75
Taxes (40%)	<480>	57.50
After-tax return on investment (6%)	10.79	69.92
Investment (year four)	190.60	1235.18
Gross income	<1200>	143.75
Taxes (40%)	<480>	57.50
After-Tax return on investment (6%)	40.24	70.67
Investment (year five)	710.84	1248.34
Gross income	<1200>	143.75
Taxes (40%)	<480>	57.50
After-tax return on investment (6%)	71.45	71.45
Total after-taxes at the end of five years	1262.29	1262.29

At the end of five years, A would have $1262.29 if A included the entire $8000 payment in gross income upon receipt or if A included it over the five-year period using an after-tax rate of return of six percent annually.

Simplifying the above example leads to a formula that is consistent with previously discussed formulas. Simplifying will also demonstrate how clearly erroneous the use of a pre-tax rate of return is in the above example. The option that the revenue procedures essentially provide is whether to include the advance payment immediately in income or to delay inclusion until a later point in time. For this purpose, the deduction each year is essentially irrelevant as it is the same amount whether or not the taxpayer elects to utilize the imputed income method of the revenue procedures. In the above example, the taxpayer's deduction is $1200 each year for five years whether under the imputed income method or simply under the *Schlude* doctrine.

Focusing solely on the income side of the automobile dealer, the above example can be generalized algebraically using the following additional assumptions: (1) the deductions to the automobile dealer are disregarded and (2) the option is to either include the prepaid service income on receipt or defer it until the end of the contract. In the case of *immediate recognition of income* under the *Schlude* doctrine, an amount A of income is reduced by tax t such that $A(1-t)$ may be invested. At an annual rate of return r, $A(1-t)$ invested will earn $rA(1-t)$ per year, which will be subject to tax at rate t equaling tax each year of $trA(1-t)$. The automobile dealer's net annual after-tax position each year will be:

$$rA(1-t) - trA(1-t) \text{ which equals } rA(1-t)(1-t).$$

In the case of imputing interest income in which prepaid service income is recognized *at the end of the contract* (not over the life of the contract), an amount A of prepaid service income is not reduced by tax t at the time of receipt. At an annual rate of return r, A invested will earn rA per year, which will be subject to tax at rate t equaling tax each year of trA. In addition, interest income is imputed each year in the amount of $rA(1-t)$, which is an after-tax rate of return. This is subject to tax at rate t equaling tax each year of $trA(1-t)$. The automobile dealer's net annual after-tax position will be:

$$rA(1-t) - trA(1-t) \text{ which equals } rA(1-t)(1-t).$$

This is equal to the automobile dealer's net annual after-tax position when immediate recognition of income is required and tax is immediately imposed.

If a pre-tax rate of return is used in imputing interest income in which prepaid service income is recognized at the end of the contract, the amount A of prepaid service income is not reduced by tax t at the time of receipt. At an annual rate of return r, A invested will earn rA per year, which will be subject to tax at rate t equaling tax each year of trA. In addition, interest income is imputed each year in the amount of rA, which is a pre-tax rate of return. This is subject to tax at rate t equaling tax each year of trA. The automobile dealer's net annual after-tax position will be $rA(1-t) - rAt$. The automobile dealer is worse off by the amount of tax that would be saved by only including imputed interest income at an after-tax rate of return.

C. Deduction Side – Mining Reclamation Expenses

The Deferral of Income with Imputed Interest Method has also been applied to the deduction side, involving mining reclamation expenses. Generally, a taxpayer establishes a reserve for mining reclamation costs that will be incurred in the future. The reserve is treated as if it were an actual fund that earns a pre-tax rate of return each year. At the end of each year, the balance of the fund is compared to the amount of estimated mining reclamation costs. The excess, if any, is income to the taxpayer.

As Professor Halperin has noted, it appears that the U.S. Congress should treat the fund as earning interest at an after-tax rate of return instead of a pre-tax rate of return.[117] If Professor Halperin is correct (which he is), then the mining reclamation reserve provision actually treats a taxpayer worse than the general rule for accruing deductions (unless the after-tax rate of return is greater than the pre-tax rate of return).

An example will best illustrate the inaccuracy of this special provision. Assume in 1994, the taxpayer deducts $1000 as a mining reclamation expense. The taxpayer will actually pay $1000 in 1997 to restore the land where the mining has taken place and the restoration will take place that same year. The currently deducted amount of $1000 is treated as being deposited in a fund earning interest at a pre-tax rate of return. Assume the pre-tax rate of return is 10 percent and therefore the after-tax rate of return is six percent. In 1994, the taxpayer will save $400 in taxes from establishing the reserve at the end of 1994 ($1000 deduction multiplied by 40 percent tax rate). The savings will earn, after-taxes, $24 ($400 multiplied by six percent) in 1995. This is the time value of money benefit of tax deferral. To eliminate this benefit, the government needs to collect $24 from the taxpayer in 1995.

If the reserve is treated as earning interest at a 10 percent pre-tax rate of return, then the reserve will be treated as earning $100 in 1995 ($1000 multiplied by 10 percent). The taxpayer will include this amount in income and will pay $40 in taxes, leaving the taxpayer with a net deficit of $16 ($40 taxes paid less $24 earned from tax savings). If, however, the reserve is treated as earning interest at a six percent after-tax rate of return, then the reserve will be treated as earning $60 in 1995 ($1000 multiplied by six percent). The taxpayer will include this amount in income and will pay $24 in taxes. The taxpayer will end up with a net amount of zero. As a result, the taxpayer will receive no time value of money benefit of tax deferral.

Professor Halperin is accurate in stating that the reserve for mining reclamation expenses should be treated as earning interest at an after-tax rate of return. The U.S. government should amend the provision dealing with mining reclamation expenses to reflect the reserve fund growing at an after-tax rate of return, not a pre-tax rate of return.

D. Comments on Deferral of Income with Imputed Interest Method

It is difficult to determine why the U.S. government would adopt the Deferral of Income with Imputed Interest Method over the Interest Charge Method. For example, it seems just as easy to require that the automobile dealers use an Interest Charge Method. To illustrate, the automobile dealers would determine what portion of the advance payment is being deferred. Second, multiply this amount by the applicable tax rate (maybe the highest marginal tax rate) and then multiply it by the applicable

[117] See Halperin, *supra* note 45, at 530–31.

interest rate. This amount would be remitted to the government as interest on deferred taxes, very similar to the interest on deferred tax liability under the Annual Method for the Interest Charge Method. Ideally, the interest would be deductible. This seems to be much easier than imputing income which, in terms of the bottom line, reaches pretty close to the same result, i.e., an additional amount is owed to the government each year.

The advantage to the Deferral of Income with Imputed Interest Method may be that the income generated is taxed at the taxpayer's marginal tax rate for the year. Under the Interest Charge Method for large installment sales, the government computes the deferred taxes using the highest tax rate in the U.S. Internal Revenue Code as opposed to the taxpayer's marginal tax rate. As a result, the Deferral of Income with Imputed Interest Method is probably a more accurate method of preventing tax deferral. The government, however, could easily correct the disparity by also using the taxpayer's marginal tax rate for the Interest Charge Method, but as previously stated, this could be an administrative nightmare.

The application of the Deferral of Income with Imputed Interest Method to automobile dealers may, however, be theoretically more sound than the use of the Interest Charge Method. The underlying principle of the *Schlude* doctrine seems to be that a prepayment of service income is in essence a loan to be repaid by the payee's performance under the contract.[118] If so, then the proper approach is to impute interest income as the Service has done in its revenue procedure. In contrast, the Interest Charge Method is one of deferred tax payment between the taxpayer and the government and not of a disguised loan between taxpayers.

V. Deposit Method

A. *Partnerships*

In the previous chapter, the Deposit Method of preventing tax deferral was briefly mentioned with respect to fiscal year partnerships. Generally, the idea behind the Deposit Method is that the taxpayer must pay to the government the amount of taxes that are being deferred, the government keeps this amount as a deposit, and returns the deposit when the tax deferral period ends. Mechanically, the government requires the taxpayer to determine the income that is being deferred and multiply it by the tax rate, and remit this amount to the government. When the tax deferral period ends, the taxpayer receives the deposit back.

As a result of the U.S. Congress' increasing concern with the time value of money and tax deferral, it enacted Section 7519, which introduced the Deposit Method for partnerships, in 1987.[119] The Deposit Method under Section 7519 is intended to eliminate the tax deferral that a partnership gives its partners when it uses a year

[118] See *Commissioner v. Schlude*, 372 U.S. 128 (1963). The Supreme Court held in *Schlude* that an accrual method dance studio had to include in gross income upon receipt advance payments for future dance lessons.

[119] Pub. L. No. 100-203, tit. X, § 10206(b)(1) (1987).

other than the taxable year being used by the partners.[120] The deposit made by the taxpayer to the government is, in essence, an interest-free loan to the government. The deposit ("required payment" is the technical term used by the U.S. government) is determined through a complex set of calculations. To calculate the amount of the deposit, the partnership must first compute its "deferral ratio." This is equal to the ratio of the number of months in the deferral period of the base year to the number of months in the partnership's taxable year.[121] The base year means the taxable year of the partnership preceding the year when the 444 election is made and the Deposit Method is applicable.[122] The deferral ratio is then multiplied by the partnership's net income for the base year.[123] This amount is then added to the excess of the deferral ratio multiplied by the aggregate of applicable payments made by the partnership during the base year over the aggregate amount of such applicable payments made during the deferral period of the base year.[124] The sum is the partnership's "net base year income."[125]

The partnership's net base year income is multiplied by the "adjusted highest section one rate."[126] The product is the required payment for the first applicable election year.[127] For subsequent applicable election years of the partnership, the required payment is the excess of the product of the net base year income multiplied by the

---

[120] H.R. Rep. No. 391, 100th Cong., 1st Sess. 1540 (1987), reprinted in [1987] U.S. Code & Cong. Ad. News. 2313-1127.

[121] I.R.C. § 7519(d)(1) flush language. The term "deferral period" means the number of months between the beginning of the taxable year elected under Code section 444 and the close of the first required taxable year ending within such year. I.R.C. §§ 7519(e)(1) and 444(b)(4). For example, if a new partnership elected under Code section 444 to use a 30 September taxable year and its required taxable year is the calendar year, the deferral period is three months and the deferral ratio is 3/12 or 1/4.

[122] I.R.C. § 7519(e)(2)(A).

[123] The net income is generally the aggregate amount of the partnership's items described in Code section 702(a) other than credits and tax-exempt income. I.R.C. § 7519(d)(2)(A). Any limitation on the amount of any partnership item that is taken into account in computing the taxable income of a partner is disregarded for purposes of computing the partnership's net income under Code section 7519(d)(2)(A). I.R.C. § 7519(d)(2)(C). In addition, the net income of the partnership is determined by disregarding any guaranteed payments (as defined in Code section 707(c)) of the partnership. I.R.C. § 7519(d)(5)(A).

If the base year is less than 12 months ("short base year"), then the net income for the short base year must be annualized. Temp. Treas. Reg. § 1.7519-1T(b)(5)(v)(A) and (B). This is accomplished by increasing the net income for the short base year by deductible applicable payments in the short base year and then multiplying this amount by 12 and dividing by the number of months in the short base year. Temp. Treas. Reg. § 1.7519-1T(b)(5)(B).

[124] Applicable payment means an amount paid by a partnership which is includible in a partner's gross income. I.R.C. § 7519(d)(3)(A). The regulations state that for an amount to be an applicable payment it must also be deductible by the partnership in the base year as well as includible in a partner's gross income. Temp. Treas. Reg. § 1.7519-1T(b)(5)(iv)(A). Applicable payment does not include gain from the sale or exchange of property between a partner and the partnership. I.R.C. § 7519(d)(3)(B)(i). It also does not include guaranteed payments under Code section 707(c). I.R.C. § 7519(d)(5).

[125] I.R.C. § 7519(d)(1).

[126] The applicable percentage for applicable election years beginning in and after 1990 is 100 percent. I.R.C. § 7519(d)(4). The adjusted highest section one rate is the highest marginal individual tax rate plus one percentage point. I.R.C. § 7519(b) flush language.

[127] If an applicable election year is the partnership's first year in existence, the required payment for such year is zero. Temp. Treas. Reg. § 1.7519-1T(b)(4)(i). If the first applicable election year ends before the last day of the partnership's required taxable year, the required payment for such year is zero. Temp.

applicable percentage of the adjusted highest section one rate over the net required payment balance.[128] The net required payment balance is the excess of the aggregate of required payments for all previous applicable election years over the aggregate amount allowable as a refund for all previous applicable election years.[129]

An example will best demonstrate the mechanics of the Deposit Method. Assume a partnership is formed on 1 January 1994. All of its partners are calendar year individuals. The partnership adopts 30 September as its taxable year.

By adopting a 30 September taxable year as opposed to a calendar year, the partnership is giving its partners three months of tax deferral. To prevent the time value of money benefit of tax deferral, the U.S. Congress requires that the partnership make a required payment (deposit) to approximate the amount of tax deferral. This is the Deposit Method. Assume the partnership's net income for each month is $10,000. The partnership's first applicable election year is the taxable year from 1 January 1994 to 30 September 1994. No payment is required for this first applicable election year because this is the partnership's first year in existence.[130] The partnership's second applicable election year is from 1 October 1994 to 30 September 1995. It must make a required payment by 15 May 1995.[131]

The deferral ratio of the partnership is 3/12 (three months of deferral divided by twelve total months) which equals 1/4. The base year is from 1 January 1994, to 30 September 1994. The net income is $90,000 for the base year and the annualized short base year income is $120,000. Therefore, the net base year income is 1/4 multiplied by $120,000 or $30,000. This amount is multiplied by the adjusted highest section one rate (39.6 percent plus one percent) to equal $12,180. This is the amount of the deposit.[132] The U.S. Treasury pays no interest to the partnership on the deposit.[133]

For the third applicable election year from 1 October 1995 to 30 September 1996, the partnership must make the calculation again. If the partnership income has remained constant, however, the applicable percentage of the adjusted highest section one rate multiplied by the net base year income will again equal $12,180. From this amount is subtracted the net required payment balance of $12,180, leaving a balance due of zero. Thus, no amount is due for the third applicable election year. If the partnership terminates its election under Section 444, then it is entitled to a refund of the deposit ("net required payment balance").[134]

Treas. Reg. § 1.7519-1T(b)(4)(ii). If the required payment for an applicable election year does not exceed $500 and the partnership has not been required to make a required payment for a previous year, then no required payment is due. I.R.C. § 7519(a)(2) and Temp. Treas. Reg. § 1.7519-1T(a)(2).

[128] I.R.C. § 7519(b). [129] I.R.C. § 7519(e)(4).

[130] Temp. Treas. Reg. § 1.7519-1T(b)(4)(i). The reason that a newly-formed partnership does not make a required payment for its first applicable election year is that it does not have a base year. *Id.*

[131] In Code section 7519(f)(2), Congress established 15 April of the calendar year following the calendar year in which the applicable election year begins as the due date for the required payment unless the Secretary establishes a later date. The Secretary has done so through regulations by establishing 15 May of the calendar year following the calendar year in which the applicable election year begins as the due date for the required payment. Temp. Treas. Reg. § 1.7519-2T(a)(4)(ii).

[132] It is assessed and collected in the same manner as a tax imposed by subtitle C. I.R.C. § 7519(f)(1). Subtitle C deals with Employment Taxes.

[133] I.R.C. § 7519(f)(3). [134] I.R.C. § 7519(c)(2).

It is interesting that Congress adopted the Deposit Method for partnerships in the 1987 Act rather than an Interest Charge Method, which it adopted for installment sales also as part of the 1987 Act. They are both intended to achieve the same goal: eliminate the time value of money benefit that accompanies tax deferral. By taking the Deposit Method one step further, however, the U.S. Congress could transform the Deposit Method into the Interest Charge Method. The U.S. Congress could simply have partnerships compute the deposit as it does under Section 7519. Then, rather than having the partnership remit this amount or subtracting the net required payment balance and remitting the difference, the partnership would multiply it by an interest rate, say the applicable federal rate, and only pay this amount to the government. This interest amount would not be refundable to the partnership.

The obvious advantage to partnerships under an Interest Charge Method is that they would not use a significant amount of their cash to make the deposit as required under Section 7519 but rather use the significantly smaller amount of the interest on the deposit. The advantage to the government (and the partnership) is that it will not have to keep track of the deposit balance from year to year and determine when to require additional deposits or refund deposits, either during the life of the partnership or its liquidation. The Interest Charge Method is a one-time payment each year. If it is used, there is no running balance to keep track of from year to year. To illustrate, assume the partnership during its second applicable election year, computes its deposit to be $12,180. Under the Deposit Method, the partnership must pay this amount to the government. If Congress were to adopt the Interest Charge Method instead of the Deposit Method, then the partnership, using an applicable federal rate of 10 percent, would pay $1218 to the government ($12,180 times 10 percent). If the deposit were $12,180 during the third applicable election year and the applicable federal rate remained at 10 percent, then the partnership would pay another $1218 to the government. This would accomplish the same result as paying the full $12,180 and receiving it back when the partnership liquidates or terminates its Section 444 election.

Under the Deposit Method, the government has the use of the partnership's money. Under the Interest Charge Method, the government receives the *benefit* of the use of the partnership's money. In terms of eliminating the benefits of tax deferral, these two concepts are identical. In addition, if the government were to adopt the Interest Charge Method, the partnership ideally should receive a deduction for the interest paid to the government, which of course would flow through to the partners because the partnership is a transparent entity. This would achieve parity with the Deposit Method. Under the Deposit Method, the deposit that the partnership pays to the government constitutes a lost rate of return for the partnership. But this is offset by the lack of requirement to pay interest to the government. By offsetting each other, the partnership, in essence, is deducting interest that would be paid to the government.

B. Variation of the Deposit Method

An unusual technique to eliminate the benefits of tax deferral can be found with respect to certain mortgage guarantee insurance companies.[135] These companies can

[135] I.R.C. § 832(e).

deduct an amount required by law to be set aside in a reserve for mortgage guarantee insurance losses resulting from adverse economic cycles. But the tax savings from the deductions must be invested in a non-interest bearing, non-transferable U.S. government bond. These bonds are called "Mortgage Guaranty Insurance Company Tax and Loss Bonds." Because these bonds are non-interest bearing, this provision is really a type of Deposit Method. In essence, the taxes being deferred are deposited with the government by purchasing non-interest bearing, non-transferable bonds, so-called tax and loss bonds.

VI. Double Inclusion in Income Method

The Double Inclusion in Income Method is quite interesting. The taxpayer establishes a reserve fund for a future liability and deducts the full amount contributed into the fund. The taxpayer is then taxed each year on the earnings of the fund (which are kept in the fund) but also *deducts* the income taxes paid on the earnings. When money is paid out of the fund to settle a liability, no additional deduction is permitted to the taxpayer. When the fund is terminated, the taxpayer includes the amount in the fund (if any) that is returned to the taxpayer.

An example, given by the U.S. government but greatly simplified, will best demonstrate the Double Inclusion in Income Method. The taxpayer X, transferred in January 1991, $9000 of cash into a fund in a transaction treated as a contested liability. Generally, X established a reserve because it was not clear how much X owed the third party and therefore the amount of the deduction could not be determined in 1991. X deducted the entire $9000 deposited in the reserve fund in 1991. During 1991, the fund earned $600, for which X paid taxes on and deducted the taxes. During 1992, X settled the contested liability for $8000. As a result, $8000 was transferred from the fund to settle the liability and the remaining $1600 in the fund was returned to X. X included the entire $1600 in income in 1992.

Many U.S. commentators believed that X was being double taxed on $600 of the fund's earnings.[136] In other words, X was taxed on $600 of the fund's income in 1991. Then X is taxed on $1600 of the fund's assets in 1992. This latter amount appears to include the $600 of income that X was previously taxed on in 1991. Several commentators argued that X should only be taxed on $1000 of income in 1992. The reason for this apparent double taxation, however, is to compensate for the fact that X took too large a deduction in 1991 at too early in time. In other words, X should have taken an $8000 deduction in 1992 or the present value of $8000 discounted by one year to 1991. Because the $9000 deduction for 1991 essentially includes an expensing of an amount returned to X in 1992, an inclusion of this returned amount and income thereon in 1992 brings X to a zero tax situation. A greater inclusion is necessary to provide the government with a tax on X's pretax income on the amount. As a result, the example is really nothing new. Rather it is a somewhat complex variation of the Cary Brown model.

[136] See, e.g., Marianne Evans, "IRS' Kempson Explains Contested Liabilities Under Economic Performance Test," 48 *Tax Notes* 1463 (1990); Christopher H. Hanna, "The Virtual Reality of Eliminating Tax Deferral," 12 *Amer. J. Tax Pol'y* 449, 500 (1995).

The methodology of the example can be seen in the following four steps:

1. At the fund's pre-tax rate of return of 6.67 percent, the $8000 payment to the creditor consumes $7500 of the $9000 payment ($8000 divided by 1.0667) and the remaining $1500 of the payment ultimately returns to X.
2. The income on the $7500 is $500 (6.67 percent multiplied by $7500). It is taxed to X at 40 percent percent (assumed tax rate) of $500 or $200. X is allowed a deduction for this tax because it is an addition to the amount ultimately pass- ing to the creditor. In other words, X pays it and the creditor gets the pre-tax amount.
3. The income on the remaining $1500 is $100 (6.67 percent multiplied by $1500). It is taxed to X at 40 percent of $100 or $40. X is allowed a deduction for this tax because it is also an addition to the amount ultimately passing to the creditor and so there is no need to distinguish between the $200 tax on the $7500 and the $40 tax on the $1500. In other words, X pays it and the creditor gets the pre-tax amount. X is taxed on a net amount of $60. Essentially, the expensing of the $1500 made X and the government partners with respect to this amount ($900 net investment by X and $600 government invest- ment). The income from X's share (6.67 percent of $900 or $60) is taxed and the income from the government share's (6.67 percent of $600 or $40) is not taxed.
4. The $1600 received by X on the liquidation of the fund is included in gross income, resulting in a tax of $640, which consists of $600 to return to the government its share of the $1500 and $40 to pay the government its share of the income on the $1500. Since the tax on the liquidation merely pays over to the government its share of the $1500 and income thereon, X in essence bears no tax at the time of the liquidation, and the tax on X's share of the income, imposed when the income is realized is essentially the only tax on X.

This four-step methodology will now be discussed in greater detail using both pre-tax and after-tax rates of return.

In the above example, ideally X should have transferred and taken an $8000 deduction in 1992 when the contest was settled. This is the amount that the creditor was actually entitled to when the contest was settled. Or possibly, X could have taken a deduction in 1991 equal to the present value of an $8000 deduction discounted by one year. Using a pre-tax rate of return of 6.67 percent, X's deduction in 1991 would be $7500 ($8000 divided by 1.0667). Taking an $8000 deduction in year two yields equivalent results to taking a $7500 deduction in year one, discounted at a pre-tax rate of return, if the taxes on the earnings of the set aside funds are deductible. But instead, X took a $9000 deduction in 1991. This is $1500 too much ($9000 minus $7500), not merely $1000 too much.

The above example can be generalized algebraically. In the case of deductibility in year two, an amount A of income is reduced by tax t such that $A(1-t)$ may be invested. At an annual rate of return r, $A(1-t)$ invested will earn $rA(1-t)$ per year, which will be subject to tax at rate t equaling tax each year of $trA(1-t)$. The net annual after-tax position each year will be:

$$rA(1-t) - trA(1-t) \text{ which equals } rA(1-t)(1-t).$$

In the case of immediate deductibility, an amount A of income is not reduced by tax t such that A may be invested. At an annual rate of return r, A invested will earn rA per year, which will be subject to tax at rate t equaling tax each year of trA. In addition, interest income is generated each year in the amount of $rA(1-t)$, which is an after-tax rate of return. This is subject to tax at rate t equaling tax each year of $trA(1-t)$. The net annual after-tax position will be:

$$rA(1-t) - rAt(1-t) \text{ which equals } rA(1-t)(1-t).$$

This is equal to the net annual after-tax position when deductibility is delayed until the following year.

If a pre-tax rate of return is used in generating interest income in which an immediate deduction is allowed, the amount A of income is not reduced by tax t at the time of receipt. At an annual rate of return r, A invested will earn rA per year, which will be subject to tax at rate t equaling tax each year of trA. In addition, interest income is generated each year in the amount of rA, which is a pre-tax rate of return. This is subject to tax at rate t equaling tax each year of trA. The deduction of the tax will be $trAt$, leaving the taxpayer with a burden of $rAt - trAt$ which equals $rAt(1-t)$. The taxpayer's net annual after-tax position will be:

$$rA(1-t) - rAt(1-t) \text{ which equals } rA(1-t)(1-t).$$

In the above example, a pre-tax rate of return of 6.67 percent was used in computing the proper amount of deduction in 1991. If an after-tax rate of return of four percent was used, X's deduction in 1991 would be $7692.31. This will also yield equivalent results to taking an $8000 deduction in year two if the taxes on the earnings of the fund are *not* deductible.

By taking a $9000 deduction in 1991, which was $1500 too much (using a pre-tax rate of return with deductibility of the taxes on the earnings), X has, in essence, expensed an asset with a cost of $1500, which is an application of the Cary Brown model. If our tax system allowed X to do this, X would achieve the equivalence of exempting the income on cash or property that was contributed to the fund. During 1992, the fund earned income of $600. This amount can be bifurcated into the earnings on the proper amount that was contributed to the fund and the remainder is attributable to the excess amount. The proper amount that was contributed into the fund is $7500. This amount generated earnings of $500. The tax at a 40 percent rate equals $200. The excess amount of $1500 generated earnings of $100. The tax on this amount equals $40.

If X could immediately deduct $1500, then X only needs to initially set aside $900 at a 40 percent tax rate. By expensing the cost of the investment, X can increase the investment to $I/(1-t)$, where I is the amount of income to be invested and t is the tax rate. In this case, it would be $900/(1 − 0.40) equaling $1500. Cary Brown would describe the government as being a partner with X, with X contributing $900 and the government contributing $600. At a pre-tax rate of return of 6.67 percent, the set aside funds of $1500 will earn $100 of which X must pay $40 in taxes. If the taxes are deductible and the original $1500 plus the investment return of $100 is included in X's gross income the beginning of the second year when the contest is settled, this is equivalent to never having set aside the excess $1500. The following chart demonstrates this, assuming $1500 of gross income in year one and zero gross income in year two:

	No set aside ($)	Set aside ($)
Gross income	1500	1500
Deduction	0	1500
Taxable income	1500	0
Taxes (40%)	600	0
Investment	900	1500
Investment return (6.67%)	60	100
Taxes (40%)	24	24 ($40 of taxes less $16 if taxes are deductible)
After-taxes	936	1576
Gross income	0	1600 (inclusion of $1600 from termination of the fund)
Deductions	0	0
Taxable income	0	1600
Taxes (40%)	0	640
Investment	936	936

By allowing X to deduct the taxes paid on the earnings of the fund of $1500 and then requiring X to include $1600 in gross income at the beginning of year two when the contest is settled, X will be in the same position as if X never contributed the $1500 to the fund. Or, in the alternative, at the beginning of year two, X by including $1600 in gross income and paying $640 in taxes on this amount is merely returning the government's portion as a partner. The government originally put up $600 for one year at a 6.67 percent rate of return and the government is getting this amount back totaling $640 ($600 plus 6.67 percent multiplied by $600). The benefits of the Cary Brown model, which X received in year one by immediately deducting $1500 into a fund that X would eventually receive back, have been recaptured by X in year two. Tax deferral has been eliminated through yet another method.

Probably, the easiest method to eliminating tax deferral in the case of contested liabilities is a wait and see approach. The funds that are set aside are earning a rate of return that is still taxed to the settler of the fund. In other words, for tax purposes, it is as if the settler still has the use of the funds because the settler is taxed on the earnings of the funds. If the U.S. Congress were to allow a deduction when the contest is settled rather than when the money (or property) is set aside into a fund, then no tax deferral is taking place and no need exists to have a Double Inclusion in Income Method when the contest is settled.

Chapter 7

Summary of the Various Methods

I. Introduction

In recent years, the U.S. government has developed and implemented at least five general methods of eliminating the benefits of tax deferral, each of which has been described in the previous chapter. Some of these general methods contained a number of sub-methods, each of which utilized the same basic principle underlying the general method but mechanically were very different. All five general methods are intended to eliminate the benefits of tax deferral, which they do. Although eliminating the benefits of tax deferral is an important goal of the government, it would be ideal if the government could select one method and utilize it on all occasions or, at least, on as many occasions as possible. Admittedly, however, it may not be possible to have one method that can apply in all situations.

II. Interest Charge Method

The interest charge method appears to be a very straightforward and in most cases a relatively simple method of eliminating tax deferral. It is a payment to the government, which the government retains. There is no need for the taxpayer to keep a balance with the government or for the government to refund money at some point in time as it does under the Deposit Method. In addition, the Interest Charge Method, at least the Annual Method, requires a relatively simple calculation to be performed once at the end of each year. The Interest Charge Method is also more direct than the other methods. It results in the amount owed to the government rather than the amount of a deposit (under the Deposit Method), or the amount of imputed income (under the Deferral of Income with Imputed Interest Method) that must then be included in income to determine the amount of additional taxes owed to the government.

The Interest Charge Method as currently implemented by the U.S. government has its disadvantages. One major disadvantage appears to be that the U.S. government uses the highest tax rate in the income tax laws instead of the taxpayer's marginal tax rate, which would be a more accurate measure, in computing the amount of deferred taxes. This problem could be easily corrected by adopting the taxpayer's marginal tax rate for each year in which the computation is made. This, of course, could lead to administrative problems but would be more accurate than simply using the highest tax rate in the income tax laws. A second disadvantage to the Interest Charge Method is that the U.S. government treats the interest as interest on a tax deficiency, which is nondeductible personal interest for a non-corporate taxpayer. As demonstrated earlier, the non-deductibility of the interest destroys the parity that the Interest Charge Method was intended to create. As a result, the interest should be deductible by all taxpayers unless the government charges interest at an after-tax rate of return, in which case the interest is, in essence, already deducted.

Finally, the rate of interest charged by the government may be substantially different than the taxpayer's rate of return. Depending on which rate is greater, this could be advantageous or disadvantageous to the taxpayer or the government. Ideally, the rate of interest charged by the government should equal the taxpayer's rate of return, either on its investments or its borrowings. Determining each taxpayer's rate of return, however, would lead to great administrative difficulties.

There are situations in which the Interest Charge Method has traditionally not been used. For example, it traditionally applies to transactions in which income is recognized but not with respect to claims for deductions. It could easily be adapted so that it would apply to deductions. If a taxpayer ultimately took too large a deduction in a particular year, the taxpayer could be forced to pay interest to the government when the correct amount of the deduction is determined in a later year, similar to the interest charge for the PFIC regime.[1] In addition, it appears that the Annual Method of the Interest Charge Method can be used for all installment sales rather than having a different method for dealers in timeshares and residential lots. Also, the Interest Charge Method appears to be adaptable for use by automobile dealers in deferring income as opposed to the Deferral of Income Imputed Interest Method. It could also be used by partnerships adopting a fiscal year instead of the Deposit Method that is currently in use.

More important than adopting and implementing one method for preventing tax deferral, however, is ensuring that each of the methods currently in place prevents tax deferral in a fair and equitable manner. Unfortunately, the current provisions of the U.S. income tax laws do not achieve this result. As previously mentioned, under the Interest Charge Method, the interest should be deductible even if paid by a non-corporate taxpayer. In addition, in computing the amount of deferred tax liability, it appears that a more accurate measure would be to use the taxpayer's marginal tax rate instead of the highest income tax rate. Finally, the rate of interest charged by the

[1] The U.S. Congress has utilized the Interest Charge Method with respect to depreciation deductions as part of the Small Business Job Protection Act of 1996, Pub. L. No. 104–188, Section 1604(a). It applies with respect to the income forecast method of depreciation. I.R.C. § 167(g). Generally, the income forecast method of depreciation applies to motion picture films, video tape, sound recordings, copyrights, books, and patents. The amount of depreciation each year is dependent upon the income earned in the current year and the estimated total income from the property for the 10 years after the year in which the property was placed in service. If it is determined in a later year that the depreciation deduction is too large in an early year, then the taxpayer owes interest to the government. If, however, the depreciation deduction is determined to be too small in an early year, then the government owes the taxpayer interest.

government should be equal to the taxpayer's rate of return on investments or borrowings.

III. Immediate Inclusion in Income Method

The Immediate Inclusion of Income Method is probably the most direct method of preventing tax deferral. If a taxpayer is forced to recognize income each year, by, for example, repealing a particular provision allowing deferral or the more radical approach of adopting mark-to-market accounting, no tax deferral is taking place except within a particular year. Implementation of a mark to market method would force the income tax system closer to the Haig–Simons model, which most tax theorists feel is the ideal definition of income. With the increasing use of derivatives in business transactions, a mark to mark method of accounting may be the only solution to preventing tax deferral in an equitable manner.

There are the obvious disadvantages to the Immediate Inclusion of Income Method, including possible lack of liquidity to pay the tax liability. In addition, valuation and administrative problems would arise under a mark-to-market regime.

IV. Deferral of Income with Imputed Interest Method

The Deferral of Income with Imputed Interest Method also does not prevent tax deferral in a completely equitable manner. In computing the amount of imputed income each year, it appears that an after-tax rate of return should be used as opposed to a pre-tax rate of return. Under the current U.S. provisions applicable to automobile dealers selling extended warranty contracts, which employ a pre-tax rate of return, the taxpayer is better off by immediately including the prepayment in gross income. This lack of parity seems to violate the objective of the Deferral of Income with Imputed Interest Method, which is to provide relief to taxpayers in terms of cash flow, yet still achieve parity in terms of tax consequences. In addition, from a strictly theoretical standpoint, using a single rate of interest to compute the amount of imputed income each year seems to lead to inaccurate results.[2] The amount of imputed income each year may be inconsistent with economic reality because short-term rates differ from long-term rates and also the term of the deferral keeps getting shorter as time passes.[3] As a practical matter, however, the use of a single rate of

---

[2] See, e.g., Joseph Bankman and William A. Klein, "Accurate Taxation of Long-Term Debt: Taking Into Account the Term Structure of Interest," 44 *Tax L. Rev.* 335 (1989); Bruce Kayle, "Where Has All the Income Gone? The Mysterious Relocation of Interest and Principal in Coupon Stripping and Related Transactions," 7 *Va. Tax Rev.* 303 (1987); Theodore S. Sims, "Long-Term Debt, the Term Structure of Interest and the Case for Accrual Taxation," 47 *Tax L. Rev.* 313 (1992).

[3] See Bankman and Klein, *supra* note 2, at 336.

interest is probably the best method based in large part because of simplicity and materiality.[4]

V. Deposit Method

The Deposit Method also has its advantages and disadvantages. The use of the highest individual rate plus one percent for determining the amount of the deposit is too high. Prior to the 1993 Act, the highest individual rate was 31 percent and the maximum corporate rate was 34 percent. As a result, the rate under the Deposit Method of Section 7519 was 32 percent (31 percent plus one percent). Use of a 32 percent rate could be justified, however, because if a partnership had corporate partners, the corporate partners could be subject to tax at a top rate of 34 percent and achieve a three percentage point deferral if the lower 31 percent individual rate was used in calculating the deposit. The 31 percent plus one percent rate presented a compromise for partnerships, which may have a combination of individual and corporate partners. After the 1993 Act, however, the rate under Section 7519 is 40.6 percent, which is one percent above the individual rate and 5.6 percent above the corporate rate.[5] This rate no longer offers a compromise but rather provides a rate that is above both the individual and corporate rates. Consequently, as a practical matter, it appears that fewer partnerships will want to make the fiscal year election under Section 444 today.

In addition, by making the deposit under Section 7519, the partnership not only loses a rate of return on the money but also does not make a direct interest payment to the government. In other words, it is as if the partnership paid the government, as a deductible interest payment, its rate of return on the deposited funds. As a result, parity is achieved because the partnership's rate of return equals the government's rate of interest charge and the partnership receives the equivalence of a deduction so that a wash takes place. Thus, the Deposit Method offers an advantage over the Interest Charge Method in which the government treats the interest payment as personal interest for non-corporate taxpayers.

VI. Double Inclusion in Income Method

The Double Inclusion Method is a relatively simple method of preventing tax deferral. It seems to be just as easy to adopt a wait-and-see approach. Under a wait-and-see approach, the government would disallow a deduction for a contested liability until the contest is settled. The U.S. Congress has adopted this approach for workers

---

[4] See Boris I. Bittker and Lawrence Lokken, Federal Taxation of Income, Estates and Gifts ¶56.2 (1994 Supplement).

[5] See Ann. 94–5, 1994-2 I.R.B. 39, in which the Service reminds partnerships and S corporations that the rate under Sections 444 and 7519 has been increased to 40.6 percent.

compensation and torts as part of the Tax Reform Act of 1984.[6] Under Section 461(h), an accrual method taxpayer cannot deduct a liability arising from workers compensation or tort until payment is made.[7] Treasury has extended this requirement for other types of liabilities of an accrual method taxpayer.[8] On the other hand, the advantage to the Double Inclusion Method, aside from the obvious fact that the taxpayer's deduction is accelerated, is that it more closely follows accrual method of accounting. A wait-and-see approach would be closer to the cash method of accounting.

VII. New Proposals

A. *Professor Alan Auerbach's Approach*

Professor Alan Auerbach, an economics professor at the University of California at Berkeley, has proposed a method for eliminating tax deferral that includes the Interest Charge Method.[9] He suggests retaining the realization doctrine but treating the asset as increasing in value by the risk-free rate of return from the date of acquisition to the date of realization. At realization, he proposes taxing the realized gain and charging interest on the deferral of the gain to the point of realization. As a result, basis is irrelevant as is the actual increase or decrease in value each year.

An example will best illustrate the Auerbach approach. Assume property is purchased for 50*u*. It is sold two years later for 1210*u*. The risk-free rate of return is assumed to be 10 percent annually. The sales proceeds of 1210*u* is treated as having been accumulated at the 10 percent risk-free rate of return from the acquisition date to the sales date. This would result in 210*u* of gain (1210*u* minus 1000*u*). The basis in the property is irrelevant. In addition, the actual timing of the increase in value of the property is irrelevant.

An interest charge based on the risk-free rate of return would also be imposed at the time the gain of 210*u* was triggered on realization. The interest charge would compensate the government for the deferral of imputed gain that took place over the previous two years. The first year, the property was deemed to increase in value by 100*u* (1000*u* multiplied by 10 percent). The second year, the property was deemed to increase in value by 110*u* (1100*u* multiplied by 10 percent). Assuming a 40% tax rate, the tax owed for the first year is 40*u*. The tax owed for the second year is 44*u*. Because the tax of 40*u* for the first year was deferred by one year, interest is charged at the risk-free rate of return of 10 percent. The interest for one year is 4*u* (40*u* multiplied by 10 percent). If the interest is deductible, then the taxpayer will have a deduction of 1.60*u*.

---

6 Pub. L. No. 98-369, Section 91(a) (1984).

7 I.R.C. § 461(h)(2)(C).

8 Treas. Reg. § 1.461–4(g) (payment constitutes economic performance for liabilities arising under a workers compensation act, tort, breach of contract, or violation of law; rebates and refunds; awards, prizes, and jackpots; insurance, warranty, and service contracts; certain taxes; and certain other liabilities).

9 See Alan J. Auerbach, "Retrospective Capital Gains Taxation," 81 *Amer. Econ. Rev.* 167 (1991).

The taxpayer will be left with 1123.60*u* (1210*u* (sales proceeds) minus 84*u* (taxes) minus 4*u* (interest on deferred tax) plus 1.60*u* (taxes saved by deducting the interest on deferred tax)) on the sales date. This would be the result whether the taxpayer originally paid 100*u*, 20*u*, or 15,000*u* for the property. The basis is irrelevant.

B. Professor David Bradford's Addition

Professor David Bradford, an economics professor at Princeton University, has proposed an addition to Professor Auerbach's method for eliminating tax deferral and also retained the use of adjusted basis.[10] Under Professor Bradford's approach, the taxpayer must select a gain reference date ("GRD") at the time the property is acquired.[11] The acquired property is treated as increasing in value by the risk-free rate of return beginning on the date of acquisition. The increase is added to the basis of the property. Then, at the GRD, the taxpayer must determine the gain or loss using a present value discounted at the risk-free rate of return. The actual tax is paid on the sales date with an interest charge on gain from the GRD to the sales date.

An example will demonstrate the Bradford addition. Assume property is purchased for 50*u*. The taxpayer selects the GRD as one year from the date of acquisition. The property is sold for 1210*u* after the taxpayer has held it for two years. The risk-free rate of return is assumed to be ten percent annually. The taxpayer is taxed on 5*u* during the first year, which is the risk-free rate of return on the purchase price. In addition, the purchase price of 50*u* is treated as increasing by the 10 percent risk-free rate of return from the acquisition date to the GRD. Therefore, on the GRD, the basis is 55*u* (50*u* purchase price plus 5*u*). On the GRD, the present value needs to be determined using the sales price discounted at the risk-free rate of return. Because the property has not been sold yet, the calculation of the present value has to be suspended.

At the end of two years, the property is sold for 1210*u*. This amount is discounted at the 10 percent risk-free rate of return to the GRD giving a present value of 1100*u*. Therefore, the amount of gain (or loss) on the GRD is 1045*u* (1100*u* minus 55*u*). As a result, the taxpayer will include 5*u* of income in year one based on the 10 percent risk-free rate of return and pay tax on that amount. In year two, the taxpayer will include 110*u* in income again based on the 10 percent risk-free rate of return applied to the present value of 1100*u* and also include gain of 1045*u*. The gain will attract an interest charge of 104.50*u*, which is based on the 10 percent risk-free rate of return for one year. The interest charge compensates the government for the deferral of the gain that was deemed to take place on the GRD. On the sales date, the taxpayer will be left with 685.30*u* (1210*u* (sales proceeds) minus 44*u* (tax on risk-free rate of return) minus 418*u* (tax on gain) minus 104.50*u* (interest charge) plus 41.80*u* (taxes saved by deducting the interest)).

---

[10] David F. Bradford, "Fixing Realization Accounting: Symmetry, Consistency and Correctness in the Taxation of Financial Instruments," 50 *Tax L. Rev.* 731, 770–82 (1995).

[11] At the time of acquisition, the tax authorities or the taxpayer also select a gain tax rate ("GTR"). This is the rate of tax that will apply to the gain (or loss) on the GRD. In the example in the text, the GTR is not relevant because of the assumption that the tax rate is 40 percent.

Chapter 8

Conclusion

The United States has been at the forefront in addressing tax deferral issues and devising methods of preventing deferral. The primary reason appears to be one of equity. For example, the U.S. Congress enacted the PFIC rules in 1986 to equalize the tax treatment of U.S. investors in domestic and offshore investment funds. The U.S. Congress also enacted the Interest Charge Method for installment sales to equalize the treatment of sellers of property for cash and sellers of property for an installment note. The downside to making the tax rules more equitable, however, is the complexity it generates. Utilizing the example with the PFIC, the U.S. Congress now has three different taxing schemes under the PFIC rules to eliminate the time value of money benefit of U.S. investors investing in an offshore investment fund. A further example of complexity to achieve equity is the two different methods of the Interest Charge Method to eliminate the tax deferral benefit in installment sales. Clearly, one method for all installment sales should suffice.

The United States should continue to eliminate the benefits of tax deferral unless a strong policy reason is advanced to permit the benefits of deferral in a given situation. But it would appear to make sense, from both an equitable and simplicity standpoint, to focus on one or two methods for eliminating deferral. Having numerous methods makes the tax laws more complex without a rational policy reason for doing so.

Japan is in the early stages of attacking tax deferral. It has utilized an Interest Charge Method since 1962 for pension plans. It is very interesting that Japan has attacked the tax deferral benefit generated by pension plans while the United States expressly endorses the benefit. Japan has also adopted mark-to-market in very limited circumstances. It will be interesting to see whether Japan expands its use of mark-to-market the way that the United States has in the last 10 years. It will also be interesting to see how Japan attacks the tax deferral benefit in many of the areas of its tax laws. Hopefully, Japan will focus on one or two methods, such as the Interest Charge Method and mark-to-market, instead of developing a number of different methods.

Appendix

History of the Japanese Income Tax System

I. Introduction

In the late 1860s, a new administration headed by Emperor Meiji overthrew the 250-year reign of the Shogun Administration. This episode, culminating in 1868, became known as the Meiji Restoration or Meiji Ishin, leading to the end of feudalism in Japan. A number of political changes took place after the Meiji Restoration, including the re-establishment of the Ministry of Finance (or Ōkura-shō) in 1869.[1] The name Ōkura-shō literally means Ministry of the Big Storehouse, deriving its name because taxes were traditionally paid in rice. The Ōkura-shō would become responsible for creating and administering the Japanese tax laws.

Until the Meiji Restoration, much of Japan's tax revenues derived from the land tax.[2] In fact, the land tax accounted for over 80 percent of Japan's total tax revenue.[3] In 1872, Japan reformed the land tax, changing the tax base from the crop to the value of the land, fixing the tax rate, and requiring payment in cash rather than in kind.[4]

In 1885, Hirobumi Ito became Japan's first official Prime Minister and headed a government that introduced the income tax system to Japan in March 1887.[5] Apparently, a dispute exists as to exactly how Japan adopted the income tax in 1887.[6] The late Hosei University Professor Isamu Abe believed that the income tax law draft prepared by Count Masayoshi Matsukata in December 1884, was the basis for Japan's adoption of an income tax system.[7] The late Kyoto University Professor Saburo Shiomi believed that a draft of the revenue tax law contained in a letter dated

---

[1] See Eamonn Fingleton, *Blindside: Why Japan is Still on Track to Overtake the U.S. by the Year 2000* 137 (1995).

[2] See Morio Uematsu, "Computation of Income in Japanese Income Taxation: A Study in the Adjustment of Theory to Reality in Law," in *Law in Japan: The Legal Order in a Changing Society* (Arthur Taylor von Mehren ed., 1963) at 567, 569 fn. 8 (citing to 6 *Meiji Taisho Zaisei Shi* (A History of Meiji-Taisho Public Finance) 530–32 (Ministry of Finance ed. 1937)); Ministry of Finance, Tax Bureau, *An Outline of Japanese Taxes 1997* at 1. The late Kyoto University Law Professor Saburo Shiomi wrote that, prior to the adoption of the income tax in 1887, "Japan had depended on her traditional taxes – land and liquor." Saburo Shiomi, *Japan's Finance and Taxation 1940–1956* (1957) at 114.

[3] See MOF 1997, *supra* note 2, at 1. [4] See *id.* [5] See Shiomi, *supra* note 2, at 114–15.

[6] See *id.* [7] *Id.* at 114.

29 November 1874, sent by a German financial advisor named Rudolff to Hirobumi Ito was the basis for Japan's income tax system.[8] As a result, Professor Shiomi believed that the Japanese income tax system owes its beginning to the Western tax system.[9]

The government introduced the income tax as a source for additional revenue in their quest of "nation building."[10] Consequently, Japan became one of the first countries in the world with an income tax system.[11] The income tax system had a very modest beginning. It was levied on the aggregate income of every individual with rates ranging from one percent to three percent with an exemption allowance of 300 yen.[12] In 1888, only 118,600 people out of a total population of 39 million paid the income tax.[13] The income tax generated about one and a half percent of total tax revenue, with the land tax generating over 50 percent of total tax revenue.[14] The land tax continued to be the most important source of government revenue until 1908, gradually being replaced by indirect taxes, e.g., liquor tax.[15] By 1935, however, the

---

[8] *Id.* [9] *Id.* at 114–15.

[10] See Uematsu, *supra* note 2, at 569. Professor Shiomi has written that "[i]ts [the income tax] immediate purpose was to alleviate the tax on certain products in Hokkaido . . . ." Shiomi, *supra* note 2, at 114.

[11] The other countries that had previously adopted an income tax system were Great Britain (1799), Switzerland (1840), Prussia (1851), the United States (1862), Italy (1864), Serbia (1884), and South Australia (1884). See Uematsu, *supra* note 2, at 569 fn. 7; see also Shiomi, *supra* note 2, at 139–41 (listing the above mentioned countries except for Prussia using Johannes Popitz: *Einkommensteur Handworterbuch der Staatswissenschaften*, 4th ed., Vol. III, secs. 437–91 as authority).

[12] See MOF 1997, *supra* note 2, at 2; see also Shiomi, *supra* note 2, at 142 (table 26). The exemption amount was 300 yen. The rate schedule was as follows:

0–300 yen	0%
300–1000 yen	1.0%
1000–10,000 yen	1.5%
10,000–20,000 yen	2.0%
20,000–30,000 yen	2.5%
Over 30,000 yen	3.0%

Shiomi, *supra* note 2, at 142 (table 26).

[13] See MOF 1997, *supra* note 2, at 1.

[14] See Uematsu, *supra* note 2, at 569 fn. 8 ("In 1887, the income tax produced 527,724 yen ($406,347) and in 1888, 1,066,894 yen ($789,502) – 0.8 percent and 1.8 percent of the total tax revenues for these years, respectively. By comparison, the revenue from the land tax in the same two years was 42,152,171 yen ($32,457,172) and 34,650,528 yen ($25,641,391).") As a result, the land tax's percentage is approximately 63.9 percent and 58.5 percent for 1887 and 1888, respectively. The figures used by Uematsu are from Ministry of Finance, 6 *Meiji Taisho Zaisei Shi* (A History of Meiji-Taisho Public Finance) 530–32. The dollar–yen exchange rate is from *Gaikoku Kawase Gairon* (A General Treatise on Foreign Exchange) appendix table 11 (1957).

The Ministry of Finance currently states that the income tax accounted for only 1.5 percent of total tax revenue in 1888 while the land tax accounted for 53.8 percent of total tax revenue in 1888. See MOF 1997, *supra* note 2, at 1.

Despite the slight discrepancies in the two authorities, the land tax was a significant source of tax revenue in the late 1880s, while the income tax generated a relatively insignificant amount of tax revenue. See Shiomi, *supra* note 2, at 136–37 (table 24).

[15] See MOF 1997, *supra* note 2, at 1. Professor Shiomi wrote that prior to the adoption of the income tax in 1887, "Japan had depended on her traditional taxes – land and liquor." Shiomi, *supra* note 2, at 114. In addition, the revenue derived solely from the liquor tax did not exceed the revenue derived from the land tax until 1909. See Shiomi, *supra* note 2, at 136.

income tax became the most important single item of tax revenue.[16] It was also the year when tax reform became a major concern.[17]

II. The Period from 1899 to 1920

The income tax system adopted in 1887 was primarily a copy of existing income tax systems of other countries.[18] In 1899, Japan started to tailor the income tax system to better suit its needs and also to raise revenue for the government in light of the Sino-Japanese War that had just taken place. The law of 1899 included five major revisions to the tax laws.[19] First, a taxpayer's tax liability became dependent on domicile, residence, and location of items of income and deductions.[20] Second, the income tax was divided into three classes thus introducing schedular taxation: Class I included the corporate income tax; Class II included interest income; and Class III included individual income other than Class II interest income.[21] Individuals were not taxed on dividends received from corporations thus preventing double taxation of corporate earnings. The third revision involved the calculation of taxable income in each class.[22] Classes I and III were calculated using a net approach (income minus deductions) while Class II was calculated using a gross approach (total amount received). The fourth revision provided proportional tax rates for Classes I and II and a number of progressive tax rates for Class III.[23] The rate on Class I was 2.5 percent, Class II was 2 percent, and Class III rates ranged from 1 percent to 5.5 percent.[24] Finally, certain procedural matters were transferred from local authorities to the Tax Affairs Supervision Bureau.[25]

The tax laws were revised again in 1904 and 1905, generally increasing the tax burden to finance the Russo-Japanese War of 1904–05.[26] But the increased tax burden fell on Class I and Class III income.[27] The Japanese government did not increase the tax rates on Class II income (interest income).[28] In fact, in 1905, the government eased the tax burden on Class II income by exempting from tax the interest income on government bonds issued after 1904 for military purposes.[29] Four years later, the government exempted interest income on all government bonds without regard to the purpose of the issuance.[30]

Several major improvements were introduced in 1913. First, the progressive nature of the rates were changed, with an increase in the number of rates and an increase in their progressivity, ranging from 2.5 percent to 22 percent for Class III income.[31] Japan also introduced an employment income deduction for the first time,

---

[16] See MOF 1997, *supra* note 2, at 1. Actually, during the years 1918 through 1922 and the year 1925, the income tax generated more tax revenue than either the land tax or the liquor tax. See Shiomi, *supra* note 2, at 136–37 (table 24). Beginning in 1935 and all subsequent years, the income tax once again generated more tax revenue than either the land tax or the liquor tax. See Shiomi, *supra* note 2, at 136–37 (table 24) and 140 (table 25).

[17] See Shiomi, *supra* note 2, at 33. [18] See *id.* at 115–16. [19] *Id.* at 118.

[20] *Id.* [21] *Id.* [22] *Id.* [23] *Id.*

[24] See MOF 1997, *supra* note 2, at 2; see also Shiomi, *supra* note 2, at 142 (table 26).

[25] See Shiomi, *supra* note 2, at 118. [26] See *id.* at 118–19. [27] *Id.*

[28] *Id.* [29] *Id.* at 119. [30] *Id.* [31] *Id.* at 120; see also *id.* at 142 (table 26).

which was equal to 10 percent of the taxpayer's employment income.[32] Five years later, Japan increased the tax rates again, in large part, due to Japan's participation in World War I.[33]

III. The Period from 1920 to 1940

After World War I, Japan entered a period of great prosperity, which led to an uneven distribution of wealth.[34] This led to the changes in the tax law revision of 1920. It should be noted that the 1920 changes were the first changes to the tax laws that were not revenue driven.[35] The corporate income tax, Class I, was substantially changed with the introduction of five components of the corporate income tax.[36] These five components included: a reserve tax on undistributed corporate earnings, a dividend tax on corporate earnings paid out in the form of dividends, a liquidation tax on any corporate surplus when a corporation liquidated, excess tax for corporate income exceeding 10 percent of the operating capital, and a corporate income tax on foreign corporations.[37] In addition, an individual was taxed on receiving dividends with partial relief from double taxation provided by allowing a 40 percent deduction of the amount of the dividends.[38] Class II income was expanded to include interest on term deposits.[39] Class III income was also substantially revised with a more targeted approach to aggregate income taxation as opposed to withholding income taxation.[40] The tax rates were increased to 0.5 percent to 36 percent.[41] In addition, an exemption amount for dependents was provided for the first time.[42]

In 1926, Japan enacted major changes to the corporate income tax.[43] The progressive reserve tax on undistributed corporate earnings was abolished thereby bringing it into line with the proportional dividend tax on earnings paid out in the form of dividends.[44] Corporations would be taxed at a proportional five percent on their earnings, regardless of whether it was retained or paid out in the form of dividends.[45] As a result, corporations would not be forced to pay out all of their earnings to avoid the punitive nature of the progressive tax rates on undistributed corporate earnings.[46] Corporations were also permitted to deduct taxes paid on Class II income to avoid double taxation on that income.[47]

IV. The 1940 Tax Reform

A number of changes were made to the income tax system culminating in major tax reform in 1940.[48] In 1940, the income tax system was divided into an individual

---

32 See MOF 1997, *supra* note 2, at 2. 33 See Shiomi, *supra* note 2, at 120–21.
34 See *id.* at 123. 35 *Id.* 36 *Id.* at 124. 37 *Id.*
38 See MOF 1997, *supra* note 2, at 2. 39 See *id.* 40 See Shiomi, *supra* note 2, at 125.
41 See *id.* at 143. 42 *Id.* at 125. 43 *Id.* 44 *Id.* at 125–26. 45 *Id.* at 126.
46 *Id.* at 125. 47 *Id.* at 126.
48 See generally Uematsu, *supra* note 2, at 571 ("Together with the subsequent alteration inspired by [Dr. Carl S.] Shoup, the 1940 changes formed one of the two most far-reaching tax reforms in modern Japanese history.").

income tax and a corporate income tax adopting a pattern used by the United States and Germany.[49] The individual income tax was divided into further parts: a schedular income tax and a comprehensive income tax, adopting a pattern used by England and France.[50] Apparently, Japan was attempting to adopt the income tax systems of various advanced countries of the world.[51] The schedular income tax categorized income into one of six categories or baskets of income: (1) real property income, (2) dividends and interest income, (3) business income, (4) employment income, (5) timber income, and (6) retirement income.[52] Different rates applied to each of the different categories of income.[53] Apparently, one reason for the schedular income tax is that the Japanese thought that "the ability to pay differs with the type of income – it is strongest with income from assets (capital), stronger with business income from assets and labor combined, and weakest with earned income."[54] A second reason was the ability of the Japanese tax authorities to increase the proportional rates of the schedular income tax to raise revenue for the war effort.[55] A basic exemption also applied to categories three, four, and five: business income, employment income, and timber income.[56] In addition, a withholding tax of six percent was imposed on employment income.[57] The comprehensive income tax applied to aggregate income at rates ranging from 10 percent to 65 percent, with the highest rate applying at income of 800,000 yen or more ($187,520).[58]

See Saburo Shiomi, The Reform of the Tax System, 15 *Kyoto U. Econ. Rev.* at 36–52 (1940) for a detailed description of the 1940 tax reform; see also Shiomi, *supra* note 2, at 33–52 for a detailed description of the 1940 tax reform based on his earlier article.

[49] See, e.g., Uematsu, *supra* note 2, at 571; MOF 1997, *supra* note 2, at 3; Shiomi, *supra* note 2, at 127.

[50] See Shiomi, *supra* note 2, at 127.

[51] See *id.* at 127.

[52] See MOF 1997, *supra* note 2, at 3.

[53] See *id.* The rates were as follows on the six categories of income:

(1) Real property income – 10 percent
(2) Dividend and interest income – 10 percent (Class A, on national bonds – 4 percent; local bonds – 9 percent; others – 10 percent; Class B – 7.5 percent)
(3) Business income – (Class A – 8.5 percent; Class B – 7.5 percent)
(4) Employment Income – 6 percent
(5) Timber income – under 1600 yen – 5 percent; over 1600 yen – 7.5 percent
(6) Retirement income – under 20,000 yen – six percent; 20,000 yen to 100,000 yen – 12 percent; 100,000 yen to 500,000 yen – 25 percent; over 500,000 yen – 40 percent

Shiomi, *supra* note 2, at 127–28 and 143 (table 26).

[54] Uematsu, *supra* note 2, at 572.

[55] See *id.*

[56] See Shiomi, *supra* note 2, at 143 (table 26); see also MOF 1997, *supra* note 2, at 3 (listing only categories three and four, business income and employment income, as having a basic exemption).

[57] See MOF 1997, *supra* note 2, at 3.

[58] See Shiomi, *supra* note 2, at 128; See also Uematsu, *supra* note 2, at 572 (fn. 23). The rate schedule was as follows:

0–5000 yen	0 percent
5001–8000 yen	10 percent
8001–12,000 yen	15 percent
12,001–20,000 yen	20 percent
20,001–30,000 yen	25 percent
30,001–50,000 yen	30 percent

The corporate income tax was imposed on normal income, liquidation income, and capital income.[59] It was imposed at a flat 18 percent tax rate if the corporation had its head office or principal places of business within the area where the corporation tax was enforced, i.e., a domestic corporation.[60] If the corporation did not have its head office or principal places of business where the corporation tax was enforced, i.e., a foreign corporation, then the rate was 28 percent.[61] The rate was 18 percent on liquidation income and 0.15 percent on capital income.[62] This was not Japan's first experience with the corporate income tax. Japan had previously introduced the corporate income tax in 1899, shortly after its victory in the Sino-Japanese War, with a tax rate of 2.5 percent.[63]

As a result of the reforms in 1940, direct taxes accounted for about 64 percent of Japan's total tax revenues in 1941.[64] The primary components of the direct taxes were the individual income tax and the corporate income tax.

V. World War II and its Immediate Aftermath

The end of World War II left the Japanese economy in shambles and also hampered it with incredibly high inflation.[65] The dual income tax system, which was adopted in 1940, was repealed in 1947 primarily due to the high inflation after the war.[66] It

50,001–80,000 yen	35 percent
80,001–120,000 yen	40 percent
120,001–200,000 yen	45 percent
200,001–300,000 yen	50 percent
300,001–500,000 yen	55 percent
500,001–800,000 yen	60 percent
Over 800,000 yen	65 percent

Shiomi, *supra* note 2, at 128 and 143 (table 26).

[59] See Shiomi, *supra* note 2, at 128.

[60] See Shiomi, *supra* note 2, at 128; See also MOF 1997, *supra* note 2, at 3.

[61] See Shiomi, *supra* note 2, at 128.

[62] See *id.* at 128. [63] See MOF 1997, *supra* note 2, at 2.

[64] See *id.* at 3. According to Professor Shiomi, in 1941, income tax and corporation tax, the two primary but not only components of direct taxes, generated tax revenues of 1,401,363 yen and 534,907 yen, respectively. As a result, the percentage of income and corporation taxes to total revenue was 39.28%. The land tax was not included in total revenue because it was transferred from national revenue to local revenue. See Shiomi, *supra* note 2, at 140 (table 25).

[65] Dr. Joseph M. Dodge, who was serving as advisor to the Allied Forces, is credited with bringing inflation under control in Japan after the end of World War II. He stressed that the maintenance of a balanced budget was necessary to control inflation. See MOF 1997, *supra* note 2, at 6. The Dodge Line is the name that was given to Dr. Dodge's program to control inflation. Although the Dodge Line was successful in controlling inflation, it led to a great depression in Japan. See Hiromitsu Ishi, *The Japanese Tax System* 28 (2d Ed. 1993).

[66] See Ishi, *supra* note 65, at 4.

was replaced with a single comprehensive income tax (or global tax) with highly progressive rates.[67] In addition, prior to 1947, tax officials calculated and assessed an income tax on business income based on the previous year's income.[68] In 1947, the government introduced the American self-assessment system thereby requiring a taxpayer to pay income tax based on the taxpayer's current year's income.[69] The tax rates ranged from 20 percent to 75 percent with the withholding tax applying to earned income, dividends, and interest.[70] In general, the 1947 tax reform was based on the American system.[71] In addition, the corporation tax was also revised based on the American model.[72] The rate for domestic corporations was set at 35 percent, and for foreign corporations, it was set at 45 percent.[73] In 1949, the government established the National Tax Administration to enforce the tax laws more efficiently and to remove this function from the Tax Bureau of the MOF.[74]

VI. The Shoup Mission

A. *Introduction*

In 1948, the Supreme Commander of the Allied Powers (SCAP), General Douglas MacArthur, asked Professor Carl S. Shoup of Columbia University to head a mission of American tax scholars to evaluate and make recommendations for an overhaul of the Japanese tax system.[75] The American tax scholars included Dean Howard R. Bowen, College of Commerce and Business Administration, University of Illinois; Professor Jerome B. Cohen, Department of Economics, College of the City of New York; Mr. Rolland F. Hatfield, Director of Tax Research, Department of Taxation, St. Paul, Minnesota; Professor Carl S. Shoup, School of Business and Graduate Faculty of Political Science, Columbia University; Professor Stanley S. Surrey, School of Jurisprudence, University of California at Berkeley; Professor William S. Vickrey, Graduate Faculty of Political Science, Columbia University; and Professor William G. Warren, School of Law, Columbia University.[76]

They studied the Japanese tax system for four months before releasing their recommendations in four volumes, both in English and Japanese, in the fall of 1949.[77] The four volumes consisted of two volumes (volumes one and two) on the revenue

---

67 See Uematsu, *supra* note 2, at 573.

68 See Ishi, *supra* note 65, at 5; see also Uematsu, *supra* note 2, at 573 (fn. 35) (In 1945, because of a shortage of government tax personnel, a self-assessment system was in effect for certain large companies).

69 See Uematsu, *supra* note 2, at 573; see also MOF 1997, *supra* note 2, at 5.

70 See Shiomi, *supra* note 2, at 131. 71 See *id.* 72 *Id.*

73 *Id.* at 146 (table 27). 74 See MOF 1997, *supra* note 2, at 5.

75 See generally Carl S. Shoup, The Tax Mission to Japan, 1949–50 in *Tax Reform in Developing Countries* (Malcolm Gillis ed., 1989) for an in-depth description of how the Shoup Mission came into existence.

76 See, e.g., Shoup Mission, *Report on Japanese Taxation* iv (1949); Uematsu, *supra* note 2, at 568; Shoup, *supra* note 75, at 179.

77 See Shoup, *supra* note 75, at 179–81.

system and two volumes (volumes three and four) of appendices. The first two volumes contained 227 pages of double spaced English text (554 pages if the Japanese text is included) focusing on income taxes, taxation of gifts and bequests, the local-inhabitants tax, the real estate tax, other local taxes, and indirect taxes.[78] The appendices in volumes three and four included: (A) Finance of Local Governments, (B) Treatment of Irregular Incomes under the Personal Income Tax, (C) Revaluation of Assets (for purposes of Income Taxation), and (D) Administration of the Individual and Corporate Income Taxes.[79] The Shoup Mission, through its recommendations, attempted to make the Japanese tax system in a few years "the best tax system in the world" through three objectives: the establishment of an equitable tax system, the improvement of tax administration, and the reinforcement of local government finance.[80] A brief summary of the Shoup Mission's recommendations was released to the public on August 26, 1949. The first two volumes were made public on 15 September 1949, and the final volumes were made public on 3 October 1949.[81]

The primary focus of the Shoup Mission was to draw up a plan for a permanent tax system for Japan.[82] The Shoup Mission emphasized that all of its major recommendations were interconnected as well as most of the minor recommendations.[83] As a result, the focus of the Japanese should be on adopting the entire tax system recommended by the Shoup Mission and not just selected provisions.[84] In fact, the Shoup Mission stressed that if some of the major recommendations were implemented while others were not, the implemented provisions would lose some of their effectiveness and may actually cause more harm than good.[85] The Shoup Mission's 1949 report overwhelmingly focused on the income tax, both individual and corporate.[86] The Shoup Mission felt that the income tax should be the largest single source of revenue and, as a result, needed to be overhauled from its present form.[87] The Shoup Mission's recommendations have been summarized a number of times, including a press release distributed on 26 August 1949.[88] The following is a description of the major income tax changes advocated by the Shoup Mission.

B. Personal Income Tax

The Shoup Mission emphasized that the personal income tax was by far the most important component in the Japanese tax system.[89] It generated between 40 and 50 percent of the annual revenue for the national government.[90] The Shoup Mission

---

[78] See *id.* at 181–83. [79] *Id.* at 183.

[80] See Shoup Mission, *supra* note 76, at volume 1 page ii; see also Hiroshi Kaneko, "The Development of the Japanese Tax System After World War II," in *A Final Draft Report from FAIR (Foundation for Advanced Information and Research) to the World Bank on "Taxation and Economic Growth" (Asian Miracle Project)* (Oliver Oldman and Hiroshi Kaneko eds., 1993) at 13.

[81] See Shiomi, *supra* note 2, at 82. [82] See Shoup Mission, *supra* note 76, at volume 1 page i.

[83] See *id.* at ii. [84] *Id.* [85] *Id.* [86] See Shoup, *supra* note 75, at 182–83.

[87] See *id.*; see also Shoup Mission, *supra* note 76, at volume 1 page 45; MOF 1997, *supra* note 2, at 6.

[88] See, e.g., *Nippon Times*, 24 August 1989; Shoup, *supra* note 75, at 184–191; Shiomi, *supra* note 2, at 82.

[89] See Shoup Mission, *supra* note 76, at volume 1 page 43. [90] See *id.*

concluded that the personal income tax should continue its dominant role in the Japanese tax system.[91] The alternative would be a return to a system relying heavily on indirect taxation, which the Shoup Mission felt was completely wrong.[92] The Shoup Mission stressed that even though the personal income tax should play the dominant role, it would take a number of years, maybe five to ten years, to have an efficiently operating system.[93]

The two primary recommendations that the Shoup Mission made for the personal income tax were a reduction in the tax rates and an increase in the personal and dependency exemptions.[94] This combination of rate reduction and exemption increase would ideally lead to less tax evasion by taxpayers and fewer arbitrary assessments by tax administrators.[95] The rate reduction and exemption increases would reduce the average taxpayer's tax liability by almost one-third.[96]

As for the actual mechanics of the recommendation, the individual income tax rates were to be reduced, with the top rate being reduced from 85 percent to 55 percent.[97] The lowest rate of 20 percent would apply to the first 50,000 yen and the top rate of 55 percent would apply to income over 300,000 yen.[98] A total of eight income brackets was proposed, with each subsequent income bracket subject to a tax rate five percent higher than the previous income bracket.[99] In setting up the rate schedule, the Shoup Mission had three goals in mind.[100] First, it wanted to reduce taxes for all individuals.[101] Second, it needed to raise the required amount of revenue for the national government.[102] Third, the Shoup Mission wanted to set the top tax rate at 55 percent (reduced from 85 percent) so as to enhance enforcement of the tax laws.[103] Too high a rate would lead to continued tax evasion.[104] In fact,

---

[91] *Id.*

[92] The reasons given by the Shoup Mission for the inadequacy of a system relying heavily on indirect taxation include the lack of awareness between a citizen and the national government, and failure to account for income, wealth, and family burdens. *Id.*

[93] *Id.* at 45. [94] *Id.* at 46.

[95] *Id.* at 45–47. The Shoup Mission commented that tax evasion was especially prevalent among small businessmen and farmers and less so with wage earners. *Id.* at 46.

[96] *Id.* at 47. The Shoup Mission felt, for a number of reasons, that revenues would only decline by about 10 percent and not one-third for the 1950–51 fiscal year. *Id.* at 47–50.

[97] *Id.* at 55–58.

[98] *Id.* at 57. The lowering of the individual income tax rates was to be partly offset by a personal net worth tax on individuals with more than five million yen. See Shoup, *supra* note 75, at 184. The rates would range from one-half of one percent to as high as three percent. See *id.*

[99] See Shoup Mission, *supra* note 76, at volume 1 page 57. The rate schedule proposed was as follows:

0–50,000 yen	20 percent
50,000–80,000 yen	25 percent
80,000–100,000 yen	30 percent
100,000–120,000 yen	35 percent
120,000–150,000 yen	40 percent
150,000–200,000 yen	45 percent
200,000–300,000 yen	50 percent
over 300,000 yen	55 percent

Id.

[100] *Id.* at 64. [101] *Id.* [102] *Id.* at 64–65. [103] *Id.* at 65–68. [104] *Id.*

the Shoup Mission expected that once its proposed net worth tax was implemented, the top personal income tax rate would decrease below 50 percent, possibly at 45 percent.[105] The net worth tax would be annually imposed on individuals whose net worth exceeded five million yen.[106] The rates ranged 0.5 percent to three percent.[107]

Personal exemptions would be increased from 15,000 yen to 24,000 yen with an additional 12,000 yen deduction for dependents (including the spouse).[108] The current personal exemption of 15,000 yen represented about one and a half times a semi-skilled worker's monthly salary of 10,000 yen. In the United States, the personal exemption of $600 was more than two times the same type of semi-skilled worker's monthly salary of between $250 and $300. As a result, the current exemption amount of 15,000 yen was not far out of line when compared to the United States. However, the Shoup Mission stated that to have the income tax continue to be the primary source of revenue, to increase enforcement, and to relieve the tax burden for low-income taxpayers, a rate of 24,000 yen would be appropriate. In addition, the 1800 yen credit for a dependent would be changed to a 12,000 yen deduction from income, a slight increase in the exemption.[109] This increase to 12,000 yen for dependents would achieve the same three objectives.

Medical expenses would be allowed as deductions to the extent they exceeded ten percent of a taxpayer's net income.[110] Similar treatment would be provided for personal casualty losses.[111] Capital gains would be fully included in income and capital losses would be deducted in full without limitation.[112] In addition, in the case of a transfer of a capital asset by gift or bequest, the gain or loss accrued on the property would be triggered and taken into account as capital gain or capital loss.[113] The net capital gain or net capital loss each year would be averaged over the next five years (or possibly 10 years) to alleviate the adverse tax consequences of a bunching of income.[114] Royalty income would also be subject to five year (or maybe as long as twenty year) averaging.[115]

An individual shareholder would be entitled to a tax credit of 25 percent of the amount of dividends included in income.[116] This was an attempt to alleviate the potential for double taxation of corporate earnings. Finally, no special treatment would be given to interest paid on bank accounts.[117]

---

[105] *Id.* at 68. [106] *Id.* at 88. [107] *Id.* at 88. The rate schedule proposed was as follows:

0–5 million yen	Exempt
5 million–10 million yen	0.5 percent
10 million–20 million yen	1.0 percent
20 million–50 million yen	2.0 percent
above 50 million yen	3.0 percent

Id.

[108] *Id.* at 51–55. [109] *Id.* at 53–55. [110] *Id.* at 103–104. [111] *Id.* at 103.

[112] *Id.* at 90–93; see also Shoup Mission, *supra* note 76, at volume III, Appendix B, Sections D and E.

[113] *Id.* at 91–92; Appendix B, Sections D and E.

[114] *Id.* at 89–90, Appendix B, Section A. [115] *Id.* at 89–90; Appendix B, Section A.

[116] *Id.* at 107–08.

[117] *Id.* at 98–101. The Shoup Mission stated that many had urged that it propose a special flat withholding tax on interest on bank deposits. *Id.* at 98. The Shoup Mission found no merit in this proposal. *Id.*

C. Corporate Tax

As to the corporate income tax, the Shoup Mission recommended that the tax rate remain at 35 percent.[118] The excess profits tax and withholding tax on dividends would be repealed.[119] A one-percent annual interest-like tax would be imposed on the retained earnings of a corporation.[120] This one-percent tax was not intended as a penalty for accumulation of earnings in the corporation.[121] Rather, it was primarily designed to partially negate the tax deferral benefits associated with retained earnings or, in the words of the Shoup Mission, "to approximately counterbalance this pressure for accumulation of earnings which arises from the income tax on shareholders."[122] The Shoup Mission was concerned that a one-percent interest charge might not be sufficient in the case of family corporations, where the desire of high bracket taxpayers to shift income to a closely held type of corporation may be great.[123] As a result, in the case of family corporations, a higher rate of possibly nine-percent, would apply.[124] Finally, no corporate level tax would be imposed on a corporate liquidation.[125] Rather, the shareholders would be subject to any dividend income and capital gain.[126]

D. Provisions Common to the Personal Income Tax and the Corporate Tax

The Shoup Mission also recommended a number of income tax provisions that applied to both corporate and noncorporate businesses. Business assets would be revalued to current fair market value with a six-percent tax imposed on the increase in book value.[127] This revaluation was due primarily to the tremendous inflation Japan had experienced in the 1940s.[128] A number of other tax accounting changes were recommended, including repeal of the inventory profit tax,[129] a two year carryback for business losses and an unlimited carryforward period for business losses,[130] several methods for inventory valuation such as FIFO (first-in, first-out) or LIFO (last-in, first-out) as opposed to the exclusive method of weighted average,[131] and several methods for depreciation of business assets including straight-line

---

118 *Id.* at 107. 119 *Id.* at 112–13. 120 *Id.* at 106–11. 121 *Id.* at 109.

122 *Id.* at 109. 123 *Id.* at 110–11. 124 *Id.* at 111.

125 *Id.* at 112–13. This should be immediately familiar to American readers as the *General Utilities* doctrine, named after the 1935 U.S. Supreme Court case *General Utilities v. Helvering*, 296 U.S. 200 (1935). It is interesting that the Shoup Mission wanted the *General Utilities* doctrine to apply to corporate liquidations in Japan as part of their ideal tax system. The U.S. Supreme Court's decision has been roundly criticized in the American tax literature, and the doctrine was finally repealed in 1986 as part of the Tax Reform Act of 1986.

126 *Id.* at 112–113. 127 *Id.* at 123–31; see also Shoup, *supra* note 75, at 186.

128 See Shoup Mission, *supra* note 76, at volume II page 123; see also MOF 1997, *supra* note 2, at 7. The Shoup Mission remarked that the depreciation on business assets purchased before 1940 was negligible in 1949 yen terms because price levels had increased 100–200 times since 1940. See Shoup Mission, *supra* note 76, at volume II page 123.

129 See *id.* at 131. The inventory profit tax was imposed at a 66 2/3 percent rate on the inventory profits of all taxpayers whenever an increase was made under the Price Control Law. *Id.*

130 *Id.* at 133–35. 131 *Id.* at 135–38.

as opposed to the exclusive method of declining balance.[132] In addition, the Shoup Mission proposed that the MOF should provide guidance to taxpayers on expenditures that are deductible versus expenditures that are capital in nature,[133] and also to determine the feasibility of allowing bad debt reserves.[134]

E. The 1950 Shoup Mission

In 1950, Professors Shoup, Surrey, Vickrey, and Warren made a second trip to Japan releasing a second report on recommendations for the Japanese tax system.[135] The second report gave no substantive recommendations on the Japanese income tax system. Rather, it focused on administration and the value-added tax.

F. One Comment on the Shoup Missions

The Shoup Mission devoted little attention to issues of the time value of money and tax deferral. As previously stated though, this was understandable because issues of time value of money and tax deferral did not achieve importance in the United States until the 1960s, with Professor Surrey's appointment as Assistant Secretary of the Treasury by President John F. Kennedy in 1961. Probably, one of the main reasons that the time value of money was not of much concern to American tax scholars is that interest rates were relatively low in the United States in the years prior to the 1960s (usually about six percent per annum) and inflation was also relatively low (about one percent per annum).

The Shoup Mission did propose one income tax provision that appears to be solely a tax deferral/time value of money issue. It proposed a one percent annual interest-like tax (as high as nine percent in the case of family corporations) on the retained earnings of a corporation. As previously stated, this one-percent tax was not intended as a penalty for accumulation of earnings in the corporation. Rather, it was primarily designed to partially negate the tax deferral benefits associated with retained earnings or, in the words of the Shoup Mission, "to approximately counterbalance this pressure for accumulation of earnings which arises from the income tax on shareholders."

VII. Tax Reform in the Immediate Aftermath of the Shoup Missions

A number of the Shoup Mission Recommendations were incorporated in the Tax Reform of 1950.[136] In fact, Dr. Shoup has written "[a]lmost all of the more important

[132] *Id.* at 138–39; see also Shoup, *supra* note 75, at 186.

[133] See Shoup Mission, *supra* note 76, at 140–41.

[134] See *id.* at 141–42.

[135] See Shoup Mission, *Second Report on Japanese Taxation* (1950).

[136] Apparently, General Douglas MacArthur's letter dated 15 September 1949, to Japanese premier Shigeru Yoshida hoping that the Japanese would adopt a tax system based on the Shoup Mission's recommendations assured quick passage of the Shoup Mission's recommendations. See Shoup, *supra* note 75, at 195.

conceptual and substantive recommendations in the report were implemented over the short run, in the year or two following publication."[137] However, the Japanese soon repealed or substantially changed a number of the previously implemented provisions. The University of Tokyo Professor Emeritus Hiroshi Kaneko has written that "[t]he basic structure of the 'Shoup tax system' was maintained until 1953."[138] The year 1953 is often seen as the year that Japan truly became independent from the United States and began its economic miracle.[139] It is probably no coincidence that 1953 was also the year that the Japanese repealed or amended the many Shoup Mission recommendations.

Japan substantially changed its tax system after 1950, the year in which it adopted many of the Shoup Mission's recommendations, because they felt that "[t]he Shoup Mission's intentions were somewhat idealistic and did not fit in with the reality of the Japanese economy and the standard of living of the Japanese people."[140] The tax reforms beginning in 1951, which began to undo the Shoup Mission's provisions, "represented the effort to readjust the taxation system to actual conditions prevailing in the country."[141] In addition, one of the primary goals of the Shoup Mission was the "equitable sharing of the burdens to meet government expenditures, avoiding arbitrary reduction of the tax burden even at the cost of economic policy goals."[142] The Japanese government felt that certain economic policies were so vital, that they should override general principles of taxation.[143] Finance Minister Hayato Ikeda, who would later become Prime Minister of Japan, conducted the negotiations with the Shoup Mission and served in a supervisory role with regard to subsequent revisions of the tax system.[144] He wrote in 1952:

> Dr. Shoup's party was composed solely of scholars who made academically logical recommendations, but, if I may say so frankly, I believe that there are some points which are overly theoretical and conceptual. One such manifestation is the assumption that the final issue is always whether or not an item is income, and that, provided it is income, any and everything without discrimination should be taxed at the same rate; such an approach fails to treat tax law as an active and living thing. To present a short example, in the building of a hydroelectric dam there are farming families who must be pushed off farm land which has been handed down from their ancestors for generations. While they receive a good price for the purchase, they have to immediately bear a sizable tax simply because it is capital gain. Rational or not, it is absolutely impossible to tax income produced under such circumstances at exactly the same rate applicable to ordinary income. A "tax law which ignores human sentiment" will not succeed. Here, in order to do away with a mere tax in name only, the law was subsequently amended, but there are still many other similar instances. Although all called "income," such items as severance income, assignment income, and forestry income differ from that income which arises from trade, and it is improper to tax them fully at the normal tax rate. It is my feeling that it is desirable to digest thoroughly the

137 See *id.* at 195.
138 See Kaneko, *supra* note 80, at 19.
139 See R. Taggart Murphy, *The Weight of the Yen*, 87(1996).
140 MOF 1997, *supra* note 2, at 8.
141 *Id.*
142 *Id.*
143 See *id.*
144 See Uematsu, *supra* note 2, at 620. Finance Minister Ikeda and Tanzan Ishibashi are often credited for starting the Japanese economic miracle in the 1950s. See Murphy, *supra* note 139, at 301–02.

peculiar circumstances and conditions under which various sorts of income have been obtained and then impose taxation fitted to the actual situation. Revision in this sense was partially enacted in a recent session of the National Diet, but many matters requiring change yet remain.[145]

The Japanese adopted the interest-like tax on a corporation's retained earnings in 1950 but utilized a two percent rate instead of the one percent rate proposed by the Shoup Mission.[146] But in 1952, the interest-like tax was repealed, except in the case of family corporations, because "of the important role of profit retention in business financing."[147]

The Japanese also initially adopted the Shoup Mission's recommendation for fully taxing capital gains. In 1953, however, the Japanese eliminated capital gains and losses from the sale of securities from the income tax base.[148] This was done because "the taxation of capital gains allegedly hampered the development of the securities market"? and "technically the tax on such gains was difficult both to assess and collect."[149]

The Japanese abolished the net worth tax in 1953. They thought that "[t]he net worth tax proved inequitable because real property owners whose net worth is easily identified bore the full brunt while others escaped to some extent."[150] The Japanese also increased the corporate tax rate from 35 percent in 1950, which was the rate suggested by the Shoup Mission, to 42 percent in 1952.[151]

VIII. Tax Reform in the Late 1950s and 1960s

By 1951, the Japanese economy had returned such that its industrial output was equivalent to that of 1935, "the last year before the economy had been put fully on a war footing."[152] In 1955, the Japanese began its economic miracle, with economic growth averaging nine percent a year over the next 20 years.[153] In fact, in 1961, the Japanese GNP grew by over 14 percent.[154]

---

145 See Uematsu, *supra* note 2, at 621 (citing to Hayato Ikeda, *Kinko Zaisei* (Balanced Public Finance) 122–23 (1952)).

146 See MOF 1997, *supra* note 2, at 8.   147 *Id.* at 8.

148 See Shoup, *supra* note 75, at 198; see also MOF 1997, *supra* note 2, at 8.

149 MOF 1997, *supra* note 2, at 8. See Shoup, *supra* note 75, at 198.

150 MOF 1997, *supra* note 2, at 8.

151 See Eiji Tajika and Yuji Yui, "Public Policies and Capital Accumulation: Japan at the Dawn of Economic Growth," in *A Final Draft Report from FAIR (Foundation for Advanced Information and Research) to the World Bank on "Taxation and Economic Growth" (Asian Miracle Project)* 39, 51 (1993); see also Shiomi, *supra* note 2, at 147 (table 27).

152 See Fingleton, *supra* note 1, at 125.

153 See *id.*; see also Shiomi, *supra* note 2, at 28 ("The year 1955 proved to be a year of remarkable prosperity in Japan. Exports registered the second highest rate of increase in the world, yielding an overall surplus of the trade balance amounting to $500 million. An economic expansion was achieved without greatly stimulating commodity prices or credit expansion. A growth of national real income by nine percent was recorded.").

154 See Fingleton, *supra* note 1, at 125. Fingleton writes that the GNP growing by 14.6 percent in 1961 was "surely the fastest growth any major nation has achieved in history." *Id.* Professor Chalmers Johnson cites Arisawa Hiromi, ed., *Showa keizai shi* (Economic History of the Showa era), Tokyo, 1976, p. 371 in

The explosive growth of the Japanese economy in the late 1950s resulted in a large increase in tax revenue to the Japanese government. As a result, the government implemented a number of tax provisions to make the income tax less progressive and also raised exemption amounts for individuals.[155] This resulted in the indirect tax revenues comprising a larger share of the government's total tax revenue.[156]

In 1956, the government established a Provisional Tax System Committee to submit reports for tax reform.[157] The government felt that the committee was needed because of the tremendous growth in the Japanese economy and wanted "to maintain the equitable sharing of the tax burden and to adapt the current tax system to the new economic conditions."[158] The committee was "to study the existing tax system and make tax policy proposals at the Prime Minister's request."[159] The committee remained in existence for two years until 1958 and "then evolved into the Tax System Research Council ["TSRC"], which became a permanent advisory council in 1962."[160] The TSRC is composed of thirty members (or less) from many different professions, including academics, journalists, former bureaucrats, and industry representatives. The TSRC submits reports on suggested reform of the tax system and most of the changes from year to year are based on the council's reports.[161]

One of the underlying themes of tax reform in the 1950s seemed to be the granting of special tax treatments, which was in direct contravention to the Shoup Mission's emphasis of an equitable tax system.[162] These special tax treatments were reflected by the Special Tax Treatments Law in 1957, which granted a number of special tax treatments.[163] Professor Kaneko has written that "[t]he purpose of most of these treatments was to promote capital formation and develop the national economy by encouraging, among other things: savings, retained profits, modernization of equipment and machinery, and promotion of exports."[164] Later, the government enacted additional special tax treatment provisions designed to protect small and medium-size enterprises, to promote development of certain regions, and to address pollution and land-use problems.[165]

---

stating that GNP grew by 14.4 percent in 1961. See Chalmers Johnson, *MITI and the Japanese Miracle* (1982) at 237 (table 18).

155 See MOF 1997, *supra* note 2, at 9. 156 *Id.*

157 *Id.* at 10. Professor Ishi writes that the Tax Advisory Commission was established in 1953. See Ishi, *supra* note 65, at 15.

158 See MOF 1997, *supra* note 2, at 9.

159 Junko Kato, *The Problem of Bureaucratic Rationality* (1994) at 94.

160 See *id.* 161 See MOF 1997, *supra* note 2, at 10.

162 See Kaneko, *supra* note 80, at 19. Special tax treatments should be identifiable to those familiar with the American tax system as comparable to the term "tax expenditures," a term made famous by Professor Stanley S. Surrey. See, e.g., *Tax Policy and Tax Reform: 1961–1969 Selected Speeches and Testimony of Stanley S. Surrey* (William F. Hellmuth and Oliver Oldman, eds., 1973) at Chapter X – Tax Expenditures and the Budget; Stanley S. Surrey, *Pathways to Tax Reform* (1973); Stanley S. Surrey and Paul R. McDaniel, *Tax Expenditures* (1985).

163 See Kaneko, *supra* note 80, at 19. These special tax treatments are referred to today as The Special Taxation Measures Law. See MOF 1997, *supra* note 2, at 22. The MOF describes this law as providing "special tax measures directed toward economic policy goals." *Id.* Examples given by the MOF include special tax rates on interest income and accelerated depreciation. *Id.*

164 See Kaneko, *supra* note 80, at 19. 165 See *id.*

In 1959, the Prime Minister requested that the TSRC suggest ways to improve the tax system and also suggest a reasonable distribution of tax revenue between the national and local governments.[166] The TSRC submitted an interim report in 1960, after examining the tax burden both before and after World War II, the tax burden relative to other countries, and the tax burden in relation to budget expenditures.[167] In the interim report, the TSRC stated that the income tax burden should be approximately 20 percent of the national income.[168] The 20 percent figure included both the national and local income tax burden.[169] Consequently, the TSRC stated that if tax revenues increased because of unexpected economic growth, then the government should reduce taxes in the following years.[170] As a result of the TSRC's recommendations, one of the major tax policies of the high economic growth era of the 1960s was a reduction of the income tax burden to taxpayers.[171]

In 1961, the TSRC issued a second report recommending enactment of a general law of national taxation.[172] Based on the report, the government enacted The General Law of National Tax in 1962, which was designed to simplify and clarify the tax laws.[173] The General Law of National Tax contains provisions that are fundamental to all areas of taxation.[174] Some of the areas covered by The General Law of National Tax include articles dealing with procedural matters, such as tax payments, refunds, and disputes, and also general provisions on additional taxes.[175] The enactment of The General Law of National Tax is considered an important event in the history of the Japanese tax system because of its purpose of making the tax laws more understandable to practitioners and taxpayers.

In 1962, the Prime Minister again requested that the TSRC study the current tax system and make recommendations based on the tremendous growth of the economy and the changes to Japanese society in general.[176] After several years of study, the TSRC presented its report in 1964. In its report, the TSRC made several primary recommendations.[177] First, the TSRC determined that a critical issue in the upcoming years was the appropriate division of the increased tax revenue from the sustained economic expansion. Generally, the projected increased tax revenue could be divided in one of two ways: tax reduction or increased public expenditures. The TSRC recommended that tax reduction for the next several years should be approximately 20 percent of the expected annual increase in tax revenue.[178]

The TSRC also believed that income taxes should continue to be the most important component of the tax system for several reasons: (1) it properly allocates resources without disturbing prices, (2) it properly redistributes income through progressive tax rates, and (3) it alleviates the swings in business cycles by acting as a stabilizer.[179] It is interesting to note that the TSRC wanted the income tax to remain

---

[166] See MOF 1997, *supra* note 2, at 10. [167] See *id.* [168] *Id.* [169] *Id.* [170] *Id.*

[171] *Id.* At the same time, indirect tax revenues had been increasing relative to income tax revenues. In 1961, the TSRC recommended that the indirect tax rate should be approximately 10 percent of consumer prices or 20 percent of producer prices. *Id.*

[172] See MOF 1997, *supra* note 2, at 10. The TSRC also recommended a self-assessment system for indirect taxes, which was quickly enacted. See *id.* at 11.

[173] *Id.* at 10–11, 22. [174] *Id.* at 22. [175] *Id.*

[176] *Id.* at 11. [177] *Id.* [178] *Id.* [179] *Id.*

the most important component of the tax system yet it also wanted future income tax reductions. The TSRC justified this apparent inconsistency by concluding that the income tax burden will get larger as the economy grows because of the high elasticity of income tax revenue.[180]

The TSRC thought that the special taxation measures should eventually be abolished.[181] This view was consistent with the Shoup Mission's recommendations. The TSRC also thought that dividend paying corporations should be subject to taxation on the earnings that generated the dividends with appropriate relief to shareholders on receipt of the dividends to avoid double taxation.[182]

In the mid-1960s, the government changed its position with respect to its fiscal policy. Prior to World War II during the first half of the 1930s, Japan had run huge budget deficits to stimulate its economy.[183] In the first half of the 1930s, Japan's manufacturing and mining output increased by 49.6 percent while during this same period, the United States' output decreased by 6.3 percent.[184] During this period prior to World War II, approximately 30 percent of the government's revenue came from borrowing and issuing new government bonds.[185] After Ambassador Dodge's arrival to Japan in February 1949, Japan maintained a balanced budget through the 1950s and the first half of the 1960s.[186]

In 1965, the government substantially revised the Income Tax Law and the Corporation Tax Law "to incorporate provisions that had been previously provided by Cabinet orders."[187] In June and July of 1965, the government approved the issuance of bonds for the first time since the end of the war, ending its fiscal policy of maintaining a balanced budget.[188] The bonds were not actually issued until January 1966.[189] The TSRC submitted an interim report in 1967 and a final report in 1968, re-examining the government's strategic tax planning in light of its new fiscal policy of deficit financing.[190] The TSRC suggested that the basic tax structure should remain the same.[191] The TSRC also recommended expansion of the employment income deduction and personal exemptions as well as reducing the degree of progressivity for individuals.[192] As for the corporation tax, the TSRC recommended establishing a more stable corporate tax system.[193]

IX. The 1970s to Present Day

By the end of the 1960s, Japan had surpassed Great Britain and West Germany to become the third largest economy in the world.[194] During the 1970s, the government

[180] *Id.* [181] *Id.* [182] *Id.* [183] See Johnson, *supra* note 154, at 119.

[184] See *id.* at 121; see also Fingleton, *supra* note 1, at 105.

[185] See MOF 1997, *supra* note 2, at 12.

[186] See *id.*; see also Ishi, *supra* note 65, at 53; Johnson, *supra* note 154, at 264.

[187] See Kaneko, *supra* note 80, at 20.

[188] See, e.g., Johnson, *supra* note 154, at 264; MOF 1997, *supra* note 2, at 12; Murphy, *supra* note 139, at 209. See also John Creighton Campbell, *Contemporary Japanese Budget Politics* (1977).

[189] See Campbell, *supra* note 188, at 236–37. [190] See MOF 1997, *supra* note 2, at 12.

[191] See *id.* [192] *Id.* [193] *Id.* [194] See Fingleton, *supra* note 1, at 127.

continued to issue bonds and engage in deficit financing.[195] The Japanese economy started to slow in the 1970s, substantially slowing down from the 10-percent plus growth rates of the late 1960s.[196] As a result of the slower growth in the Japanese economy and the recession of 1974–1975, the government continued to issue bonds to cover the revenue shortfall.[197] The government became concerned about the continuing deficits it was incurring and tried to limit the annual growth of expenditures.[198] In addition, beginning in 1976, the government cut back and repealed a number of the special taxation measures.[199]

During the 1980s, it became apparent that a number of problems existed in the Japanese tax system. First, the system was too complicated.[200] Substantial simplification was needed to make it easier for taxpayers to comply with the rules.[201] Second, in addition to simplification, the tax system needed to be equitable and neutral in its treatment of taxpayers.[202] This meant cutting back or simply repealing a number of the various special tax measures, improving taxpayer compliance by eliminating the 9-6-4 problem, and, with respect to indirect taxes, changing from a selective consumption tax system to a comprehensive one.[203]

Japan also needed to address the budget deficits it was continually incurring and also address the issue of financing the expenditures that would be needed to care for its rapidly aging population.[204] The solution seemed to be a comprehensive consumption tax as a way of raising a steady amount of revenue.[205] Finally, Japan needed to have a tax system that addressed the globalization of business activities.[206]

On 20 September 1985, Prime Minister Nakasone requested that the TSRC review the entire tax system in light of "equity, fairness, simplicity, choice, vitality of the private sector economy, neutrality, and internationality."[207] On 28 October 1986, the TSRC submitted its report titled, "Report on Overall Review of the Tax System," which recommended substantial reform to the existing tax system with a combination of income tax reduction and introduction of a value-added tax.[208] As a result of this report, the government passed tax legislation on 25 September 1987.[209]

---

[195] See MOF 1997, *supra* note 2, at 13. [196] See Murphy, *supra* note 139, at 130.

[197] See MOF 1997, *supra* note 2, at 13. [198] See *id.* at 13–14.

[199] *Id.* at 14; see also Tajika and Yui, *supra* note 151, at 50.

[200] See Kaneko, *supra* note 80, at 21. [201] See *id.* [202] *Id.*

[203] *Id.* The 9-6-4 problem, referred to in Japanese as the "ku-ro-yon" problem, is shorthand describing the tax evasion issues among the three major groups of taxpayers subject to the individual income tax. Salaried workers, represented by "9," are believed to be about ninety percent compliant. In other words, about ninety percent of all salaried workers' income is taxed. Self-employed workers are believed to only have about sixty percent of their income taxed by the Government. This is represented by "6." Farmers are believed to only have about forty percent of their income taxed by the Government. This is represented by "4." See Ishi, *supra* note 65, at 67–75. The compliance issue is sometimes referred to as 10-5-3-1, referred to in Japanese as "to-go-san pin." The 10-5-3 correspond to the 9-6-4 and the 1 represents politicians, meaning that politicians are believed to only have about 10 percent of their income taxed by the Government.

[204] See Kaneko, *supra* note 80, at 21; see also MOF 1997, *supra* note 2, at 14.

[205] See Kaneko, *supra* note 80, at 21. [206] See *id.*; See *also* MOF 1997, *supra* note 2, at 14.

[207] See Kaneko, *supra* note 80, at 22; see also Ishi, *supra* note 65, at 318.

[208] See Ishi, *supra* note 65, at 318. [209] See MOF 1997, *supra* note 2, at 14.

One of the changes made by the government was the repeal of the exemption for interest income from personal savings (referred to as the "Maruyu").[210] It was replaced by a flat withholding tax of 15 percent plus an additional five percent local tax resulting in a total withholding tax of 20 percent.[211]

On 12 November 1987, Prime Minister Takeshita asked the TSRC to again make recommendations for an "optimal tax system, balancing income [taxes], consumption [taxes], and property [taxes], and other taxes."[212] After conducting a number of public hearings in early 1988, the TSRC submitted its "Interim Report on Tax Reform" and "Report on Tax Reform."[213] As a result of these reports, the government passed tax legislation on 24 December 1988, referred to as the Tax Reform of 1988.[214]

The Tax Reform of 1988 included a number of major changes. First, a consumption tax was introduced in the form of a value-added tax. The rate was set at three percent and it was to take effect on 1 April 1989. The MOF has stated that two of the goals for the consumption tax were: "(1) to facilitate the shifting of the tax burden and to prevent excessive price increases and (2) to reduce and rationalize compliance costs of small and medium-sized enterprises."[215] The consumption tax resulted in a "fundamental change of the structure of the Japanese tax system."[216] The 1988 Act also reduced and flattened the income tax brackets. Prior to the 1988 Act, the income tax system had 12 income brackets with rates ranging from 10.5 percent to 60 percent.[217] The 1988 Act reduced the number of brackets to five and reduced the rates to ranges of 10–50 percent.[218] The 1988 Act also repealed the exemption of capital gains from the sale or transfer of securities.[219] In addition, the corporate tax rate was reduced slightly and the reduced rate on corporate income distributed as dividends was repealed.[220] Finally, a number of significant changes were made to the inheritance tax to take into account inflation and the increase in land value.[221]

In 1991, the Diet passed the Land Tax Reform of 1991. This legislation attempted to address the problems created by the dramatic rise in land prices, resulting in widening disparity between the upper and lower classes.[222] The legislation included a new land tax which was designed to (1) promote the effective utilization of land, (2) control land prices, and (3) impose a reasonable tax burden on holding land.[223] The legislation also raised the tax rate on capital gains from land transactions.[224]

By the middle of 1990, the Japanese economy entered into a recession that would persist for the first half of the 1990s. The TSRC released the first of two reports on

---

210 See Hiroshi Kaneko and Yoshihiro Masui, "Taxation of Interest Income in Japan – History and Current Situation," in *A Final Draft Report from FAIR (Foundation for Advanced Information and Research) to the World Bank on "Taxation and Economic Growth" (Asian Miracle Project)* 85, 110 (1993).

211 See *id.* 212 See MOF 1997, *supra* note 2, at 14. 213 See *id.* 214 See *id.*

215 *Id.* at 301. 216 See Kaneko, *supra* note 80, at 22.

217 See MOF 1997, *supra* note 2, at 299. 218 See *id.*

219 See Kaneko, *supra* note 80, at 22.

220 See *id.* at 22; see also MOF 1997, *supra* note 2, at 302–03.

221 See Kaneko, *supra* note 80, at 23.

222 See *id.* at 23; see also MOF 1997, *supra* note 2, at 15.

223 See Kaneko, *supra* note 80, at 23. 224 See MOF 1997, *supra* note 2, at 15.

19 November 1993, titled "Report on Taxation for the Coming Years." It released its second report on 21 June 1994, titled "Outline on Tax Reform." Based largely on these reports, the Diet passed the Tax Reform of 1994 on 25 December 1994. Generally, the reform provided for an immediate income tax reduction for all taxpayers, partly as a means of stimulating the economy. To partly offset the income tax cuts, however, the 1994 Reform also raised the consumption tax rate from three percent to four percent with an additional one percent local consumption tax resulting in a total consumption tax rate of five percent. The rise in the consumption tax rate would not take effect until 1 April 1997, in hopes that the economy would be sufficiently stimulated by the immediately implemented income tax cuts.

Bibliography

Alpert, H.H. and van Raad, K. (Eds.). 1993. *Essays on International Taxation*. Kluwer Law and Taxation, Netherlands.

Andrews, W.D. 1974. A consumption-type or cash flow personal income tax. *Harvard Law Review* 87(6).

Andrews, W.D. 1975. Fairness and the choice between a consumption-type and accretion-type personal income tax: a reply to Professor Warren. *Harvard Law Review* 88(5).

Andrews, W.D. 1983. The Achilles' heel of the comprehensive income tax, in: C.E. Walker and M.A. Bloomfield (Eds.). *New Directions in Federal Tax Policy for the 1980s*. Ballinger Pub. Co., Cambridge, MA.

Andrews, W.D. 1991. *Basic Federal Income Taxation*, 4th edn. Little, Brown & Company, Boston, MA.

Arnold, B.J. 1993. The taxation of investments in passive foreign investment funds in Australia, Canada, New Zealand and the United States, in: H.H. Alpert and K. van Raad (Eds.). *Essays on International Taxation*. Kluwer Law and Taxation, Netherlands.

Auerbach, A.J. 1991. Retrospective capital gains taxation. *American Economic Review* 81(1).

Ault, H.J. (principal author). 1997. *Comparative Income Taxation: A Structural Analysis*. Kluwer Law International, Boston, MA.

Bankman, J. and Klein, W.A. 1989. Accurate taxation of long-term debt: taking into account the term structure of interest. *Tax Law Review* 44(2).

Bird, R.M. and Head, J.G. (Eds.). 1972. *Modern Fiscal Issues: Essays in Honor of Carl S. Shoup*. University of Toronto Press, Toronto.

Bittker, B.I. 1967. A "comprehensive tax base" as a goal of income tax reform. *Harvard Law Review* 80(5).

Bittker, B.I. 1974. Tax reform and tax simplification. *University of Miami Law Review* 29(1).

Bittker, B.I. and Lokken, L. 1989. *Federal Taxation of Income, Estates and Gifts*. Warren, Gorham & Lamont, Boston, MA.

Bittker, B.I. and McMahon, M.J. 1995. *Federal Income Taxation of Individuals*, 2nd ed., Warren, Gorham & Lamont, Boston, MA.

Bradford, D.F. 1995. Fixing realization accounting: symmetry, consistency and correctness in the taxation of financial instruments. *Tax Law Review* 50(4).

Bradford, D.F. and the U.S. Treasury Tax Policy Staff. 1984. *Blueprints for Basic Tax Reform*, 2nd ed., Tax Analysts, Arlington, VA.

Break, G.F. and Pechman, J.A. 1975. *Federal Tax Reform: The Impossible Dream?* Brookings Institution, Washington, DC.

Brown, E.C. 1948. Business income taxation and investment incentives, in: *Income, Employment and Public Policy: Essays in Honor of Alvin H. Hansen*. W.W. Norton, New York, NY.

Brown, F.B. 1996. "Complete" accrual taxation. *San Diego Law Review* 33(4).

Campbell, J.C. 1977. *Contemporary Japanese Budget Politics*. University of California Press, Berkeley, CA.

Canellos, P.C. 1995. Commentary. *Tax Law Review* 50(4).

Canellos, P.C. and Kleinbard, E.D. 1983. The miracle of compound interest: interest deferral and discount after 1982. *Tax Law Review* 38(4).

Cantrell, J.P. et al. 1989. Notice 89-21 crashes the interest rate swap party. *Tax Notes* 45(3).

Chirelstein, Marvin A. 1997. *Federal Income Taxation*, rev. 8th ed., Foundation Press, Westbury, NY.

Cunningham, N.B. 1985. A theoretical analysis of the tax treatment of future costs. *Tax Law Review* 40(3).

Cunningham, N.B. 1996. The taxation of capital income and the choice of tax base. *Tax Law Review* 52(1).

Cunningham, N.B. and Schenk, D.H. 1992. Taxation without realization: a "revolutionary" approach to ownership. *Tax Law Review* 47(4).

Darcy, J.W. 1994. *Japan-U.S. International Tax Transactions*. CCH Japan Limited, Tokyo.

Dodge, J.M. 1995. A combined mark-to-market and pass-through corporate-shareholder integration proposal. *Tax Law Review* 50(3).

Engen, E.M. and Gale, W.G. 1996. The effects of fundamental tax reform on saving, in: H.J. Aaron and W.G. Gale (Eds.), *Economic Effects of Fundamental Tax Reform*. Brookings Institution, Washington, DC.

Evans, M. 1990. IRS' Kempson explains contested liabilities under economic performance test. *Tax Notes* 48(12).

Evans, T.L. 1989. The evolution of federal tax accounting – a growing trend towards mark-to-market? *Taxes* 67(12).

Evans, T.L. 1992. The realization doctrine after Cottage Savings. *Taxes* 70(12).

Fellows, M.L. 1990. A comprehensive attack on tax deferral. *Michigan Law Review* 88(4).

Fingleton, E. 1995. *Blindside: Why Japan is Still on Track to Overtake the U.S. by the Year 2000*. Houghton Mifflin Company, Boston, MA.

Fried, B.H. 1992. Fairness and the consumption tax. *Stanford Law Review* 44(5).

Fujitani, S. 1995. Tax aspects of derivative financial investments: Japan, in: 80b *Cahiers De Droit Fiscal International [Studies on International Fiscal Law]*. Kluwer Law International, Netherlands.

Gentry, W.M. and Hubbard, R.G. 1997. Distributional implications of introducing a broad-based consumption tax, in: J.M. Poterba (Ed.), *Tax Policy and the Economy*. NBER and MIT Press Journals, Cambridge, MA.

Gergen, M.P. 1994. The effects of price volatility and strategic trading under realization, expected return and retrospective taxation. *Tax Law Review* 49(2).

Ginsburg, M.D. 1990. Teaching tax law after tax reform. *Washington Law Review* 65(3).

Ginsburg, M.D. 1997. Taxing the components of income. *Georgetown Law Journal* 86(1).

Gomi, Y. 1996. *Japan Corporation Tax Law*. Sozeishiryokan, Tokyo.

Gomi, Y. 1998. *Guide to Japanese Taxes 1998–99*. Zaikei Shoho Sha, Tokyo.

Graetz, M.J. 1979. Implementing a progressive consumption tax. *Harvard Law Review* 92(8).

Graetz, M.J. and Schenk, D.H. 1995. *Federal Income Taxation*, 3rd edn., Foundation Press, Westbury, NY.

Gravelle, J.C. 1997. The economics of taxing capital income, in: R. Klever (Ed.), *Tax Conversations: A Guide to the Key Issues in the Tax Reform Debate*. Kluwer Law International, London.

Gunn, A. 1984. Matching of costs and revenues as a goal of tax accounting. *Virginia Tax Review* 4(1).

Haig, R.M. 1921. The concept of income – economic and legal aspects, in: R.M. Haig (Ed.), *The Federal Income Tax*. Columbia University Press, New York, NY.

Hall, R.E. and Rabushka, A. 1995. *The Flat Tax*, 2nd edn., Hoover Press, Stanford, CA.

Halperin, D.I. 1984. The time value of money – 1984. *Tax Notes* 23(7).

Halperin, D.I. 1986. Interest in disguise: taxing the "time value of money". *Yale Law Journal* 95(3).

Halperin, D.I. 1996. Assumption of contingent liabilities on sale of a business. *Florida Tax Review* 2(12).

Halperin, D.I. 1997. Saving the income tax: an agenda for research. *Tax Notes* 77(8).

Hanna, C.H. 1992. A partnership's business purpose taxable year: a deferral provision whose time has passed. *The Tax Lawyer* 45(3).

Hanna, C.H. 1993. Partnership distributions: whatever happened to nonrecognition? *Kentucky Law Journal* 82(2).

Hanna, C.H. 1995. The virtual reality of eliminating tax deferral. *The American Journal of Tax Policy* 12(2).

Hanna, C.H. 1997. Initial thoughts on classifying the major Japanese business entities under the check-the-box regulations. *SMU Law Review* 51(1).

Hanna, C.H. 1999. Demystifying tax deferral. *SMU Law Review* 52(2).

Hanna, C.H. and Olchyk, S. 1992. Interest under section 453A(c): is it or isn't it? *Tax Notes* 56(10).

Hariton, D.P. 1991. New rules bifurcating contingent debt – a mistake? *Tax Notes* 51(2).

Hariton, D.P. 1996. The accrual of interest on derivative investments: where do we go from here? *Taxes* 74(12).

Hartman, D.G. 1984. Tax policy and foreign direct investment in the United States. *National Tax Journal* 37(4).

Hellmuth, W.F. and Oldman, O. 1973. *Tax Policy and Tax Reform: 1961–1969 (Selected Speeches and Testimony of Stanley S. Surrey).* Commerce Clearing House, Chicago, IL.

Institute for Fiscal Studies. 1978. *The Structure and Reform of Direct Taxation.* George Allen & Unwin, London.

Isenbergh, J. 1990. *International Taxation.* Little Brown & Company, Boston, MA.

Ishi, H. 1993. *The Japanese Tax System*, 2nd edn., Oxford University Press, Oxford.

Johnson, C.H. 1990. Soft money investing under the income tax. *Illinois Law Review* 1989(4).

Johnson, C.H. 1995. The illegitimate "earned" requirement in tax and nontax accounting. *Tax Law Review* 50(3).

Johnson, C.H. 1995. Three errors in the neutral cost recovery system proposal. *Tax Notes* 67(9).

Johnson, C.H. 1996. Taxing the income from writing options. *Tax Notes* 73(2).

Johnson, C. 1982. *MITI and the Japanese Miracle.* Stanford University Press, Stanford, CA.

Joint Committee on Taxation. 1982. *General Explanation of the Revenue Provisions of the Tax Equity and Fiscal Responsibility Act of 1982.*

Joint Committee on Taxation. 1984. *General Explanation of the Tax Reform Act of 1984.*

Kaneko, H. 1993. The development of the Japanese tax system after World War II, in: O. Oldman and H. Kaneko (Eds.), *A Final Draft Report from FAIR (Foundation for Advanced Information and Research) to the World Bank on "Taxation and Economic Growth" (Asian Miracle Project).* Foundation for Advanced Information and Research, Tokyo.

Kaneko, H. and Gomi, Y. 1998. Outlook for Japan, in: H. Stein (Ed.), *Tax Policy in the Twenty-First Century.* JohnWiley & Sons, New York, NY.

Kaneko, H. and Masui, Y. 1993. Taxation of interest income in Japan – history and current situation, in: O. Oldman and H. Kaneko (Eds.), *A Final Draft Report from FAIR (Foundation for Advanced Information and Research) to the World Bank on "Taxation and Economic Growth" (Asian Miracle Project).* Foundation for Advanced Information and Research, Tokyo.

Kato, J. 1994. *The Problem of Bureaucratic Rationality: Tax Politics in Japan.* Princeton University Press, Princeton, NJ.

Kayle, B. 1987. Where has all the income gone? The mysterious relocation of interest and principal in coupon stripping and related transactions. *Virginia Tax Review* 7(2).

Kawakami, E. 1997. The taxation of investment funds: Japan, in: 82b *Cahiers De Droit Fiscal International [Studies on International Fiscal Law]*. Kluwer Law International, Netherlands.

Kitagwa, Z. 1989. *Doing Business in Japan*. Matthew Bender, New York, NY.

Kleinbard, E.D. and Evans, T.L. 1997. The role of mark-to-market accounting in a realization-based tax system. *Taxes* 75(12).

Koffey, R.S. and Umbrecht, R.L. 1989. Japanese cross-border leasing into the United States. *The Tax Lawyer* 43(1).

Kuboi, T. and Asakawa, Y. 1996. Partnering in Japan: form of entry and recent tax issues. *Tax Notes International* 13(6).

Kuntz, J.D. and Peroni, R.J. 1992. *U.S. International Taxation*. Warren, Gorham & Lamont, Boston, MA.

Land, S.B. 1996. Defeating deferral: a proposal for retrospective taxation. *Tax Law Review* 52(1).

Landau, T.M. 1996. Japan's new wave of advantages. *International Tax Review* 7(3).

Lokken, L. 1986. The time value of money rules. *Tax Law Review* 42(1).

Lokken, L. 1991. New rules bifurcating contingent debt – a good start. *Tax Notes* 51(4).

Louie, M.L. 1982. Realizing appreciation without sale: accrual taxation of capital gains on marketable securities. *Stanford Law Review* 34(4).

Malman, L.L. 1981. Treatment of prepaid income – clear reflection of income or muddied waters. *Tax Law Review* 37(1).

McLure, Jr., C.E. and Zodrow, G.R. 1998. The economic case for foreign tax credits for cash flow taxes. *National Tax Journal* 51(1).

Miller, D.S. 1998. Taxpayers' ability to avoid tax ownership: current law and future prospects. *The Tax Lawyer* 51(2).

Murphy, R.T. 1996. *The Weight of the Yen*. W.W. Norton & Company, New York, NY.

Musgrave, R.A. 1959. *The Theory of Public Finance*. McGraw-Hill, New York, NY.

Musgrave, R.A. 1996. Clarifying tax reform. *Tax Notes* 70(6).

National Commission on Economic Growth and Tax Reform. 1996. Unleashing America's Potential. *Tax Notes* 70(4).

Nolan, J.S. 1995. Erwin N. Griswold lecture: the merit of an income tax versus a consumption tax. *The American Journal of Tax Policy* 12(2).

Oldman, O. and Kaneko, H. (Eds.). 1993. *A Final Draft Report from FAIR (Foundation for Advanced Information and Research) to the World Bank on "Taxation and Economic Growth" (Asian Miracle Project)*. Foundation for Advanced Information and Research, Tokyo.

Organisation for Economic Co-operation and Development. 1996. *Controlled Foreign Company Legislation: Studies in Taxation of Foreign Source Income*. OECD, Paris.

Organisation for Economic Co-operation and Development. 1998. *Harmful Tax Competition*. OECD, Paris.

Otsuka, I. 1995. International income tax problems of partnerships: Japan, in: 80a *Cahiers De Droit Fiscal International [Studies on International Fiscal Law]*. Kluwer Law International, Netherlands.

Otsuka, M. and Watanabe, K. 1994. *Butterworths International Taxation of Financial Instruments and Transactions: Japan*, 2nd edn. Butterworths, London.

Plambeck, C.T. et al. 1995. Tax aspects of derivative financial instruments: general report, in: 80b *Cahiers De Droit Fiscal International [Studies on International Fiscal Law]*. Kluwer Law International, Netherlands.

Rubenfeld, S.I. and Rubin, J.R. 1987. Passive foreign investment companies: the pentapus becomes the sextapus, or does it? *Tax Notes* 36(2).

Rubin, B.D. 1990. Taxable dispositions of real estate: planning under the passive loss and installment sale rules, in: 48 *N.Y.U. Institute on Federal Taxation*. Matthew Bender, New York, NY.

Samuelson, P.A. 1964. Tax deductibility of economic depreciation to insure invariant valuation. *Journal of Political Economy* 72(12).

Scarborough, R.H. 1991. Payments in advance of performance. *Taxes* 69(12).

Schenk, D.H. 1995. Taxation of equity derivatives: a partial integration proposal. *Tax Law Review* 50(4).

Scholes, M.S. and Wolfson, M.A. 1992. *Taxes and Business Strategy: A Planning Approach.* Prentice Hall, Englewood Cliffs, NJ.

Seago, W.E. and Callihan, D. 1997. Toward a sound (neutral) tax policy for prepaid income from services. *Tax Notes* 74(3).

Shakow, D.J. 1986. Taxation without realization: a proposal for accrual taxation. *University of Pennsylvania Law Review* 134(5).

Shaviro, D.N. 1992. An efficiency analysis of realization and recognition rules under the federal income tax. *Tax Law Review* 48(1).

Shaviro, D.N. 1995. Risk-based rules and the taxation of capital income. *Tax Law Review* 50(4).

Sheppard, L.A. 1985. Ginsburg discusses taxing the privilege of tax deferral in installment sales. *Tax Notes* 27(5).

Sheppard, L.A. 1993. The Goldberg variations, or: giving away the store. *Tax Notes* 58(5).

Shibata, T. (Ed.). 1986. *Public Finance in Japan.* University of Tokyo Press, Tokyo.

Shiomi, S. 1957. *Japan's Finance and Taxation, 1940–1956.* Columbia University Press, New York, NY.

Shoup. C.S. 1969. *Public Finance.* Aldine Publishing Company, Chicago, IL.

Shoup, C.S. 1989. The tax mission to Japan, 1949–1950, in: M. Gillis (Ed.), *Tax Reform in Developing Countries.* Duke University Press, Durham, NC.

Shuldiner, R. 1992. A general approach to the taxation of financial instruments. *Texas Law Review* 71(2).

Simon, K.W. 1990. Revenue or religion? issues and answers on tax deferral. *Taxes* 68(12).

Simons, H.C. 1938. *Personal Income Taxation.* University of Chicago Press, Chicago, IL.

Sims, T.S. 1992. Long-term debt, the term structure of interest and the case for accrual taxation. *Tax Law Review* 47(2).

Slawson, D. 1967. Taxing as ordinary income the appreciation of publicly held stock. *Yale Law Journal* 76(4).

Steuerle, C.E. 1996. Zero tax rates on returns to new investment and learning. *Tax Notes* 72(10).

Strnad, J. 1986. Tax timing and the Haig-Simons ideal: a rejoinder to Professor Popkin. *Indiana Law Journal* 62(1).

Strnad, J. 1990. Periodicity and accretion taxation: norms and implementation. *Yale Law Journal* 99(8).

Strnad, J. 1994. Taxing new financial products: a conceptual framework. *Stanford Law Review* 46(3).

Strnad, J. 1995. Taxing new financial products in a second-best world: bifurcation and integration. *Tax Law Review* 50(4).

Strnad, J. 1995. The taxation of bonds: the tax trading dimension. *Virginia Law Review* 81(1).

Surrey, S.S. 1941. The Supreme Court and the federal income tax: some implications of the recent decisions. *Illinois Law Review* 35(7).

Surrey, S.S. 1971. The Tax Reform Act of 1969 – tax deferral and tax shelters. *Boston College Industrial and Commercial Law Review* 12(3).

Surrey, S.S. 1973. *Pathways to Tax Reform*. Harvard University Press, Cambridge, MA.

Surrey, S.S. and McDaniel, P.R. 1985. *Tax Expenditures*. Harvard University Press, Cambridge, MA.

Tajika, E. and Yui, Y. 1993. Public policies and capital accumulation: Japan at the dawn of economic growth, in: O. Oldman and H. Kaneko (Eds.), *A Final Draft Report from FAIR (Foundation for Advanced Information and Research) to the World Bank on "Taxation and Economic Growth" (Asian Miracle Project)*. Foundation for Advanced Information and Research, Tokyo.

Tax Bureau of the Ministry of Finance. 1997. *An Outline of Japanese Taxes 1997*.

Thomas, G.M. 1992 (January). Structure of Japanese operations and other selected Japanese tax issues. *Intertax*.

Uematsu, M. 1963. Computation of income in Japanese income taxation: a study in the adjustment of theory to reality, in: A.T. von Mehren (Ed.), *Law in Japan: The Legal Order in a Changing Society*. Harvard University Press, Cambridge, MA.

United States Department of the Treasury. 1984. *Report to the President, Tax Reform for Fairness, Simplicity, and Economic Growth*.

van Wolferen, K. 1989. *The Enigma of Japanese Power*. MacMillan, London.

Walker, C.E. and Bloomfield, M.A. (Eds.). 1984. *New Directions in Federal Tax Policy for the 1980s*. Ballinger Publishing Company, Cambridge, MA.

Warren, A.C. 1975. Fairness and a consumption-type or cash flow personal income tax. *Harvard Law Review* 88(5).

Warren, A.C. 1980. Would a consumption tax be fairer than an income tax? *Yale Law Journal* 89(6).

Warren, A.C. 1985. Accelerated capital recovery, debt, and tax arbitrage. *The Tax Lawyer* 38(3).

Warren, A.C. 1987. The timing of taxes. *National Tax Journal* 39(4).

Warren, A.C. 1993. Financial contract innovation and income tax policy. *Harvard Law Review* 107(2).

Warren, A.C. 1996. How much capital income taxed under an income tax is exempt under a cash flow tax? *Tax Law Review* 52(1).

Way, G. et al. 1990. *Business Operations in Japan*. BNA Tax Management Portfolios, 51–7th, Washington, DC.

Weisbach, D.A. 1995. Tax responses to financial contract innovation. *Tax Law Review* 50(4).

Weisbach, D.A. 1999. A partial mark-to-market tax system. *Tax Law Review* 53(1).

White, M. and White, A. 1972. Tax neutrality of instantaneous versus economic depreciation, in: R.M. Bird and J.G. Head (Eds.), *Modern Fiscal Issues: Essays in Honour of Carl S. Shoup*. University of Toronto Press, Toronto.

White, P.D. 1990. Realization, recognition, reconciliation, rationality and the structure of the federal income tax system. *Michigan Law Review* 88(4).

Yoost, D.A. and McGinnis, R.R. 1996. Using Japan's tokumei kumiai. *International Tax Review* 7(11).

Zelinsky, E.A. 1997. For realization: income taxation, sectoral accretionism, and the virtue of attainable values. *Cardozo Law Review* 19(3).

Index

www.ingramcontent.com/pod-product-compliance
Lightning Source LLC
Chambersburg PA
CBHW071244230926
51849CB00001B/228
9789041197719